Joseph George Greenwood

The Elements of Greek Grammar

Including accidence, irregular verbs, and principles of derivation and composition;

adapted to the system of crude forms

Joseph George Greenwood

The Elements of Greek Grammar
Including accidence, irregular verbs, and principles of derivation and composition; adapted to the system of crude forms

ISBN/EAN: 9783337319724

Printed in Europe, USA, Canada, Australia, Japan

Cover: Foto ©Paul-Georg Meister /pixelio.de

More available books at **www.hansebooks.com**

THE ELEMENTS

OF

GREEK GRAMMAR,

INCLUDING

ACCIDENCE, IRREGULAR VERBS, AND PRINCIPLES
OF DERIVATION AND COMPOSITION;

ADAPTED TO THE SYSTEM OF CRUDE FORMS,

BY

J.^o G.^o GREENWOOD,

FELLOW OF UNIVERSITY COLLEGE, LONDON;
PRINCIPAL OF OWENS COLLEGE, MANCHESTER.

SEVENTH EDITION.

London:
MACMILLAN AND CO.
1880.

PREFACE.

THAT method of teaching the Accidence of the Classical Languages which, under the name of the "Crude-Form System," discards the fiction under which the nominative case of a noun, or the 1st person of the present tense of a verb, is treated as, in some peculiar sense, *the word*, from which the other cases or tenses are deduced, has so far made good its ground as no longer to stand in need of defence or apology. That the nominative case is as much a *formed word* as the accusative or genitive, that is, made like the other cases by addition of a suffix, or by some equivalent process, from a stem or declinable form called in this Grammar the *Crude Form*,* and that the present tense of a verb is also very generally made in like manner from a verbal stem; that the various cases and tenses are easily made from the stem or crude form, but only by most artificial and sometimes grotesque devices from the nominative case and present tense respectively; that the otherwise perplexing diversities of declension and conjugation are thus simply explained, regard being paid to the different terminations of the crude form; that analogies, real and not arbitrary, are readily seized and pursued to their legitimate consequences, even by young students, so that an effort of memory is converted into a reasoning process; and that the science of tracing the derivation of

---

* Crude forms are indicated in this Grammar by a hyphen affixed thus, ἵππος being the nom. sing. of the Greek word signifying *horse*, ἵππον, the accus. sing., etc., the crude-form state of the word is written ἱππο-.

one word from another, either in the same or a kindred language, (which, when the nominative case or the present tense is taken for the starting-point, often seems to the beginner little else than a succession of lucky guesses, in which he chiefly admires the ingenuity, perhaps the audacity, of his tutor,) is brought under obvious and easily stated rules, scarcely less rigorous than those which govern mathematical operations;—all this will scarcely be questioned as matter of theory;* and it is believed that the experience of those who have made fair trial of the system would shew that it has succeeded well in practice. Yet while the admirable Latin Grammar of Professor Key has been in use for more than ten years, and though Exercise Books, both Greek and Latin, have been published on this system,† no corresponding Greek Grammar, so far as the writer knows, has yet appeared, although the system is perhaps still better adapted to the Greek than to the Latin language. To supply this deficiency the present Grammar is offered. It has been in a great measure compiled, but with many changes and considerable additions, from the Elementary Grammars of Professor G. Curtius‡ and Dr. H. L. Ahrens,§ which, like many other approved Greek Grammars in Germany, are founded on the system of Crude Forms.

The writer's especial thanks are due to his friends and former Tutors, Professors Key and Malden, of University

---

* On the Crude-form System see the Preface to Professor Key's (larger) Latin Grammar, and articles by the same author in Bell's *English Journal of Education*, Nos. 48 and 49; also an article by Mr. John Robson, B.A., in the *Classical Museum*, vol. iv., p. 388.

† *Constructive Greek Exercises*, and *Constructive Latin Exercises*, by John Robson, B.A., published by Walton and Maberly.

‡ *Griechische Schulgrammatik*, von Dr. G. Curtius. Prag.

§ *Griechische Formenlehre des Homerischen und Attischen Dialektes*, von Dr. H. L. Ahrens. Göttingen.

College, London. In common with all who have made the Greek and Latin languages their special study, he is under great obligations to Professor Key for his critical researches in classical philology, and for the many important and original additions he has made to it as a science. It was, moreover, at Mr. Key's suggestion that the compilation of this book was at first undertaken; much valuable assistance and advice have been received from him during its progress;* and, in many points of form and arrangement, free use has been made of his Latin Grammar: but the references contained in the notes to the Grammar, and the other philological writings of Professor Key, furnish no adequate measure of the extent to which this book is indebted to him.

Had the excellent but brief fragment of a Greek Grammar for Schools, printed many years ago by Professor Malden, been completed, this attempt would never have been made. While the sheets were passing through the press, the writer was favoured with the perusal, in MS., of the earlier portion (on Letter-changes and on the Substantives) of a much more extended Grammar by the same distinguished scholar.† From this source, as well as from sundry criticisms kindly communicated from time to time,‡ some valuable improvements were derived; and very frequently, when the writer found the methods he had adopted corroborated by Mr. Malden's MS., he was reminded how much of what was most accurate

---

* Particularly in the §§ on Letter-changes, and on the laws of Verbal formations. Many of the illustrations given in the foot-notes are founded on suggestions from Prof. Key.

† "Ex pede Herculem."—It is impossible not to express a hope that this Grammar may be in due time completed: it would leave little to be desired in this department of Greek learning.

‡ Particularly on some portions of the detailed conjugation of γράφ-, §§ 353 etc. The rules in §§ 115—120 are principally taken with the author's leave, from the fragment mentioned in the text.

in his knowledge of the Greek language was due, directly or indirectly, to the Professor of Greek in University College.

It is intended shortly to publish a brief Syntax, with chapters on the Dialectical Varieties, and on Accents.*

OWENS COLLEGE, MANCHESTER,
May 15, 1857.

---

* The marks of accent are not printed in the body of this Grammar, except in a very few instances to distinguish between identical forms. Until the laws which govern them are understood they are of little use to the learner, and by their omission space is gained for marking the quantity of all doubtful vowels,—a matter, it is believed, of much greater importance to a beginner.

GREEK GRAMMAR.

INTRODUCTION.

1. THE Greek language was spoken by the ancient Hellenes (Ἕλληνες), the inhabitants of Greece, its islands, and colonies. It is akin to the Sanscrit, Persian, and Latin languages, and to those of the Slavonic, the Lithuanian, the German, and the Celtic nations, etc. All these are sister tongues, and together form the Indo-Germanic family of languages.

2. The Greek people was divided at an early period into tribes, each of which spoke a distinct dialect. The principal dialects of the Greek language are the Æolic, the Doric, and the Ionic.

3. The Ionic dialect was spoken by the Ionian Greeks in Attica, in many islands, and in the Ionian colonies in Asia Minor. Of all the dialects it was the first which was cultivated in poetry. It gave rise to three distinct but closely related dialects, viz.:—

a. The *old Ionic*, or *Epic*, dialect, which is preserved in the poems of Homer, Hesiod, and their successors.

b. The *new Ionic* dialect, known to us principally from the History of Herodotus.

c. The *Attic* dialect, in which were written the numerous works in poetry and prose which Athens produced in her prime. The principal writers of the Attic dialect are the tragic poets Æschylus, Sophocles, and Euripides; the comic poet Aristophanes; the historians Thucydides and Xenophon; the philosopher Plato; and the great orators Lysias, Demosthenes, and Æschines.

Through the pre-eminence of Athens in Greece, and the excellence of the Athenian literature, the Attic became the principal dialect: it has since been made the acknowledged standard of the language; and when *Greek* simply is spoken of, *Attic* Greek is commonly meant.

4. Varieties of the *Æolic* dialect were spoken by the Æolians in Asia Minor, Bœotia, and Thessaly. The poet Alcæus, and the poetess Sappho, in the island of Lesbos, wrote in the Æolic dialect.

5. The *Doric* dialect was spoken by the Dorians in North Greece, Peloponnesus, and Crete, and in the numerous Dorian colonies, especially in Sicily and Lower Italy. Doric is the dialect of the lyric poet Pindar and of the bucolic poet Theocritus. The choral odes of the Attic tragedians also contain individual Doric forms.

6. When Athens had ceased to be the leading city of Greece, the Attic dialect still continued to be the speech of all cultivated Greeks. It soon began, however, to fall away from its ancient purity; and from the third century before Christ, the *common* dialect (ἡ κοινη διαλεκτος) was distinguished from the older Attic.

7. Mid-way between the older Attic and the common dialect stands the great philosopher Aristotle. Among the later authors the most important are the historians Polybius, Plutarch, Arrian, and Dio Cassius; the geographer Strabo; and the rhetoricians Dionysius of Halicarnassus, and Lucian.

ACCIDENCE.

8. The letters of the Greek alphabet are as follows:—

Large letters.	Small letters.	Name.	Pronunciation.
A	α	Alpha	a (short or long,
B	β ϐ	Beta	b.
Γ	γ ϝ	Gamma	g (as in *gun*).
Δ	δ	Delta	d.
E	ε	E psilon	e (short).
Ϝ	ϝ	Vau	w.
Z	ζ ς	Zeta	(z).
H	η	Eta	e (long).
Θ	θ ϑ	Theta	th (as in *thin*).
I	ι	Iota	i (short or long)
K	κ	Kappa	k.
Λ	λ	Lambda	l.

Large letters.	Small letters.	Name.	Pronunciation.
Μ	μ	Mu	m.
Ν	ν	Nu	n.
Ξ	ξ	Xi	x.
Ο	ο	O micron	o (short).
Π	π ϖ	Pi	p.
Ϙ		Koppa	k (before o).
Ρ	ρ	Rho	r.
Σ	σ ς	Sigma	s (as in *sun*).
Τ	τ ϟ	Tau	t.
Υ	υ	U psilon	u (short or long).
Φ	φ	Phi	ph or f.
Χ	χ	Chi	ch (as in German).
Ψ	ψ	Psi	ps.
Ω	ω	O mĕga	o (long).

9. The characters of the Greek alphabet do not differ materially from those of the Latin, or of modern languages. All are derived from the Phœnician alphabet.

10. Γ γ before the gutturals γ, κ, χ, ξ, was pronounced as *n* in *long*: hence in Latin words derived from the Greek *n* is substituted for it. Τεγγω was pronounced *tengo*; Αγχῑσης, *Anchises*; φορμιγξ, *phorminx*.

11. The letter *vau*, Ϝ ϝ (called also, from its shape, *digamma*), was entirely rejected in Ionic and Attic. It has even disappeared from the manuscripts of the Homeric poems; though it is plain, from metrical considerations, that when those poems were composed, the letter had not yet become obsolete, at least in pronunciation. Its existence is, besides, sufficiently attested by ancient inscriptions. For these reasons, and from its use in explaining the inflections of words, and the connection of the Greek with kindred languages,* *vau* has been restored to its place in the alphabet.

12. The most ancient Greek seems to have possessed a consonantal ι, equivalent to the English *y* (consonant). Though this letter has disappeared from the classical Greek, traces of it are

---

* Compare, for instance, the Greek words οινος, ἰδειν, ωον (i. e. Ϝοινος, Ϝιδειν, ωϜον), with the Latin *vinum*, *vĭdēre*, *ŏvum*; and εργον (Ϝεργον) with the English *work*, and German *Werk*.

found in the changes arising out of its combination with the several consonants.*

13. The precise sound of ζ has been lost. It is very commonly pronounced as *ds* or *dz;* yet in many forms it is more accurately represented by *sd,* or perhaps by the sounds heard in both parts of *judge.* Hence it occupies the same place in the alphabet as our *g,* which before *i* and *e* often has this sound.

14. Ϙ was used only before *o*: as, Ϙορινθος, Συρᾱϙοσιοι, on coins, for Κορινθος, Συρᾱκοσιοι. Hence its name *koppa,* as opposed to *kappa,* which was once used only before *a,*† as was the case always with the Latin *k*—*kalumnia, Karthago, kalendæ;* while the Latin *q* was used only before *u,* which in the old Latin alphabet represented the Greek *o.* Observe, also, that the Latin *q* (Q) occupies the same place in the Latin alphabet as Ϙ in the Greek.

15. The character σ is used at the beginning and in the middle of words, ς at the end: thus, σῠν, σειω, ησᾰν; but πονος, κερᾰς. In compound words ς is sometimes used at the end of the first element of the compound: as, προς-ερχομαι, δυς-βᾰτος.

16. Υ υ was probably pronounced nearly as the French *u* or German *ü:* τυπτω as *tüptō,* approaching *typtō.*

17. In addition to the letters already given, the Greek language possesses the character ' (*spiritus asper,* the *aspirate* or rough breathing), which is pronounced like the English *h,* and is written over the vowel to which it belongs: thus, ἑξ is pronounced *hex;* Ἑκτωρ, *Hector.* The aspirate is usually written over the second vowel of a diphthong: as, οὑτος, *houtos.* Every initial ρ takes the aspirate; and when double ρ occurs in the middle of a word, ' is sometimes placed over the second: thus, ῥαψῳδος, *rhapsōdus;* Πυρρος, *Pyrrhus.* With this exception, ' is only found at the beginning of words.

18. The sign, ' (*spiritus lenis,* the smooth breathing), is usually placed over all initial vowels and diphthongs which do not take

---

* It is plain, however, that the so-called consonantal ι, υ, and *w* (ϝ), are merely the vowels *i* (as in French) and *u* (*oo*) uttered with great rapidity.

† An ancient inscription contains the word ⊦ΥϘΟΔΟRΚΑΣ, *i. e.* Αυϙοδορκας, thus exhibiting *kappa* and *koppa* in one and the same word before *a* and *o* respectively (Rose, Inscr. Gr. Tab. viii.).

'; but as this sign only denotes the absence of the rough breathing, it has not been thought necessary to use it in this grammar.

19. The sign ', at the end of a word, signifies that a vowel or diphthong has been thrown away: thus, πάρ' ἐκείνῳ, for πάρα ἐκείνῳ, *by the side of yonder man;* ἐπ' ἀριστερᾷ, for ἐπὶ ἀριστερᾷ, *on the left hand.* The sign ', when so used, is called the *apostrophe*.

20. The same sign is employed to signify that a *crasis* (κρᾶσις, *mixing*), or contraction, has taken place of two words into one: thus, τοὔνομᾰ, for τὸ ὄνομᾰ; κἀγᾰθός, for καὶ ἀγᾰθός. In this case, the letters are written close together.

21. The mark ˉ over a vowel denotes that that vowel is long; ˘, that it is short; ⁓, that it is common, *i.e.* variably long or short. But, as the length of the vowels *e* and *o* is already denoted by the character (ε or η, ο or ω), the signs of quantity are only used with *a*, *ι*, and *v*.

22. For the division of sentences and periods, the *comma* and *full stop* are employed in Greek. If the point is placed above the line, it is equivalent to our colon or semicolon: as. ἑσπέρα ἦν· τότε ἦλθεν ἄγγελος, *it was evening; then came a messenger.* The sign of interrogation was ;: as, τί εἶπας; *what did you say?*

OF SOUNDS AND LETTER-CHANGES.

23. The natural order of the vowels has been ascertained to be ι, ε, α, ο, υ, pronounced as on the continent. The three intermediate vowels, ε, α, ο, which are nearly akin, are sometimes called the *strong*, and the extreme vowels, ι, υ, as partaking in some degree of the nature of consonants (§ 12, *n.*), the *weak* vowels.

24. The consonants are divided, accordingly as they are or are not audible without the aid of a vowel, into *mutes* and *semivowels*.

25. The mutes are classified, according to the part of the mouth by which they are produced, into *throat-sounds* (gutturals), *teeth-sounds* (dentals), and *lip-sounds* (labials). They are again distinguished, according to the strength with which they are uttered, as *hard* (tenues), *soft* (mediæ), and *aspirated* (aspiratæ).

	Hard (tenues).	Soft (mediæ).	Aspirated (aspiratæ).	
Throat-sounds (gutturals)	κ	γ	χ	k-sounds.
Teeth-sounds (dentals)	τ	δ	θ	t-sounds.
Lip-sounds (labials)	π	β	φ	p-sounds.

26. The semivowels are ρ, λ, γ (nasal), ν, μ, σ, and ϝ. The three nasal sounds, γ (nasal), ν, μ, correspond to the three classes of mutes, guttural, dental, and labial*: σ and ϝ are dental and labial *spirants*, and the consonant-ι (y) would have been the corresponding guttural: ρ, λ, μ, ν, are sometimes called *liquids*, and σ the *sibilant*.

27. From the union of σ with certain of the mutes, arise the double consonants, ψ, ξ, ζ: ψ is only a shorter symbol for πσ or φσ, ξ for κσ or χσ, ζ for the union of δ with a spirant (σ or consonant-ι).† But ξ is not written for κσ in compounds of the preposition ἐκ: as, ἐκσωζω, *I rescue;* not ἐξωζω.

28. *Vowels.*—The strong (intermediate) vowels followed by either of the weak (extreme) vowels form diphthongs: thus, ε-ῠ becomes ευ, *well;* πα-ῐδ- becomes παιδ-, *boy;* γενε-ῐ becomes γενει, *to the race.* The diphthongs are as follows: ει, ῃ, αι, ᾳ, οι, ῳ, ευ, ηυ, αυ, ου. In diphthongs compounded of η, ᾱ, or ω, and ι, the ι was not at all, or but slightly, audible, and hence in our editions of Greek authors it is usually written underneath the long vowels (ῃ, ᾳ, ῳ; *iota subscript*).

29. The Greek diphthongs were probably formed by the rapid succession of the several sounds. In England they are generally pronounced as the same combinations of letters would be pronounced in English.

30. If two vowels which usually form a diphthong are to be pronounced separately, the sign of *diæresis* (¨, διαιρεσῖς, *separation*) is placed over the latter: thus, παϊδ-, *boy*, is pronounced *pa-id;* ἀϋπνο-, *sleepless*, *a-upno-*.

31. The (so-called) diphthong υι arises from the union of υ with the consonant-ι; hence it is found only before vowels, and

---

* Hence the combinations γκ, γγ, etc., ντ, νδ, etc., and μπ, etc., are very frequent: αμπελος, αμφι, αγκῦρᾰ, αγγελος, αντι, ανδρος; ampelos, amphi, ankūra, angelos, anti, andros.

† Compare *Jupiter* for *Diu-piter, diurnal* and *journal*, etc.

should be pronounced *u-y*: as, μυια (moo-ya), *a fly;* υἱος, (hoo-yos), *a son.* Compare *musca* (French, *mouche*), and *filius* (Spanish, *hijo*.)

32. The (weak) vowels, ι, υ, before ε, η, α, ο, ω, generally remain unchanged, each vowel retaining its separate sound: as, σοφι-α-, *wisdom;* λυ-ω, *I loosen;* ὑ-ει, *it rains.*

33. Vowels identical with, or akin to, each other, are rarely allowed to stand together. To prevent their juxtaposition, contraction is resorted to. The following rules are observed:—

I. In the contraction of like vowels,

αα	becomes ᾱ:	thus γεραᾰ becomes	γερᾱ.
εε	ει	αιτεε	αιτει.
εη	η	αιτεητε	αιτητε.
εει	ει	αιτεει	αιτει.
ιι	ῑ	Χιιος	Χῑος.
οο	ου	πλοος	πλους.
οω	ω	ζηλοω	ζηλω.
οοι	οι	ζηλοοις	ζηλοις.
οου	ου	πλοου	πλου

II. In the contraction of unlike vowels,

a. ο prevails over α or ε.

αο	becomes ω:	thus τῑμαομεν becomes	τῑμωμεν.
αω	ω	τῑμαω	τῑμω.
αοι	ῳ	αοιδη	ῳδη.
αου	ω	τῑμαου	τῑμω.
οα	ω*	αιδοᾰ	αιδω.
εο	ου	γενεος	γενους.
εω	ω	φιλεω	φιλω.
εοι	οι	χρῡσεοι	χρῡσοι.
εου	ου	φιλεου	φιλου.
οε	ου	ζηλοε	ζηλου.
οη	ω	ζηλοητε	ζηλωτε.
οει	οι	ζηλοεις	ζηλοις.
οη	οι	ζηλοης	ζηλοις.

* But in crasis, οα becomes ᾱ: thus,
        ὁ ἀνηρ   becomes 'ᾱνηρ.
        αυτο- 'ᾱδης   αυθᾱδης.

In Ionic Greek, however, ω appears: as, ὠνηρ, ἱππωναξ, from ἱππο-αναξ.

OF SOUNDS AND LETTER-CHANGES.

b. When *a* comes into contact with ε (η), the vowel which precedes preponderates.

αε	becomes	ᾱ :	thus αεκων	becomes	ἄκων.
αη		ᾱ	τῑμαητε		τῑμᾶτε.
αει		ᾳ	αειδω		ᾳδω.
αῃ		ᾳ	τῑμαῃς		τῑμᾳς.
εα		η*	κεἄρ		κηρ.
εαι		ῃ	λυεαι		λυῃ.
ηαι		ῃ	λυηαι		λυῃ.

In the contraction of εαι, however, ει is sometimes found for ῃ : thus, λυεαι is contracted into λυει as well as λυῃ. Similarly, αικης is written as the contracted form of αεικης, *unseemly,* not ᾳκης.

34. The short vowel of a root is often lengthened, either in the inflection and derivation of words, or in compensation for the loss of a dropped consonant.

I. In the inflection and derivation of words,

ᾰ generally	becomes	η :	thus τῑμα-, *honour,*	fut. tense	τῑμησ-.
sometimes		αι	φᾰν-, *shew,*	pres. impf.	φαιν-.
ε generally		η	αιτε-, *ask,*	fut.	αιτησ-.
sometimes		ει	σπερ-, *sow,*	pres. impf.	σπειρ-.
ο always		ω	ζηλο-, *envy,*	fut.	ζηλωσ-.
ῐ either		ῑ	κρῐν-, *judge,*	pres. impf.	κρῑν-.
or		ει	λῐπ-, *leave,*	pres. impf.	λειπ-
ῠ either		ῡ	λυ-, *loosen,*	fut.	λῡσ-.
or		ευ	φῠγ-, *flee,*	pres. impf.	φευγ-.†

But after ε, ι, or ρ, ᾰ is lengthened into ᾱ, instead of η : as, εα-, *permit,* fut. εᾱσ- ; ιᾱ-, *heal,* ιᾱτρο-, *physician ;* ὁρα-, *see,* ὁρᾱ-μᾰτ-, *spectacle.* Generally, the Attic dialect avoids the combinations εη, ιη, ρη ; employing, instead, εᾱ, ιᾱ, and ρᾱ.

II. When the short vowel is lengthened in compensation for the loss of a consonant, ᾰ is for the most part changed into ᾱ even when not preceded by ε, ι, or ρ : thus, from παντ-, *all,* is made N. S. πᾱς for παντς ; ε frequently becomes ει, not η : as,

---

* But in the plurals of neuters of the second declension, εᾰ becomes ᾱ: οστεᾰ=οστᾱ, χρῡσεᾰ=χρῡσᾱ. Also, if ε or ι precedes, εα regularly becomes ᾱ, not η : as, κλεεᾰ=κλεᾱ, ὑγιεᾰ=ὑγιᾱ; but ὑγιη is also found.

† See, however, § 45 *d.* on the consonant-ι.

εἰμί, *I am*, for ἐσ-μι ; ο frequently becomes ου: as, ὀδούς fo. ὀδοντς, N. S. from ὀδοντ-, *tooth ;* ῐ and ῠ always become ῑ and ῡ.

35. The three short strong vowels, ε, ᾰ, ο, are often interchanged in one and the same root. In this case, ε must usually be regarded as the original vowel: thus, τρεπ-, *turn,* ἐτράπον, *I turned,* τροπο-, *a turning ;* γενεσ-, *a race,* N. S. γενος (compare, in Latin, *gener-is* with the N. S. *genus)* ; φλεγ-, *burn,* φλογ-, *a flame.* Sometimes η becomes ω : as, ἄρηγ-, *assist,* ἄρωγο-, *helper.*

36. *Consonants.*— Consonants are subject, on their concurrence, to yet greater restrictions and changes than vowels.

A guttural or labial mute cannot precede a dental mute, except it be of the same order. Thus the allowable combinations are κτ, πτ, γδ, βδ, χθ, φθ ; and if, through inflection or derivation, a mute of a different order is brought before the dental, the former must be assimilated to the latter. Thus, from the roots

πλεκ-, *twist,*   κλεπ-, *steal,*   γραφ-, *scratch, write,*

with the adverbial suffix -δην, are formed the adverbs

πλεγδην,   κλεβδην,   γραβδην,

for πλεκδην, etc. ; from

λεγ-, *say,*   διωκ-, *pursue,*   βλαβ-, *hurt.*

with the suffix -θηναι, of the infin. pas. 1 aor., are formed

λεχθηναι,   διωχθηναι,   βλαφθηναι,

for λεγθηναι, etc. ; and from

δεχ-, *receive,*   τρῐβ-, *rub,*   γράφ-, *write,*

with the suffix -το, are formed the verbal adjectives

δεκτο-,   τριπτο-,   γραπτο-.

Compare, in Latin, the participles *scripto-, tracto-, acto-,* from *scrib-, trah-, ag-.*

But the preposition ἐκ, *out, from,* remains unchanged in all combinations : as, ἐκθεσι-, *a putting forth ;* ἐκδοτο-, *betrayed ;* not ἐχθεσι-, ἐγδοτο-.

37. Dental mutes before dental mutes pass into the semivowel σ : thus,

from ἀνῠτ-, *accomplish,* is derived ἄνυστο-, for ανυττο, *accomplished.*
from ᾳδ-, *sing,*   ᾳστεο-, for ᾳδτεο-, *canendo-.*
from πειθ-, *persuade,*   πεισθηναι, for πειθθηναι, *to be persuaded.*

Similarly, the dental liquid, ν, sometimes passes into σ before a dental: as, μιαστορ-, *one who pollutes*, from μιαν-, *pollute* (see § 42).

38. Before μ, any guttural becomes γ, any dental (or ν) becomes σ, any labial becomes μ: thus,

From διωκ-, *pursue*   is derived διωγμο-, *pursuit*.
βρεχ-, *make wet*,   βεβρεγμαι, *I am wetted*.
ἰδ-, *know*,   ισμεν, *we know*.
πειθ-, *persuade*,   πεπεισμενο-, *persuaded*.
φᾰν-, *shew*,   φασμᾰτ-, *an apparition*.
κοπ-, *cut, beat*,   κομμο-, *a beating*.
βλᾰβ-, *hurt*,   βεβλαμμαι, *I am hurt*.
γρᾰφ-, *write*,   γραμμᾰτ-, *a letter*.

Sometimes, however, gutturals and dentals remain unchanged before μ: as, ακμα-, *point, edge;* ἀριθμο-, *number;* and in the older language ιδμεν, *we know;* αφραδμον-, *senseless;* ορχηθμυ- *dancing*, occur against ισμεν, αφρασμον-, ορχησμο-.

The preposition εκ is not changed before μ: as, εκμαθ-, *learn thoroughly*.

39. Gutturals and labials followed by σ:—

κσ ⎫
γσ ⎬ all become ξ
χσ ⎭

πσ ⎫
βσ ⎬ all become ψ:
φσ ⎭

thus, σ being the future tense suffix,

From ἀγ-, *lead*,   is formed αξ-, for αγσ-, *will lead*.
δεχ-, *receive*,   δεξ-, for δεχσ-, *will receive*.
τρῐβ-, *rub*,   τριψ-, for τριβσ-, *will rub*.
γρᾰφ-, *write*,   γραψ-, for γραφσ-, *will write*.

Compare the Latin *rexi* and *scripsi*, from *reg-* and *scrib-*.

40. Before σ, the dental mutes are dropped without compensation.* The dental liquid ν, before σ, is dropped with compensa-

---

* But in the older Greek a dental before σ was often not dropped, but assimilated to it, producing σσ: hence such forms, so frequent in Homer, as the 1 aorists εφρασσατο, εκομισσε (in later Greek, εφρᾰσατο, εκομῐσε), from the C. F. φρᾰδ-, *tell*, and κομῐδ-, *carry;* and ποσσί (i. e. ποδ-σί, in later Greek ποσί), dat. plur. from ποδ-, *foot*. Similarly, in such forms as ορεσ-σί, Epic dat. plur. of ορεσ-, *mountain*, σ of the C. F.

OF SOUNDS AND LETTER-CHANGES.

tion in a final syllable, without compensation in the middle of a word, unless σ has been substituted for τ. In like manner, ν is lost before ζ. Thus,

From ἀνῠτ-, *accomplish*, is formed ἄνῠσι-, for ἄνυτσι-, *accomplishment*.

φρᾰδ-, *tell*,	ἐφρᾰσᾰ, for ἐφραδσᾰ, *I told*.
κόρῠθ-, *helmet*,	κόρῠσἴ, for κόρυθσἴ, dat. plur.
μελᾰν-, *black*,	μελᾱς, for μελανς, nom. sing.
δαιμον-, *deity, destiny*,	δαιμόσἴ, for δαιμονσἴ, dat. plur.
λυ-, *loosen*,	λυουσἴ, for λυονσἴ (from λυοντι), *they loosen*.
σύν, *together*, and	
ζῠγο-, *yoke*,	συζῠγο-, for συνζῠγο-, *yoked together*.

The preposition ἐν in compounds remains unchanged before σ. So ν of παν-, *all*, and πᾰλιν, *back*, before σ, either remains unchanged, or is assimilated to the following letter: as, πανσοφο-, *all-wise*; πᾰλισσῡτο-, *rushing backward*. The ν of σύν, *with*, which is dropped before ζ or before σ followed by a consonant, is assimilated before simple σ: thus, συ-ζῠγο-, *yoked together*; συ-στρᾰ-τιωτα-, *fellow-soldier*; but συσ-σῑτο-, *messmate*.

41. In like manner, ντ, νδ, νθ, are dropped before σ; but the preceding vowel is always lengthened in compensation: thus,

γῐγαντ-, *giant*,	dat. plur.	γῐγᾱσἴ, for γῐγαντσἴ.
τίθεντ-, *placing*,	nom. sing.	τίθεις, for τίθεντς.
γεροντ-, *old man*,	dat. plur.	γερουσἴ, for γεροντσἴ.
σπενδ-, *pour libation*,	fut. indic.	σπεισ-, for σπενδσ-.
πενθ-, *suffer*,	fut. indic.	πεισ-, for πενθσ-.

42. N remains (generally) unchanged before dental mutes, becomes γ (nasal) before gutturals, and μ before labials. Before liquid consonants, ν is assimilated to the liquid. Thus,

συνθεσἴ-, *a placing together*,	
συγκᾰλε-, *call together*,	for συνκᾰλε-.
εμπειρο-, *experienced*,	for ενπειρο-.

---

is retained, whereas in later Greek (ορε-σἴ), it disappears, as a dental (spirant), before σ of the case-ending. Compare, also, τελεσ-σω and ετελεσ-σᾰ, fut. and 1 aor. of τελεσ-, *fulfil*, with the later τελε-σω and ετελε-σᾰ.

ἐλλῖπεσ-, *defective*, for ἐνλῖπεσ-.
συρρᾰφ-, *stitch together*, for συνρᾰφ-.
ἐμμεν-, *abide in*, for ἐνμεν-.

But the preposition ἐν remains unchanged before ρ: as, ἐυρυθμο-, *in measure*, not ἐρρυθμο-.

For euphony—that is, facility of pronunciation—δ is inserted between ν and ρ in the declension of ἄνερ-, *man*; G. S. ανδρος, for αν'ρος. Similarly, β is inserted between μ and ρ in μεσημβρια-, for μεσημ'ρια-, *midday*, from μεσο-, *mid*, and ἡμερα-, *day*.*

43. A hard mute at the end of a word, if the word following begin with the rough breathing, is changed into the corresponding aspirate; if two hard mutes come together both are changed: thus,

οὐχ ὁρῶ, for ουκ ὁρῶ, *I do not see*.
ἀφ' ἑστιᾶς, for ἄπ' (ἄπο) ἑστιᾶς, *from the hearth*.
κᾰθ' ἡμερᾰν, for κᾰτ' (κᾰτᾰ) ἡμερᾰν, *day by day*.
νυχθ' ὁλην, for νυκτ' (νυκτᾰ) ὁλην, *the whole night long*.

The same change takes place in compound words: thus,

From δεκᾰ, *ten*, and ἡμερα-, *day*, is derived δεχημερο-, *lasting ten days*.
From αντῐ, *in place of*, and 'ὑπᾰτο-, *consul*, is derived ανθῠπᾰτο-, *proconsul*.

It will be observed that in these cases the words are intimately connected.

44. If two consecutive syllables of the same word both properly begin with an aspirate, the first aspirate is, in certain cases, changed into the corresponding *tenuis* or hard consonant. If the second aspirate disappears in any of the forms, the first is restored. This change takes place,

a. If both aspirates originally belong to the root: thus,

θρῐχ-, *hair of the head*, G. S. τρῐχος, for θρῐχος; but N. S. θρῐξ.
θρεφ-, *nourish*, τρεφω, *I nourish*; but θρεψω, *I will nourish*.
ἐχ-, *hold, have*, εχω, *I have* (without the aspirate); but ἑξω, *I shall have*.

---

* Compare the French *cendre, tendre, chambre, nombre*, etc., with the Latin *cinis, tener, camera, numerus*; and *combler, humble, dissembler* with *cumulare, humilis*, and *dissimulare*.

b. In the reduplicated forms of verbs: thus,
χωρε-, *go*, perfect tense κεχωρη-, for χεχωρη-.
φυ-, *grow*, perf. πεφῡ-, for φεφῡ-.
c. In the 1 aor. indic. pass. of θε-, *place*, and θυ-, *sacrifice*,—ετεθε- and ετῠθε-, for εθεθε- and εθῠθε-; so, αμπεχ-, for αμφεχ-, *put round*, from αμφί, *round*, and ἐχ-. In the 2 p. sing. of the 1 aor. imper. pass., the second aspirate is changed: as
σωθητί, for σωθηθί, *save thyself*.

Otherwise, when the second aspirate does not belong to the same root as the first, but is due to inflection or composition, both are suffered to remain: thus, from θελγ-, *soothe*, and -θε, the suffix of the 1 aor. pas., is formed εθελχθε-, *was soothed*, not ετελχθε-; from Κορινθο-, *Corinth*, and the adverbial ending -θί, is formed Κορινθοθί, *at Corinth*; and from αμφί, *round*, and χε-, *pour*, αμφίχε-, *pour round*.

45. *Consonant-ι*.—It has been said (§ 12), that, though this letter has disappeared from the classical Greek, having passed into the vowel ι, traces of it remain in certain forms arising out of its combination with the several consonants. The most important of the changes which seem to admit of explanation from this principle, are as follows :—

a. From any guttural followed by ι cons., arises σσ (late Attic ττ) : thus,

From μᾱκ-, *long*,   is formed μασσον-, for μάκιον, *longer*.
    τᾰγ-, *arrange*,   τασσω, for τάγιω, *I arrange*.
    ἐλᾰχ-, *little*,   ελασσον-, for ελάχιον, *less*.

σσ arises, less frequently, from dentals with ι cons.: thus,

From root of κρᾰτ-εσ-, *strength*, is formed κρεισσον-, *stronger*.
    λῐτ-, *pray*, is formed λισσομαι, *I pray*.

b. From δ with ι cons. arises ζ: thus,

From φρᾰδ-, *tell*, is formed φραζω, for φράδιω, *I tell*.
    ΔιϜ- or ΔιεϜ-, *Jupiter*, is formed Ζευς, for Διευς, N. S.

ζ arises, less frequently, from γ with ι cons.: thus,

From μεγ-, *great*, is formed μεζον- (Ion.), for μεγιον, *greater*
    κρᾰγ-, *cry*,   κραζω, for κράγιω, *I cry*.

c. From λ with ι cons. arises λλ: thus,

From μᾰλ-, *much*, is formed μαλλον, for μαλιον, *more*.
    ἅλ-, *leap*,   ἁλλομαι, for ἁλιομαι, *I leap*.

d. If ν or ρ precedes the ι cons., the liquid is transposed, and a diphthong or long vowel results: thus,

From φᾰν-, *shew*, is formed φαινω, for φᾰνιω, *I shew*.
[ἄμεν-], ἄμεινον-, for ἄμενιον-, *better*.
[χερ-], χειρον-, for χεριον-, *worse*.*

46. The liquids, especially ρ and λ, are often transposed: †
thus,

From C. F. θορ-, *leap*, are derived ἐθορον, *I leaped*, and θρωσ-κω, *I leap*.
Βᾰλ-, *throw*, ἐβᾰλον, *I threw*, and βεβλη-κᾰ, *I have thrown*.
θᾰν-, *die*, ἐθᾰνον, *I died*, and τεθνηκᾰ, *I am dead*.
τεμ-, *cut*, τεμ-νω, *I cut*, and τμησῐ-, *the act of cutting*.

Hence also are to be explained the double forms, κρᾰτεσ- and καρτεσ-, *strength*; καρδια- and κρᾰδια-, *heart*, etc.

47. Certain consonants are sometimes softened. Thus,

a. τ before ι, especially when another vowel follows, is very frequently softened into σ: hence, from ἀναισθητο-, *unfeeling*, is derived ἀναισθησια-, *want of feeling*, for ἀναισθητια- ; φησῐ, *he says*, is used for φητῐ; and φᾱσῐ, *they say*, τρεπουσῐ, *they turn*, (i. e. φανσῐ, τρεπονσῐ, § 40), for φαντῐ, τρεποντῐ.

b. Initial σ is softened to the rough breathing: as, ὑ-, *hog*, as well as συ-; ἱστα-, *place*, for σιστα-. Compare the Latin *su-*, *sist-*, and such forms as *sex, septem, serp-*, with ἑξ, ἑπτᾰ, ἑρπ-.

48. Σ standing between two consonants is always struck out: thus, the suffix of the perf. infin. pass. being -σθαι, from τῠπ-, *strike*, is derived τετυφθαι, for τετυπσθαι. In like manner, σ be-

---

* Compare such forms as μασσον-, μᾱκιστο-, and θασσον-, τᾰχιστο- (from τᾰχ-υ-, *swift*), with ἡδῑον-, ἡδιστο-, from ἡδ-υ-, *sweet*; and words like μαλλον, ἀλλομαι, αλλο-, *other*, φυλλο-, *leaf*, with the Latin *melius, salio, alio-, folio-*; χειρον- is χερειον- in Epic Greek.

† Such, under the name of *metathesis*, is the explanation usually given. It has, however, been rendered probable that many of the forms in question are the result of compression, rather than of transposal of the liquid; that τεθνηκᾰ, for instance, is a contraction from τεθᾰνηκᾰ (compare θᾰνᾰτο-, *death*); that θαρσεσ- and θρᾰσεσ-, *daring*, are both due to a fuller form, θαρασεσ-, etc. See T. H. Key, *Transactions of the Philological Society*, vol. vii. p. 211.

tween two vowels is very frequently rejected, especially if the former vowel is short: thus,

From λεγ-, *say*, 2 sing. pres. indic. pass. is λεγεαι (Att. λεγῃ), for λεγεσαι.

γενεσ-, *race*, gen. sing. is γενεος (Att. γενους), for γενεσος.

σ before ν is sometimes assimilated to it: thus, from φαεσ-, *light*, with the adj. termination -νο, is made φαεννο-, for φαεσ-νο-, *shining*.

49. A short vowel is sometimes rejected from between two consonants (*syncope*), especially in the second of several short syllables: thus,

From πετ-, *fly*,   is formed επτομην, for επετομην, *I flew*.

γεν-, *become*,   γιγνομαι, for γίγενομαι, *I become*.

50. The liquid ρ is doubled in some derivatives, principally from verbs: thus,

From ῥιφ-, *throw*, is formed ερριψᾰ, for εριψᾰ,* *I threw*.

ῥηγ-, *break*,   αρρηκτο-, for ἄρηκτο-, *unbreakable*.

ῥοδο-, *rose*,   πολυρροδο-, *abounding in roses*.

51. If a word which ends with a vowel is followed by another beginning with a vowel, *hiatus* is produced. Hiatus is often endured in Greek prose: it is, however, frequently avoided, especially when the first word is short and unemphatic; and this is effected in three ways—either by *elision*, or *crasis*, or *synizesis*.

52. Elision, or the rejection of a final vowel, takes place in the case of any short vowel except υ; it is most frequent, however, with the final vowel of prepositions, conjunctions, and adverbs of two syllables: επ' αυτῳ, for επι αυτῳ, *on him;* ουδ' εδῠνᾰτο, for ουδε εδῠνᾰτο, *nor was he able;* αλλ' ηλθεν, for αλλα ηλθεν, *but he came*.

But the prepositions περῐ, *about;* αχρῐ and μεχρῐ, *until;* and the conjunction ὁτῐ, *because*, do not suffer elision in the ordinary writers.

Elision is also used in compound words, but the sign of elision (') is not then written: επερχομαι, for επι-ερχομαι, *I come towards;* but περιερχομαι, *I go round*.

---

* Rather, for εϝριψα, αϝρηκτο-. See § 286, n. So, in such compounds as πολυρροδο-, πολυρριζο-, the existence of an initial consonant may be traced in the Æolic forms βροδρ-, βριζα-, and in the English *wort*, or German *Wurzel*.

53. Crasis (κρᾶσις, *a mixing*), or the blending of the two vowels into one, is for the most part regulated by the rules already given (§ 33) for the contraction of vowels. It is chiefly resorted to after the forms of the article and relative pronoun, the preposition προ, and the conjunction και. The resulting syllable is necessarily long. The sign of crasis is the *coronis* (᾽): τᾱ᾽γᾰθᾰ, for τᾰ ἀγᾰθᾰ, *blessings*; τοὔνομᾰ, for τo ονομᾰ, *the name*; ταὐτο, for το αυτο, *the same*; 'ἇνηρ, for ὁ ἀνηρ, *the man*; θοἰμᾱτιον, for το 'ἱμᾰτιον, *the garment*.

The resulting syllable takes an ι subs. only when an ι belongs to the latter of the two syllables: κᾳ᾽τᾰ, for και ειτᾰ, *and then*; but from και ετῐ, *and likewise*, arises κᾱ᾽τῐ.

54. Sometimes the two vowels are, in pronunciation, drawn together into one long vowel, while no change is made in the writing. This is called synizesis (σὐνιζησῖς, *a sinking into one*); it is most frequent after the pronoun εγω, *I*, and the conjunctions επει, *when*; ἤ, *or*; ἤ; *num?* and μη, *not:* thus, εγω͡ ου, επεί͡ ου, μη͡ αλλοι. The cases of Θεο-, *God*, and genitives like πολεως, *of a city*, were often pronounced with synizesis.

55. No Greek word ends in any other consonant than one of the semivowels ν, ρ, ς (including ξ and ψ). The only exceptions to this rule are the negative ουκ (before consonants ου, before aspirated vowels ουχ), and the preposition εκ (before vowels εξ), which are closely joined in pronunciation to the words which follow them.

If any other consonant than ν, ρ, or ς, would appear at the end of a word, it is usually rejected: thus, μελῐ and σωμᾰ are found in the N. S. for μελῐτ and σωμᾰτ; παι and Αιᾰν in the voc. for παιδ and Αιαντ. But mute dentals are sometimes changed into the kindred semivowel ς: thus we find

> προς, for προτ, from προτῐ, *to.*
> δος, for δοθ, from δοθῐ, imperative of δο-, *give.*
> τερᾰς, for τερᾰτ, N. S. from τερᾰτ-, *portent.*

Sometimes τ final is changed into ν, as in the 3rd singular of verbs, ετυπτεν, *he was striking*, for ετυπτετ (compare ετυπτετο); or into ρ, as ἡπᾰρ, for ἡπᾰτ, N.S., from C.F. ἡπᾰτ-, n. *liver.* Similarly, μ becomes ν: as, ετυπτον, *I was striking*, for ετυπτομ (compare ετυπτομην).

56. Certain words and forms end in a moveable ν. This ν is retained before words beginning with a vowel, to avoid hiatus, and before the longer stops. In poetry it is found before consonants also.* The words and forms which exhibit this moveable ν are,

a. The dative plural in σῐ(ν) : πᾶσῐν ἐδωκᾰ, *I gave to all;* but πᾶσῐ δοκει ούτως ειναι, *it seems to all to be so.*

b. The words εικοσῐ(ν), *twenty,* and περῠσῐ(ν), *last year.*

c. The 3rd person singular in ε(ν): εσωσεν αυτους, *he rescued them;* but εσωσε τους Ἀθηναιους, *he rescued the Athenians.*

d. The 3rd person, both singular and plural, in σῐ(ν) : λεγουσῐν ευ, *they say well;* δεικνῡσῐν εκεισε, *he points in that direction.†*

In the same manner, ούτως, *thus,* εξ (i. e. εκs), *out,* retain their final consonant before a vowel only.

Of the Quantity of Syllables.

57. A syllable is said to be *long by nature,* when it contains a long vowel or a diphthong : 'ῡμεῖς, *ye;* κρῑνῶ, *I decide;* ᾁδῶ, *I sing.* Contracted syllables are obviously long : ᾱκοντ-, for αεκοντ-, *unwilling;* 'ῑρο-, for ιερο-, *sacred.*

58. A syllable is said to be *long by position,* when the vowel is followed by two or more consonants, or by a double consonant : χᾱρμᾰτ-, *joy;* 'ἕξῐ-, *condition;* Κᾱστορ-, *Castor;* ἐν τουτῳ, *meanwhile;* τᾱ κτημᾰτᾱ *the possessions.*

59. If a vowel short by nature stand before a mute consonant followed by ρ, λ, ν, or μ, as the mute and liquid admit of being sounded either separately or together, the syllable may be either long or short : thus, πατρος, *of a father,* may be pronounced either as πᾱτ-ρος, or as πᾰ-τρος ; similarly, τε͞-κνο-, *child;* τῠ͞-φλο-, *blind;* τῐ͞ δρᾱs ; *what doest thou?* Such syllables are said to be *common.‡*

---

* In the more ancient MSS. of the New Testament this ν is also found before consonants, invariably in the 3rd persons of verbs, singular and plural, in -εν and -σῐν, and very frequently in the dat. plural (see Tischendorf, *Proleg. ad Nov. Test. Gr.* p. xxiii.).

† This removeable ν was formerly treated as a suffix foreign to the word, and arbitrarily added to prevent hiatus. Hence the name by which it is generally known in grammars — ν εφελκυστῐκον, or πᾰρᾰγωγῐκον.

‡ Syllables consisting of a short vowel followed by a mute and liquid are almost invariably long in Homer, and (with the exceptions men-

60. The syllable is, however, necessarily long,

a. If the mute and liquid belong to two different words, or to the different elements of a compound word: as, ἐκ νηῶν, *from the ships;* ἐκ-λέγω, *I pick out.*

b. Before the combination of the soft mutes (β, γ, δ) with λ, ν, or μ: as, βῐβλο-, *book;* τᾱγμᾰτ-, *ordinance;* ἐχῐδνα-, *viper;* but ἄγρο-, *land.**

SUBSTANTIVES.

61. In the declension of nouns, substantive or adjective, the Greeks distinguished,

a. Three numbers: the *singular* for one, the *dual* for two, and the *plural* for more than two.

b. Five cases:

The *nominative,* denoting the source of an action, the case of the subject.

The *vocative,*† which is used in addressing persons.

The *accusative,* denoting the place *whither,* the case of the object.

The *genitive,* denoting the place *whence.*

The *dative,* denoting the place *where.*

These cases are formed by the addition of certain terminations, called *suffixes,* to the stem, or *crude form,*‡ of the substantive.

---

tioned in § 60) short in the comic poet Aristophanes: in the tragedians such syllables are used as common, yet more frequently short than long.

* Of the Greek vowels ε, η, ο, ω, the quantity is already expressed in the character: over these, therefore, and over diphthongs, no mark of quantity is placed. One vowel before another, and not forming a diphthong with it, is to be understood as short, unless the contrary is signified.

† The vocative is not, strictly speaking, *a case;* i.e. it expresses no modification of the simple notion conveyed by the word. Hence it has no special suffix. See § 71.

‡ Care must be taken not to confound the crude form with the nominative singular. The crude form is the *invariable,* as the suffix is the *variable,* part of a noun or verb; the former signifying the bare notion conveyed by the word, the latter appended to it for the expression of the various relations of number, place, time, or person. The nomina

c. Two genders, *masculine* and *feminine:* nouns of neither gender are called *neuter*.

62. The gender of nouns is distinguished partly by their meaning, partly by the termination of their crude form.

Names of male persons, of rivers, winds, and months, are masculine.

Names of female persons, of trees, countries, and islands, and of most towns, also of most abstract substantives, are feminine.

Many names of fruits, most diminutives, and all nouns or other parts of speech contemplated as words merely, are neuter.

On the determination of gender by the termination, see §§ 515—518.

63. Neuter nouns are broadly distinguished from masculines and feminines in their declension: they do not admit *s* as the case-ending of the nom. singular; they have no form for the nom. or voc. distinct from that of the accus.; and they have no other suffix for the nom., voc., or accus. plural, than ă.

64. The dual number has but two forms—one for the nominative and accusative, and one for the genitive and dative.

65. Greek nouns are usually divided into three declensions: the *first* consisting of nouns with crude forms ending in *a*; the *second*, of nouns with crude forms ending in *o*; and the *third*, of nouns with crude forms ending in ι, υ, or any consonant. They may, however, be arranged under two principal declensions— the *separable* (or *strong*) declension, and the *inseparable* (or *weak*) declension. In words of the separable declension, (which corresponds to the *third* according to the ordinary arrangement), the case-endings are distinctly marked, and easily separable from the crude form; in the inseparable declension, (which includes the *first* and *second* of the ordinary arrangement), the case-endings are not so distinctly marked, and do not so well admit of separation, as they merge into one syllable with the final vowel of the crude form.

---

tive is itself a case made by inflexion, and generally quite distinct from the crude form: thus, ποιμην is the N. S. of the crude form ποιμεν-, *shepherd*; λογος, the N. S. of λογο-, *word*. See the Preface to Professor Key's (larger) Latin Grammar.

SEPARABLE (THIRD) DECLENSION.

66. This declension consists of nouns whose crude forms end in some consonant (including the semivowel F), or in either of the weak vowels $ι$ or $υ$.

67. The following is a tabular view of the suffixes of the several cases in this declension:—

	Masculines and Feminines.	Neuters.
Singular. *Nominative* *Vocative* *Accusative* *Genitive* *Dative*	ς, or long vowel in compensation no ending ᾰ, or ν ος ῐ	no ending no ending no ending ος ῐ
Dual. *Nom. Voc. Acc.* *Gen. Dat.*	ε οιν	ε οιν
Plural. *Nominative* *Vocative* *Accusative* *Genitive* *Dative*	ες ες ᾰς, or νς, i. e. ˉς ων σῐ(ν)	ᾰ ᾰ ᾰ ων σῐ(ν)

Remarks on the Suffixes.

68. *Nominative Singular.*—The suffix for the N. S. of masculine and feminine nouns is ς. In adding this suffix to crude forms ending in a consonant, attention must be paid to the changes required by the laws of euphony (§§ 23—55).

69. In many words ending in a consonant, from reasons of euphony, ς is not added; in that case, the final vowel of the crude form, if short, is lengthened.

SEPARABLE (THIRD) DECLENSION.

70. Thus, the masc. and fem. nouns ending in a consonant fall into two classes:

  a. Nouns which take the suffix ς in the nom. sing.: as,

Crude Form.	Nom. Sing.
ἁλ-, sea,	ἅλς.
φλεβ-, vein,	φλεψ, for φλεβς.
κορᾰκ-, crow,	κοραξ, for κορακς.
λαμπαδ-, lamp,	λαμπᾰς, for λαμπαδς.
γῐγαντ-, giant,	γῐγᾶς, for γῐγαντς.
δελφῑν-, dolphin,	δελφῑς, for δελφινς.
βοϜ-, ox,	βυυς, for βοϜς.

  b. Nouns which reject the ς in the nom. sing.; but, in compensation, have the final vowel of the crude form lengthened, if it is short (§ 34): as,

C. F.	N. S.
ποιμεν-, shepherd,	ποιμην.
λεοντ-, lion,	λεων.
ῥητορ-, orator,	ῥητωρ.
αιδοσ-, shame,	αιδως.

In the following, the vowel is already long; the crude form, therefore, becomes the nom. case:

C. F.	N. S.
θηρ-, wild beast,	θηρ.
χειμων-, winter,	χειμων.
ἡρωσ-, hero.	ἡρως.

This rejection of ς in the N. S. takes place in all nouns ending in ρ and σ, except μαρτῠρ-, witness, N. S. μαρτῠς, and in most words in ν, including all nouns in οντ, except οδοντ-, a tooth, N. S. οδους.

71. *Vocative Singular.*—The vocative has no suffix. The crude form, therefore, subject to the rules which regulate the termination of Greek words (§ 55), constitutes the vocative in the singular. The nominative is, however, very generally used for the vocative. The true vocative is found,

  a. In words (substantives and adjectives) whose crude forms end in ν, ντ, ρ, and εσ: as,

C. F.	N. S.	V. S.
δαιμον-, deity,	δαιμων,	δαιμον.
γεροντ-, old man,	γερων,	γερον.

There are, however, many exceptions: as, ποιμεν-, *shepherd*, voc. ποιμην, as in the nom. On the other hand, Ἀπολλων-, *Apollo*; Ποσειδων-, *Poseidon*; and σωτηρ-, *saviour*, are found with a short vowel in the voc.—Ἄπολλον, Πόσειδον, σῶτερ. Participles make the voc. the same as the nom.

b. Nouns in ι and υ, including those in ϝ: as,

μαντι-, *seer*,   N. S. μάντις,   V. S. μάντῐ.

In other cases usually, and always in the plural, the nom. is employed as a voc. But from γυναικ-, *woman*, and παιδ-, *boy*, (with a few other words ending in ιδ), we have the regular vocatives, γύναι and παι; ἄνακτ-, *king*, has both ἄναξ and (in early Greek) ἄνᾰ.

72. *Accusative Singular.*—The accus. sing. takes the suffix ν in words whose crude forms end in ι, υ, or ϝ (with the exception of words in εϝ): as,

C. F.	A. S.
πολι-, *city*,	πόλιν.
ναϝ-, *ship*,	νευν.

If the C. F. end in any consonant (except ϝ), or in εϝ, the suffix *a* is preferred: as,

C. F.	A. S.
φλεβ-, *vein*,	φλέβᾰ.
βᾰσῐλεϝ-, *king*,	βᾰσῐλέᾱ.

But some words ending in a t-sound, preceded by ι or υ, take ν in prose, the t-sound being dropped: as,

C. F.	A. S.
ἐρῐδ-, *strife*,	ἔρῐν.
ὀρνῑθ-, *bird*,	ὄρνῐν.

The form in *a* is, however, sometimes found in prose, and that in ν in verse. Monosyllables, and other words in which the accent falls on the last syllable, as in such words the t-sound was not so readily dropped, have only the form in *a*. Thus, ποδ-, m. *foot*, A. S. πόδᾰ; but τρῐποδ-, *three-footed*, A. S. τρῐπόδᾰ and τρίπουν: ἐλπῐδ-, f. *hope*, A.S. ἐλπῐ́δᾰ (not ἐλπῖν, like ἔρῐν for ἐρῐδᾰ); but the compound εὐελπῐδ-, *hopeful*, makes εὔελπιν as well as εὐελπῐ́δᾰ : κλειδ-, *key* (originally κληῐδ-), makes κλειν more frequently than κλειδᾰ.

73. *Dative Plural.* — In adding the suffix σῐ(ν) of the dat. plur. to the crude form, the same rules must be observed as in the formation of the nom. sing. in *s*.

EXAMPLES.

74. A. Nouns whose crude forms end in a consonant.

I. Masc. and fem. nouns in which *s* is added in the nom. sing.*

If the C. F. end in a labial or guttural mute, *s* will combine with the mute to form ψ or ξ.

If the C. F. end in a dental mute, the dental will disappear before *s*.

74*.

Greek C.F. Gender. English.	ἁλ- masc. *salt.*	λαιλᾰπ- fem. *hurricane.*	φλεβ- fem. *vein.*	κᾰτηλῐφ- fem. *upper story.*	κηρῡκ- masc. *herald.*
Singular.					
Nom.	ἅλς	λαιλαψ	φλεψ	κατηλιψ	κηρυξ
Voc.	ἅλς	λαιλαψ	φλεψ	κατηλιψ	κηρυξ
Acc.	ἅλᾰ	λαιλᾰπᾰ	φλεβᾰ	κατηλῐφᾰ	κηρῡκᾰ
Gen.	ἅλος	λαιλᾰπος	φλεβος	κατηλῐφος	κηρῡκος
Dat.	ἅλῐ	λαιλᾰπῐ	φλεβῐ	κατηλῐφῐ	κηρῡκῐ
Dual					
N. V. A.	ἅλε	λαιλᾰπε	φλεβε	κατηλῐφε	κηρῡκε
G. D.	ἅλοιν	λαιλᾰποιν	φλεβοιν	κατηλῐφοιν	κηρῡκοιν
Plural.					
Nom.	ἅλες	λαιλᾰπες	φλεβες	κατηλῐφες	κηρῡκες
Voc.	ἅλες	λαιλᾰπες	φλεβες	κατηλῐφες	κηρῡκες
Acc.	ἅλᾰς	λαιλᾰπᾰς	φλεβᾰς	κατηλῐφᾰς	κηρῡκᾰς
Gen.	ἅλων	λαιλᾰπων	φλεβων	κατηλῐφων	κηρῡκων
Dat.	ἁλσῐ(ν)	λαιλαψῐ(ν)	φλεψῐ(ν)	κατηλιψῐ(ν)	κηρυξῐ(ν)

* For nouns in ϝ-, see § 81.

SUBSTANTIVES.

Greek C.F. Gender. English.	ορτυγ- masc. *quail.*	διωρυχ- fem. *canal.*	χαριτ- fem. *favour.*	παιδ- masc.&fem. *child.*	κορυθ- fem. *helmet.*
Singular.					
Nom.	ορτυξ	διωρυξ	χἄρῐs	παις	κορῠs
Voc.	ορτυξ	διωρυξ	χἄρῐs	παι	κορῠs
Acc.	ορτῠγᾰ	διωρῠχᾰ	χἄρῐτᾰ or χἄρῐν	παιδᾰ	κορῠθᾰ or κορῠν
Gen.	ορτῠγος	διωρῠχος	χἄρῐτος	παιδος	κορῠθος
Dat.	ορτῠγῐ	διωρῠχῐ	χἄρῐτῐ	παιδῐ	κορῠθῐ
Dual.					
N.V.A.	ορτῠγε	διωρῠχε	χἄρῐτε	παιδε	κορῠθε
G.D.	ορτῠγοιν	διωρῠχοιν	χἄρῐτοιν	παιδοιν	κορῠθοιν
Plural.					
Nom.	ορτῠγες	διωρῠχες	χἄρῐτες	παιδες	κορῠθες
Voc.	ορτῠγες	διωρῠχες	χἄρῐτες	παιδες	κορῠθες
Acc.	ορτῠγᾰs	διωρῠχᾰs	χἄρῐτᾰs	παιδᾰs	κορῠθᾰs
Gen.	ορτῠγων	διωρῠχων	χἄρῐτων	παιδων	κορῠθων
Dat.	ορτυξῐ(ν)	διωρυξῐ(ν)	χἄρῐσῐ(ν)	παισῐ(ν)	κορῠσῐ(ν)

Greek C.F. Gender. English.	ἀνακτ- masc. *king.*	οδοντ- masc. *tooth.*	γῐγαντ- masc. *giant.*	ῥῑν- fem. *nose.*	ἑλμινθ- fem. *worm.*
Singular.					
Nom.	ἄναξ	οδους	γῐγᾱs	ῥῑs	ἑλμινs
Voc.	ἄναξ or ἄνᾰ	οδους	γῐγᾰν	ῥῑs	ἑλμινs
Acc.	ἄνακτᾰ	οδοντᾰ	γῐγαντᾰ	ῥῑνᾰ	ἑλμινθᾰ
Gen.	ἄνακτος	οδοντος	γῐγαντος	ῥῑνος	ἑλμινθος
Dat.	ανακτῐ	οδοντῐ	γῐγαντῐ	ῥῑνῐ	ἑλμινθῐ
Dual.					
N.V.A.	ἄνακτε	οδοντε	γῐγαντε	ῥῑνε	ἑλμινθε
G.D.	ἄνακτοιν	οδοντοιν	γῐγαντοιν	ῥῑνοιν	ἑλμινθοιν
Plural.					
Nom.	ἄνακτες	υδοντες	γῐγαντες	ῥῑνες	ἑλμινθες
Voc.	ἄνακτες	οδοντες	γῐγαντες	ῥῑνες	ἑλμινθες
Acc.	ἄνακτᾰs	οδοντᾰs	γῐγαντᾰs	ῥῑνᾰs	ἑλμινθᾰs
Gen.	ἄνακτων	οδοντων	γῐγαντων	ῥῑνων	ἑλμινθων
Dat.	ἀναξί(ν)	οδουσῐ(ν)	γῐγᾱσῐ(ν)	ῥῑσῐ(ν)	ἑλμῑσῐ(ν)

SEPARABLE (THIRD) DECLENSION. 25

75. So are declined γῦπ-, m. *vulture;* Ἀράβ-, m. *an Arab;* φύλακ-, m. *sentinel;* ἀλωπεκ-, f. *fox* (N. ἀλώπηξ); φλογ-, f. *flame;* λάρυγγ-, m. *throat;* ὀνυχ-, m. *nail, claw;* βηχ-, f. *cough;* ὀρθοτητ-, f. *straightness;* γελωτ-, m. *laughter;* λαμπάδ-, f. *lamp;* κρηπῐδ-, f. *basement;* ὀρνῑθ-, m. and f. *bird* (A. ὀρνῑθἄ and ὀρνῑν); νυκτ-, f. *night;* πλᾰκοεντ- and πλᾰκουντ-, m. *a flat cake* (N. πλᾰκοεις and πλᾰκους); Κερᾰσοεντ- and Κερᾰσουντ-, f. *the town Cerasus;* τῑμηεντ- and τῑμηντ-, adj. *prized* (N. τῑμηεις and τῑμης, not τῑμης). Μαρτυρ-, m. *witness,* has N. μαρτῠς, A. μαρτῠρἄ and μαρτῠν, D. pl. μαρτῠσῐν. The monosyllable ποδ-, m. *foot,* has the vowel lengthened in the N. S., πους. Κτεν-, m. *comb,* and ἑν-, m. adj. *one,* which, unlike most words in ν, take ς in the nom., also have the vowel lengthened (§ 40), κτεις, εἱς.

II. Masc. and fem. nouns which reject ς in the nom. sing., and lengthen the final vowel of the crude form if it be short.*

75*.

Greek C.F. Gender. English.	φρεν- fem. heart, breast.	δαιμον- masc. deity, fate.	λεοντ- masc. lion.	ῥητορ- masc. orator.	μητερ- fem. mother.
Singular.					
Nom.	φρην	δαιμων	λεων	ῥητωρ	μητηρ
Voc.	φρην	δαιμον	λεον	ῥητορ	μητερ
Acc.	φρενᾰ	δαιμονᾰ	λεοντᾰ	ῥητορᾰ	μητερᾰ
Gen.	φρενος	δαιμονος	λεοντος	ῥητορος	μητρος
Dat.	φρενῐ	δαιμονῐ	λεοντῐ	ῥητορῐ	μητρῐ
Dual.					
N. V. A.	φρενε	δαιμονε	λεοντε	ῥητορε	μητερε
G. D.	φρενοιν	δαιμονοιν	λεοντοιν	ῥητοροιν	μητεροιν
Plural.					
Nom.	φρενες	δαιμονες	λεοντες	ῥητορες	μητερες
Voc.	φρενες	δαιμονες	λεοντες	ῥητορες	μητερες
Acc.	φρενᾰς	δαιμονᾰς	λεοντᾰς	ῥητορᾰς	μητερᾰς
Gen.	φρενων	δαιμονων	λεοντων	ῥητορων	μητερων
Dat.	φρεσῐ(ν)	δαιμοσῐ(ν)	λεουσῐ(ν)	ῥητορσῐ(ν)	μητρᾰσῐ(ν)

* For nouns in σ-, see § 84.

In the following words the final vowel of the crude form is already long.

Greek C.F. Gender. English.	παιαν- masc. pæan, hymn.	ἀγων- masc. contest, games.	Ξενοφωντ- masc. Xenophon.	θηρ- masc. wild beast.	Ἑλλην- masc. a Greek.
Singular.					
Nom.	παιάν	ἄγων	Ξενοφων	θηρ	Ἕλλην
Voc.	παιάν	ἄγων	Ξενοφων	θηρ	Ἕλλην
Acc.	παιᾶνᾰ	ἀγῶνᾰ	Ξενοφωντᾰ	θηρᾰ	Ἕλληνᾰ
Gen.	παιᾶνος	ἀγῶνος	Ξενοφωντος	θηρος	Ἕλληνος
Dat.	παιᾶνῐ	ἀγῶνῐ	Ξενοφωντῐ	θηρῐ	Ἕλληνῐ
Dual.					
N. V. A.	παιᾶνε	ἄγωνε		θηρε	Ἕλληνε
G. D.	παιάνοιν	ἀγώνοιν		θηροιν	Ἑλλήνοιν
Plural.					
Nom.	παιᾶνες	ἀγῶνες		θηρες	Ἕλληνες
Voc.	παιᾶνες	ἀγῶνες		θηρες	Ἕλληνες
Acc.	παιᾶνᾰς	ἀγῶνᾰς		θηρᾱς	Ἕλληνᾰς
Gen.	παιάνων	ἀγώνων		θηρων	Ἑλλήνων
Dat.	παιᾶσῐ(ν)	ἀγῶσῐ(ν)		θηρσῐ(ν)	Ἕλλησῐ(ν)

76. So are declined ποιμεν-, m. *shepherd;* ἡγεμον-, m. *guide,* (V. ἡγεμων); γεροντ-, m. *old man,* (and all nouns and participles in οντ-, except οδοντ-, *tooth,* and the participles γνοντ-, διδοντ-, δοντ-, and ἁλοντ-, all which form their N. S. masc. in -ους*); πρακτορ-, m. *exacter;* αιθερ-, m. *sky* (G. αιθερος, etc.); λειμων-, m. *meadow;* σωτηρ-, m. *saviour;* χην-, m. f. *goose.* Εικον-, f. *image;* αηδον-, f. *nightingale;* χελιδον-, f. *swallow,* throw out ν in some of the cases, and undergo contraction: as, A. εικονᾰ and εικω, G. εικονος and εικους, etc.†

* Observe that in these five words ο belongs to the root.

† These forms should perhaps be rather explained as deduced from older crude forms in οι-, εικοι-, αηδοι-, χελιδοι- (§ 99); whence the V. αηδοι and χελιδοι, and the N. εικω (in Hesychius). Similarly Γοργοι- and Γοργον-, *Gorgon,* coexist; N. S. Γοργω and rarely Γοργων G. Γοργους and Γοργονος, etc. (Ahrens.)

77. The following words in τερ, viz. πᾰτερ-, *father*; μητερ-, *mother*; θῠγᾰτερ-, *daughter*; γαστερ-, f. *belly*; and Δημητερ-, *the goddess Demeter*, drop ε in the G. and D. sing.; in the D. pl. τερσῐ(ν) is changed into τρᾰσῐ(ν); Δημητερ- has also Δημητρᾰ in the A. S.: αστερ-, m. *star*, retains ε in the G. and D. sing., but the D. pl. is αστρᾰσῐ(ν): ἄνερ-, *man*, drops ε throughout, except in the N. and V. sing., and δ is then inserted between ν and ρ (§ 42): thus, N. ἀνηρ, V. ἄνερ, A. ανδρᾰ, and so on; the D. pl. is ανδρᾰσῐ(ν).

III. Masc. and fem. nouns whose crude forms end in ϝ (αϝ, εϝ, οϝ), or σ.

78. Before those suffixes which begin with a vowel the ϝ or σ is dropped. Before the suffixes which begin with a consonant ϝ becomes υ.

79. In the Attic declension of nouns in εϝ the vowel of the suffix is lengthened in the A. and G. sing. and A. pl.: thus, εᾱ, εως, etc., appear in place of ηᾰ, ηος, etc., of the old declension. If a vowel precede, εᾱ, εᾱς, εως, εων, are contracted. All nouns in εϝ are masculine.

80. Words in σ do not take the suffix ς in the N. sing.; consequently, if the final vowel of the crude form be short, it is lengthened. In the D. pl. one σ is dropped. If a vowel precede, εᾰ in the A. sing. is contracted into ᾱ instead of η.

81.

Greek C.F. Gender. English.	βăσĭλεϝ- masc. *king.*	Δωριεϝ- masc. *a Dorian.*	γρᾱϝ- fem. *old woman.*	βοϝ-* masc. & fem. *ox.*
Singular.				
Nom.	βăσĭλευς	Δωριευς	γραυς	βους
Voc.	βăσĭλευ	Δωριευ	γραυ	βου
Acc.	βăσĭλεᾱ	Δωριεᾱ, Δωριᾱ	γραυν	βουν
Gen.	βăσĭλεως	Δωριεως, Δωριως	γρᾱος	βοος
Dat.	(βăσĭλεῖ) βăσĭλει	Δωριει	γρᾱϊ	βοΐ
Dual.				
N. V. A.	βăσĭλεε	Δωριεε	γρᾱε	βοε
G. D.	βăσĭλεοιν	Δωριεοιν	γρᾱοιν	βοοιν
Plural.				
Nom.	(βăσĭλεες) βăσĭλης or βăσĭλεις	Δωριης, Δωριεις	γρᾱες	βοες
Voc.	βăσĭλεις	Δωριεις	γρᾱες	βοες
Acc.	βăσĭλεᾱς, βăσĭλεις†	Δωριεᾱς, Δωριᾱς	γραυς	βους
Gen.	βăσĭλεων	Δωριεων, Δωριων	γρᾱων	βοων
Dat.	βăσĭλευσΐ(ν)	Δωριευσΐ(ν)	γραυσΐ(ν)	βουσΐ(ν)

82. So are declined γραμμᾰτεϝ-, *scribe*; ἱερεϝ-, *priest*; ἱππεϝ-, *horseman*; κλοπεϝ-, *thief*; νομεϝ-, *herdsman*; Μεγᾰρεϝ-, *a Megarian*; Πειραιεϝ-, *the harbour of Athens*; Πλᾰταιεϝ-, *a Platæan*; ἁλιεϝ-, *fisherman* (generally without contraction).

83. The Attic poets occasionally make the G. sing. of nouns in εϝ to end in εος: as, Θησεϝ-, *Theseus*, G. Θησεος, as well as Θησεως. The poets sometimes contract εᾱ of the A. sing. into η: as, ἱερεϝ-, *a priest*, A. ἱερεᾱ and ἱερη. The N. pl. in -ης (from -ηες) is characteristic of the older Attic writers.

---

* Compare the declension of the Latin bov-, *ox*.

† i. e. βăσĭλεᾱς or βăσĭλεις. It will be seen that βασιλεις is not regularly contracted from βασιλεᾱς: generally, when the forms of both the N. and A. pl. are contracted, the acc. is not made from the uncontracted form of the case, but assimilated to the contracted nom.

SEPARABLE (THIRD) DECLENSION.

84.

Greek C.F. Gender. English.	τριηρεσ- fem. trireme.	Περικλεεσ- masc. Pericles.	αιδοσ- fem. shame.	ηρωσ- masc. hero.
Singular.				
Nom.	τριηρης	*N. Περικλεης, -κλης ; V. Περικλεες, -κλεις ; A. Περικλεεα, -κλεα ; G. Περικλεετος, -κλεους ; D. Περικλεεϊ, -κλει.*	αιδως	ηρως
Voc.	τριηρες			ηρως
Acc.	(τριηρεα) τριηρη		(αιδοα) αιδω	ηρωα or ηρω
Gen.	(τριηρεος) τριηρους		(αιδοος) αιδους	ηρωος
Dat.	(τριηρεϊ) τριηρει		(αιδοϊ) αιδοι	ηρωϊ
Dual.				
N. V. A.	τριηρεε			ηρωε
G. D.	τριηρεοιν or τριηροιν			ηρωοιν
Plural.				
Nom.	(τριηρεες) τριηρεις			ηρωες
Voc.	τριηρεις			ηρωες
Acc.	(τριηρεας) τριηρεις			ηρωας or ηρως
Gen.	τριηρεων or τριηρων			ηρωων
Dat.	τριηρεσϊ(ν)			ηρωσϊ(ν)

85. Like τριηρεσ- (which is strictly an adjective) are declined all adjectives in εσ (m. and f.); also Σωκρατεσ-, *Socrates*, and many proper names ending in -κρατεσ, -σθενεσ, -γενεσ, -φανεσ, and -κλεεσ. These proper names and Ἄρεσ-, *the god Ares*, also form the A. sing. as from a crude form in -α, after the analogy of nouns of the inseparable (1st) declension: thus, from Σωκρατεσ- we find A. Σωκρατη and Σωκρατην. Plato prefers the form in -η, Xenophon that in -ην: other writers use both; but of nouns in -γενεσ and -φανεσ the form in -ην is preferred, while of nouns in -κλεεσ this form is only found in the later writers. Ἄρεσ- has a gen. Αρεως in good prose. When these nouns have a plural, it follows the A- declension.

86. Like αιδοσ- are declined ηοσ-, f. *daybreak*, and χροσ-, m. *the skin* (for the most part uncontracted, as being a monosyllable). These words are not found in the voc. nor in the dual and plural. Instead of ηοσ- and χροσ-, in Attic εω- (§ 131) and χρωτ- (N. χρως, A. χρωτα) are used. On the other hand, γελωτ-, m. *laughter*, and ἱδρωτ-, m. *sweat*, have in the acc. γελω (also γελων) and ἱδρω as well as γελωτα and ἱδρωτα.

87. Like ἡρωσ- are declined Τρωσ-, *Tros, a Trojan;* θωσ-, m. and f. *a jackal* (these without contraction); πἄ̄τρωσ-, m. *an uncle by the father's side;* μητρωσ-, m. *an uncle by the mother's side;* Μῑνωσ-, *Minos*: the last three words have also πἄ̄τρων, etc., in the acc. and πἄ̄τρῳ in the gen., as if from crude forms πἄ̄τρω-, etc. (see § 131).

IV. Neuter nouns whose crude forms end in a consonant.

88. Neuter nouns of this declension take no suffix for the N. or A. singular; these cases, therefore, do not differ from the crude form. When the crude form ends in τ, the τ is either thrown away or changed into ς, less frequently into ρ.

89. Neuter substantives in εσ, a very numerous class, change ε of the C. F. into ο in the N., V., and A. sing.; but this change does not extend to the neuter of adjectives in εσ. In the other cases σ is dropped, and contraction ensues (§ 33).

90.

Greek C.F. Gender. English.	σωμἄτ- neut. *corpse, body.*	τερἄτ- neut. *portent.*	ημἄτ- neut. *day.*	κερἄσ- neut. *horn.*	γενεσ-* neut. *race.*
Singular.					
Nom.	σωμἄ	τερἄς	ημἄρ	κερἄς	γενος
Voc.	σωμἄ	τερἄς	ημἄρ	κερἄς	γενος
Acc.	σωμἄ	τερἄς	ημἄρ	κερἄς	γενος
Gen.	σωμᾰτος	τερᾰτος	ημᾰτος	(κεραος) κερως	(γενεος) γενους
Dat.	σωμᾰτῐ	τερᾰτῐ	ημᾰτῐ	(κεραϊ) κερᾳ	(γενεϊ) γενει
Dual.					
N. V. A.	σωμᾰτε	τερᾰτε	ημᾰτε	(κεραε) κερᾱ	γενεε, γενη
G. D.	σωμᾰτοιν	τερᾰτοιν	ημᾰτοιν	(κεραοιν) κερῳν	γενεοιν, γενοιν
Plural.					
Nom.	σωμᾰτᾰ	τερᾰτᾰ	ημᾰτᾰ	(κεραᾰ) κερᾱ̃	(γενεᾰ) γενη
Voc.	σωμᾰτᾰ	τερᾰτᾰ	ημᾰτᾰ	(κεραᾰ) κερᾱ̃	(γενεᾰ) γενη
Acc.	σωμᾰτᾰ	τερᾰτᾰ	ημᾰτᾰ	(κεραᾰ) κερᾱ̃	(γενεᾰ) γενη
Gen.	σωμᾰτων	τερᾰτων	ημᾰτων	(κεραων) κερων	γενεων, γενων
Dat.	σωμᾰσῐ(ν)	τερᾰσῐ(ν)	ημᾰσῐ(ν)	κερᾰσῐ(ν)	γενεσῐ(ν)

* Compare the Latin declension of neuter nouns in *ĕs:* e. g. ŏpĕs-, task, gĕnĕs-, *race*, N. S. ŏpŭs, gĕnŭs (γενος), G. ŏpĕrĭs, etc., where s o! the crude form is not dropped, as in Greek, but changed into r.

91. Like σωματ- are declined μελῐτ-, *honey*; γᾰλακτ-, *milk* (N. and A. sing. γᾰλᾰ, § 55); πραγμᾰτ-, *deed*; θαυμᾰτ-, *wonder*; κτημᾰτ-, *possession*; αἱμᾰτ-, *blood*; and all neuters in μᾰτ.

92. Like τερᾰτ- are declined περᾰτ-, *end, goal*; σταιτ-, *dough*. In Homer occur such forms as τεραος, τεραων, from C. F. τερασ-.

93. Like ημᾰτ- are declined ἡπᾰτ-, *liver*; ἀλειφᾰτ-, *oil*; φρεᾰ̄τ-, *well*; σκᾰτ-, *dung*; and ὑδᾰτ-, *water*. The last two have in the N. and A. sing. σκωρ and ὕδωρ; but by some grammarians both ρ and τ in these words are considered to be radical, so that the crude forms would be ημαρτ-, ὑδαρτ-, etc.

94. Like κερᾰσ- are declined κρεᾰσ-, *flesh*; γερᾰο-, *gift, honour*; γηρᾰσ-, *old age*; some of these words are also declined from crude forms in ᾱτ: as, κερᾱτ-, N. κερᾰς, G. κερᾱτος, etc. Σελᾰσ-, *blaze*, and δεπᾰσ-, *goblet*, are declined in the same way, but often without contraction, G. σελᾰος, etc.: βρετᾰσ-, *image*; κωᾰσ-, *fleece*; and οὐδᾰσ-, *ground* (poetical words), change α of the crude form into ε, except in the nom. and acc. sing., G. βρετεος, βρετους, etc.: κνεφᾰσ-, *darkness*, has both κνεφαος and κνεφους. The D. S. of these words was in the old language written κεραι, γεραι, etc.; more correctly, as the α is short.

95. Like γενεσ- are declined τειχεσ-, *wall* (of a fortress); ανθεσ-, *flower*; πᾰθεσ-, *suffering*; αλγεσ-, *pain*; νεφεσ-, *cloud*; κλεεσ-, *rumour*; ορεσ-, *mountain*; and all neuters in εσ. The N., V., and A. pl. of κλεεσ- is κλεᾱ, not κλεη; but ορεσ- retains η. The G. pl. and the forms of the dual are sometimes found uncontracted.

96. A few neuters in ρ, νεκτᾰρ-, *nectar*; θενᾰρ-, *palm of the hand*, etc., are declined regularly: εᾰρ-, *spring* (ϝεαρ-, Latin *vēr-*), and κεᾰρ-, *heart*, contract εα into η in G. and D. sing., and κεᾱρ- also in N. and A.

B. Nouns whose crude forms end in a vowel (ι or υ).

97. In the Attic declension of nouns in ι, ι passes into ε in all the cases except the N., V., and A. sing.; and in the G. sing. masculine and feminine nouns take the Attic termination ως instead of ος. In the D. sing. and N. and A. plur. contraction is used. Adjectives in ι, such as ιδρι-, *experienced*, and some substantives in ι, which are in great measure poetical, are declined without the change of ι into ε.

98. A few substantives in υ change υ into ε in all the cases except the N., V., and A. sing.: they thus take the same termina-

tions as the Attic declension in ι : εγχελυ,-*eel*, retains υ through the whole of the singular.

99. All nouns in οι are feminine. In the N. sing. οι becomes ω (originally ῳ) : the crude form remains unchanged in the voc., but in the other cases ι between two vowels disappears, and contraction ensues. These words are seldom found in the dual and plural, the forms of which, when they occur, are made as from a crude form in ο, after the analogy of the second or O- declension. Except in the nom., the forms of the plural in the older language would be the same, whether made from a crude form in *o* or in οι.*

100.

Greek C.F. Gender. English.	πολι- fem. *city.*	πορτι- masc. and fem. *a young ox.*	ιχθυ- masc. *a fish.*	πηχυ- masc. *cubit.*
Singular.				
Nom.	πολῖς	πορτῖς	ιχθῦς	πηχῠς
Voc.	πολῐ	πορτῐ	ιχθῠ	πηχῠ
Acc.	πολῐν	πορτῐν	ιχθῦν	πηχῠν
Gen.	πολεως	πορτιος	ιχθυος	πηχεως
Dat.	(πολεϊ) πολει	πορτιῐ & πορτῐ	ιχθυῐ	(πηχεϊ) πηχει
Dual.				
N. V. A.	πολεε	πορτιε	ιχθυε	πηχεε
G. D.	πολεοιν	πορτιοιν	ιχθυοιν	πηχεοιν
Plural.				
Nom.	(πολεες) πολεις	πορτιες & πορτῖς	ιχθυες	(πηχεες) πηχεις
Voc.	(πολεες) πολεις	πορτιες & πορτῖς	ιχθυες	(πηχεες) πηχεις
Acc.	(πολεᾰς) πολεις	πορτιᾰς & πορτῖς	ιχθῦς	(πηχεᾰς) πηχεις
Gen.	πολεων	πορτιων	ιχθυων	πηχεων
Dat.	πολεσῐ(ν)	πορτισῐ(ν)	ιχθῠσῐ(ν)	πηχεσῐ(ν)

* On these words see a paper in the Transactions of the Philological Society, vol. vi. p. 155, translated from the German of H. L. Ahrens, who cites (§§ 1, 7) ἡ Λητῳ, ἡ Σαπφῳ, on the authority of the grammarian Herodian, and such nominatives as ΑΡΤΕΜΩΙ, ΦΙΛΥΤΩΙ, etc., from inscriptions (Bœckh, Corp. Inscr. No. 696, 2310); and, again, ΞΑΝΘΟΙ from an ancient vase, apparently a nom. fem. Ξανθῳ, the name of a nymph (otherwise Ξανθη) corresponding to the masc. river-god Ξανθο-ς.

SEPARABLE (THIRD) DECLENSION.

Greek C.F. Gender. English.	εγχελυ- masc.&fem. eel.	σῐνᾰπῐ- neut. mustard.	αστυ- neut. town.	ηχοι- fem. echo.
Singular.				
Nom.	εγχελῠς	σῐνᾱπῐ	αστῠ	ηχω
Voc.	εγχελῠ	σῐνᾱπῐ	αστῠ	ηχοι
Acc.	εγχελῠν	σῐνᾱπῐ	αστῠ	(ηχοᾰ) ηχω
Gen.	εγχελυος	σῐνᾱπεος	αστεος	(ηχοος) ηχους
Dat.	εγχελυῐ	(σῐνᾱπεῐ) σῐνᾱπει	(αστεῐ) αστει	(ηχοϊ) ηχοι
Dual.				
N. V. A.	εγχελεε	σῐνᾱπεε	αστεε	
G. D.	εγχελεοιν	σῐνᾱπεοιν	αστεοιν	
Plural.				
Nom.	εγχελεις	(σῐνᾱπεᾰ) σῐνᾱπη	(αστεᾰ) αστη	
Voc.	εγχελεις	(σῐνᾱπεᾰ) σῐνᾱπη	(αστεᾰ) αστη	
Acc.	εγχελεις	(σῐνᾱπεᾰ) σῐνᾱπη	(αστεᾰ) αστη	
Gen.	εγχελεων	σῐνᾱπεων	αστεων	
Dat.	εγχελεσῐ(ν)	σῐνᾱπεσῐ(ν)	αστεσῐ(ν)	

101. Like πολι- are declined μαντι-, m. *seer*; οφι-, m. *serpent*; and all feminine nouns in -σι (-τι, -ξι, -ψι), derived from verbs and denoting *an act*: as, πραξι-, *doing*; ληψι-, *seizing*; λῠσι-, *loosening*.

102. Like πορτι- are declined μηνι- (also, later, μηνῐδ-*), f. *wrath*; οι- (or οϊ-, i. e. οϝι-, Latin *ovi*-), m. and f. *sheep*; ποσι-, *husband* (in the dat. ποσει, not ποσῑ: ποσι-, f. *act of drinking*, is declined like πολι-); and some proper names, as Συεννεσι-, *Syennesis*.

103. Like ιχθυ-† are declined δρυ-, f. *oak*; πῐτυ-, f. *pine*; οφρυ-, f. *eyebrow*; στᾰχυ-, m. *ear of corn*; συ-, m. and f. *hog*. In the old poets, and again in late prose, but not in Attic, the A. pl. is found in ᾰς, as ιχθυᾱς, νεκυᾱς. Forms of the plur. of εγχελυ- retaining the υ are sometimes found.

104. Like πηχυ- and αστυ- are declined πρεσβυ-, *old man, am*-

---

* So Πᾰρι-, *Paris*, is declined later from Πᾰρῐδ-, while Θετῐδ- in Homer (acc. Θετῐν) becomes Θετι- in some later writers.

† On the varying quantity of υ in the nom. and acc. singular of these nouns, see Ahrens, *Phil. Soc. Trans.* vi. pp. 167, 168.

D

bassador; πελεκυ-, m. *axe;* πωυ-, n. *herd* (poet.); also adjectives in υ (m. and n.), except that in the G. sing. they take ος, not ως and that εα of the neut. plur. is not contracted.

105. The Attic poets occasionally make the gen. of nouns in ι, masc. and fem., to end in ος, as πολεος; while, on the other hand, such forms as αστεως are found.

106. Like ηχοι- are declined πειθοι-, *persuasion;* πευθοι-, *tidings;* ευεστοι-, *well-being;* χρειοι- (Ep.), *need;* and many feminine proper names, as Λητοι-, *Latona;* Σαπφοι-, *Sappho.*

INSEPARABLE DECLENSION.

107. Words of this declension fall into two classes:

A. Masculines and Feminines in *a* (first declension).

B. Masculines, Feminines, and Neuters in *o* (second declension).

108. The following is a tabular view of the suffixes added in this declension:—

	Feminines in *a*.	Masculines in *a*. Masc. & Fem. in *o*.	Neuters in *o*.
Singular. *Nom.* *Voc.* *Acc.* *Gen.* *Dat.*	no ending same as nom. ν ς ι (subscript)	ς no ending ν ο ι (subscript)	ν same as nom. ν ο ι (subscript)
Dual. *N. V. A.* *G. D.*	vowel lengthened ιν	vowel lengthened ιν	vowel lengthened ιν
Plural. *Nom.* *Voc.* *Acc.* *Gen.* *Dat.*	ι same as nom. ˉς (νς) ων ις	ι same as nom. ˉς (νς) ων ις	ἄ same as nom. ἄ ων ις

Remarks on the Suffixes.

109. Voc. Sing.—Of feminines in α, and in all plurals, the nominative is used as a vocative. Of masculines in α, the crude form is, according to the rule, the vocative case; but the vowel is most frequently lengthened. The crude form of masc. and fem. nouns in ο also constitutes the vocative; but the final ο is changed into ε.

110. Gen. Sing.—αο becomes ου in Attic (from the Ionic εω): in Doric this case ends in αο and ᾱ: οο is also contracted into ου.

111. Dat. Sing.—The α and ο of the crude form are lengthened, and the ι becomes subscript (§ 28).

112. Accus. Plur.—ανς and ονς become ᾱς and ους (§ 40).

113. Gen. Plur.—αων (Ion. εων) and οων are both contracted into ων in Attic.

114. Dat. Plur.—The original forms of this case in αισι(ν) and οισι(ν) are frequently found in the poets and in some prose writers.

Examples

A. Masculine and feminine nouns in α.

(First Declension.)

115. Some difficulty arises from the modification to which the final vowel of the crude form is subject in the singular. In feminine nouns it varies between ᾰ, ᾱ, and η; in masculines between ᾱ and η. Attention should be paid to the following rules:—

116. a. *If the vowel be long*, it is, in Attic, ᾱ after ε, ι, and ρ; otherwise η (§ 34).

If the vowel be short, it is, of course, ᾰ.

Exceptions to this general rule are the fem. nouns κορα-, *maiden*, and δερα-, *neck*, in the inflection of which η is used throughout the singular, not ᾱ. On the other hand, the fem. nouns γυα-, *field*; ελαα-, *olive-tree*; ποα-, *grass*; στοα-, *porch*; and χροα-, *skin, complexion*, which, according to the rule, should exhibit η, are inflected in ᾱ; but these words originally ended in ια- (γυια-, ελαια-, etc.), so that ā in the singular is only an apparent exception to the rule.

In the Doric declension of these nouns the long vowel is always ā, in the Ionic always η; words, therefore, which, being introduced into the Attic from those dialects, retain their original spelling, have not been cited as exceptions.

117. *b. The vowel is always long* in the nom., acc., and dat. of masculine nouns, which cases, therefore, end in ᾱς, ᾱν, and ᾳ after ε, ι, and ρ, otherwise in ης, ην, and η.

118. *c. The vowel is always long* in the gen. and dat. of feminine nouns, which cases, therefore, end in ᾱς and ᾳ after ε, ι, and ρ, otherwise in ης and η.

119. *d.* There remain to be considered the nom. and acc. of feminine nouns. In these *the vowel remains short* in the following cases :—

(1.) After λλ, νν, σσ (ττ), ξ, ψ, and ζ; that is, after the double letters and repeated letters: as, N. sing. θυελλᾰ, *hurricane;* γεννᾰ, *offspring;* γλωσσᾰ, *tongue;* δοξᾰ, *opinion;* διψᾰ, *thirst;* τρᾰπεζᾰ, *table.*

(2.) After σ preceded by a diphthong or long vowel: as, N. sing. μουσᾰ, *muse.*

(3.) After ρ preceded by ῠ, or by any diphthong (except αυ): as, N. sing. σφυρᾰ, *hammer;* πειρᾰ, *attempt;* μᾰχαιρᾰ, *knife:* but θῠρᾱ, *gate;* χωρᾱ, *country;* λαυρᾱ, *alley.* Exceptions are ἑταιρᾱ, *female companion;* πᾰλαιστρᾱ, *wrestling-school;* κολλῡρᾱ, *roll of bread;* Αιθρᾱ, *Æthra;* Φαιδρᾱ, *Phædra.*

(4.) In all words ending in *-αινα*, and in many others in *-να*: as, N. sing. λεαινᾰ, *lioness;* εχιδνᾰ, *viper.*

(5.) In all words in *-τρια*, signifying feminine agents: as, N. sing. ποιητριᾰ, *poetess;* and in the three feminine adjectives μιᾰ, *one;* δῐᾰ, *godlike;* ποτνιᾰ, *mistress, worshipful.*

(6.) In all words, including the feminine of all perfect participles active, in which *a* is preceded by υι: as, N. sing. μυιᾰ, *fly;* τετῠφυιᾰ, *having struck:* μητρυιᾱ, *step-mother*, is an exception.

(7.) In disyllables in which *a* is preceded by the diphthong αι, and in some proper names of places of more than two syllables: as, N. sing. γαιᾰ, *earth;* 'Ιστιαιᾰ, *Histiæa.*

INSEPARABLE (FIRST) DECLENSION.

(8.) In words of more than two syllables in which a is preceded by the diphthongs ει and οι: as, N. sing. ἱερειᾰ, *priestess*; ἄνοιᾰ, *folly*: except that nouns in -εια denoting *a condition*, and connected with verbs in -ευ, have ᾱ: thus, N. sing. βᾰσῐλειᾰ, *a queen*, but βᾰσῐλειᾱ, *royal power*.

(9.) In some isolated words: as, N. sing. διαιτᾰ, *way of life*; ἄκανθᾰ, *thorn*. From πεινα-, *hunger*; τολμα-, *daring*, and some others, two forms are found—N. sing. πεινᾰ and πεινη, τολμᾰ and τολμη, etc.

In all these cases, therefore, the nom. and acc. sing. end in ᾰ and ᾰν.

120. In other combinations the vowel is long, and (with the exceptions already given) the nom. and acc. sing. end in ᾱ and ᾱν after ε, ι, and ρ; otherwise in η and ην.

121. Throughout the dual and plural the vowel is invariably .

122.

Greek C. F. Gender. English.	νῑκα- fem. victory.	ἀσα- fem. satiety.	θεα- fem. goddess.	σκια- fem. shadow.	χωρα- fem. place, country.
Singular. *Nom.* *Voc.* *Acc.* *Gen.* *Dat.*	νῑκη νῑκη νῑκην νῑκης νῑκῃ	ἄση ἄση ἄσην ἄσης ἄσῃ	θεᾱ θεᾱ θεᾱν θεᾱς θεᾳ	σκιᾱ σκιᾱ σκιᾱν σκιᾱς σκιᾳ	χωρᾱ χωρᾱ χωρᾱν χωρᾱς χωρᾳ
Dual. *N. V. A.* *G. D.*	νῑκᾱ νῑκαιν	ἄσᾱ ἄσαιν	θεᾱ θεαιν	σκιᾱ σκιαιν	χωρᾱ χωραιν
Plural. *Nom.* *Voc.* *Acc.* *Gen.* *Dat.*	νῑκαι νῑκαι νῑκᾱς νῑκων νῑκαις	ἄσαι ἄσαι ἄσᾱς ἄσων ἄσαις	θεαι θεαι θεᾱς θεων θεαις	σκιαι σκιαι σκιᾱς σκιων σκιαις	χωραι χωραι χωρᾱς χωρων χωραις

Greek C.F. Gender. English.	μουσα- fem. muse.	ἄνοια- fem. folly.	δοξα- fem. opinion.	λεαινα- fem. lioness.	γλωσσα- fem. tongue.
Singular.					
Nom.	μουσᾰ	ἄνοιᾰ	δοξᾰ	λεαινᾰ	γλωσσᾰ
Voc.	μουσᾰ	ἄνοιᾰ	δοξᾰ	λεαινᾰ	γλωσσᾰ
Acc.	μουσᾰν	ἄνοιᾰν	δοξᾰν	λεαινᾰν	γλωσσᾰν
Gen.	μουσης	ἄνοιᾱς	δοξης	λεαινης	γλωσσης
Dat.	μουσῃ	ἄνοιᾳ	δοξῃ	λεαινῃ	γλωσσῃ
Dual.					
N. V. A.	μουσᾱ	ἄνοιᾱ	δοξᾱ	λεαινᾱ	γλωσσᾱ
G. D.	μουσαιν	ἄνοιαιν	δοξαιν	λεαιναιν	γλωσσαιν
Plural.					
Nom.	μουσαι	ἄνοιαι	δοξαι	λεαιναι	γλωσσαι
Voc.	μουσαι	ἄνοιαι	δοξαι	λεαιναι	γλωσσαι
Acc.	μουσᾱς	ἄνοιᾱς	δοξᾱς	λεαινᾱς	γλωσσᾱς
Gen.	μουσων	ἄνοιων	δοξων	λεαινων	γλωσσων
Dat.	μουσαις	ἄνοιαις	δοξαις	λεαιναις	γλωσσαις

123. So are declined ἀδικια-, *injustice*; ἀληθεια-, *truth*; ἁμαξα-, *waggon*; ἁρπυια-, *harpy*; γεφῡρα-, *bridge*; γνωμα-, *judgement*; δικα-, *justice*; θάλασσα-, *sea*; θεράπαινα-, *maid-servant*; λῡρα-, *lyre*; ῥιζα-, *root*; σοφια-, *wisdom*; τῑμα-, *honour*; φῠγα-, *flight*; χλαινα-, *cloak*—all feminine. Further examples for declension will be found in § 119.

124. Some nouns in -εα contract εα into η: as, σῡκεα-, *fig-tree*, N. σῡκεᾱ or σῡκη.

125. The vocative of masculines in α retains ᾰ (1) in nouns ending in τα; (2) in national names: as, Περσα-, *a Persian*, V. Περσᾰ; but Περσα-, *Perses*, V. Περση; (3) in some compounds of the verbs πωλε-, *sell*; μετρε-, *measure*; τριβ-, *rub*: as, γεωμετρα-, *a geometer*, V. γεωμετρᾰ.

INSEPARABLE (FIRST) DECLENSION.

126.

Greek C.F. Gender. English.	πολῖτα- masc. citizen.	τελωνα- masc. farmer of customs.	νεανια- masc. young man.	(Ἑρμεα-) Ἑρμη- masc. Hermes.
Singular.				
Nom.	πολίτης	τελώνης	νεανίας	Ἑρμῆς
Voc.	πολῖτᾰ	τελώνη	νεανίᾰ	Ἑρμῆ
Acc.	πολίτην	τελώνην	νεανίαν	Ἑρμῆν
Gen.	πολίτου	τελώνου	νεανίου	Ἑρμοῦ
Dat.	πολίτῃ	τελώνῃ	νεανίᾳ	Ἑρμῇ
Dual.				
N. V. A.	πολίτᾱ	τελώνᾱ	νεανίᾱ	Ἑρμᾶ
G. D.	πολίταιν	τελώναιν	νεανίαιν	Ἑρμαῖν
Plural.				
Nom.	πολῖται	τελῶναι	νεανίαι	Ἑρμαῖ
Voc.	πολῖται	τελῶναι	νεανίαι	Ἑρμαῖ
Acc.	πολίτᾱς	τελώνᾱς	νεανίᾱς	Ἑρμᾶς
Gen.	πολιτῶν	τελωνῶν	νεανιῶν	Ἑρμῶν
Dat.	πολίταις	τελώναις	νεανίαις	Ἑρμαῖς

127. So are declined Ατρειδα-, *son of Atreus*; γεωμετρα-, *geometer*; ὁπλῑτα-, *heavy-armed soldier*; Σκύθα-, *Scythian*; τᾰμια-, *dispenser*; τοξοτα-, *archer*—all masculine.

128. Some nouns in -ρα and many proper names, mostly Doric, retain the Doric contract genitive in ᾱ: as, Βορρα- (Βορεα-), *north wind*, G. Βορρᾶ.

B. Masculine, Feminine, and Neuter Nouns in o.

(Second Declension.)

129. In some words in which o or ε precedes the final vowel of the crude form, contraction takes place.

SUBSTANTIVES.

Greek C.F. Gender. English.	λογο- masc. word.	νησο- fem. island.	σῡκο- neut. fig.	πλοο- masc. voyage.	οστεο- neut. bone.
Singular.					
Nom.	λογος	νησος	σῡκον	(πλοος) πλους	(οστεον) οστουν
Voc.	λογε	νησε	σῡκον	(πλοε) πλου	(οστεον) οστουν
Acc.	λογον	νησον	σῡκον	(πλοον) πλουν	(οστεον) οστουν
Gen.	λογου	νησου	σῡκου	(πλοου) πλου	(οστεου) οστου
Dat.	λογῳ	νησῳ	σῡκῳ	(πλοῳ) πλῳ	(οστεῳ) οστῳ
Dual.					
N. V. A.	λογω	νησω	σῡκω	(πλοω) πλω	(οστεω) οστω
G. D.	λογοιν	νησοιν	συκοιν	(πλοοιν) πλοιν	(οστεοιν) οστοιν
Plural.					
Nom.	λογοι	νησοι	σῡκᾰ	(πλοοι) πλοι	(οστεᾰ) οστᾱ
Voc.	λογοι	νησοι	σῡκᾰ	(πλοοι) πλοι	(οστεᾰ) οστᾱ
Acc.	λογους	νησους	σῡκᾰ	(πλοους) πλους	(οστεᾰ) οστᾱ
Gen.	λογων	νησων	σῡκων	(πλοων) πλων	(οστεων) οστων
Dat.	λογοις	νησοις	σῡκοις	(πλοοις) πλοις	(οστεοις) οστοις

130. So are declined αγγελο-, m. *messenger*; ἀδελφο-, m. *brother*; αμπελο-, f. *vine*; δουλο-, m. *slave*; εργο-, n. *work*; θεο-, m. *god* (voc. θεος); ιππο-, m. and f. *horse, mare*; κᾰνεο-, n. *basket*; νοο-, m. *mind*; νοσο-, f. *disease*; ξῠλο-, n. *piece of wood*; ὁδο-, f. *road*; ροδο-, n. *rose*; ῥοο-, m. *stream*.

131. There are a few nouns with a crude form ending in ω (apparently contracted from ωο or αο): these are declined as follows :—

(Attic Declension.)

Greek C.F. Gender. English.	λεω- masc. *people.*	λᾰγω- masc. *hare.*	ἀνωγεω- neut. *upper room.*
Singular. Nom. Voc. Acc. Gen. Dat.	λεως λεως λεων λεω λεῳ	λᾰγως λᾰγως λᾰγων and λᾰγω λᾰγω λᾰγῳ	ἀνωγεων ἀνωγεων ἀνωγεων ἀνωγεω ἀνωγεῳ
Dual. N. V. A. G. D.	λεω λεων	λᾰγω λᾰγῳν	For the Dual and Plural neuter of this declension, see *Adjectives*, § 150.
Plural. Nom. Voc. Acc. Gen. Dat.	λεῳ λεῳ λεως λεων λεῳς	λᾰγῳ λᾰγῳ λᾰγως λᾰγων λᾰγῳς	

132. So are declined Ἀθω-, m. *Mount Athos;* ἐω-, f. *dawn* (§ 86); κᾰλω-, m. *rope;* Κω-, f. *the island Cos;* Μενελεω-, m. *Menelaus;* νεω-, m. *temple;* and some adjectives. Many of these words sometimes throw away ν in the accus. sing.: compare the regular Greek acc. in the separable declension with the Latin,—λεοντ-ᾰ with *leon-e-m.* Some of them, as λεω-, νεω-, Μενελεω-, coexist with crude forms in āo,—λᾱο-, νᾱο-, Μενελᾱο-, etc., which are declined regularly.

133. On a comparison of the two principal declensions, the separable and the inseparable, they will be found to have the following features in common:—

(1.) In the N. sing., masculines and, though less uniformly, feminines, either take the suffix ς, or have the final vowel of the crude form lengthened in compensation.

(2.) In the A. sing., masc. and fem. nouns ending in a vowel take the suffix ν.

(3.) In the D. sing. of all nouns the suffix is ι, subscript in nouns of the inseparable declension.

(4.) In the N. and A. dual, either ε is added, or, which is equivalent, the final vowel of the crude form is lengthened.

(5.) In the G. and D. dual of all nouns the suffix is ιν (οιν).

(6.) In the A. pl. of masculine and feminine nouns the suffix is ς added to the acc. sing. The original ending of the accus. plur. in the inseparable declension, then, was νς: ν was dropped, the vowel being lengthened; hence ᾱς, ους.

(7.) In the N., V., and A. pl. of all neuter nouns the suffix is ᾰ.

(8.) In the G. pl. of all nouns the suffix is ων.

(9.) In the D. pl. of all nouns the suffix was, originally, σῐ(ν).*

134. The principal points of difference between these two declensions are:—

(1.) In the N. and A. sing. of neuters the separable declension admits no suffix, the inseparable takes ν.

(2.) In the G. sing. the separable declension has the suffix ος (ως); the inseparable has ο, except that feminines in α take ς.

(3.) In the N. pl. of masculine and feminine nouns the separable declension has the suffix ες, the inseparable takes ι.

135. In addition to the regular case-endings there are certain suffixes which partake of the nature of case-endings, though in the ordinary language their use is limited to a few words, and they retain only the original signification of relations of place. In the older language they were much more freely used. These are,—

-δε, answering to the question *whither*: (acc.) οἰκᾰδε, *to one's house.*

-θεν, „ „ *whence*: (gen.) οἰκοθεν, *from one's house.*

-θι „ „ *where*: (dat.) αλλοθι, *elsewhere.*

136. The suffixes -θεν and -θι are appended to the crude form of the noun: as, Ἀθηνη-θεν, *from Athens*; κυκλο-θεν, *from the circle*; ο is, however, sometimes substituted for α, as ῥιζο-θεν, *from the roots* (ῥιζα-, *root*), or inserted as connecting-vowel, as παντ-ο-θεν, *from all sides*. The suffix -δε is usually appended to the accusative form: as, Μεγᾰρᾱ-δε, *to Megara*; Ἐλευσῑνᾰ-δε, *to Eleusis*; οἰκᾰδε, from οἰκο-, is irregular, but οἰκονδε is found in Homer.

---

* Compare the so-called adverbs of the place *where*, Ἀθηνησι(ν) Πλᾰται ᾱσι(ν), θυρᾱσι(ν), etc. (§ 137).

-Δε sometimes combines with ς of the acc. plural to form -ζε: thus, Ἀθήναζε, *to Athens*, for Ἀθήνασ-δε; Θήβαζε, *to Thebes*.

137. Besides this adverbial dative in θι, we find in some words, with the same meaning, a modification of the ordinary dative: as, οικοι (οικῳ), *at home* (poet. οικοθῖ); Πῡθοι, *at Pytho*; Ισθμοι, *at the Isthmus*; Ἀθήνησῐ(ν), *in Athens*; Πλᾰταιᾱσῐ(ν), *in Platææ*; θῠρᾱσῐ(ν), *at the doors*.

Peculiarities of Declension.

138. Many foreign proper names, the cardinal numbers from πεντε, *five*, to ἑκᾰτον, *one hundred*, inclusively, θεμῐς (in the sense of *fas*), and a few neuters, as ονᾰρ, *dream*; ὑπᾰρ, *waking vision*; δεμᾰς, *body*; οφελος, *use*, are undeclined, or are used only in the nom. or acc.

139. Some proper names of places have no singular: as, Ἀθηνα-, f. N. pl. Ἀθηναι, *the city Athens*; Μεγᾰρο-, n. N. pl. Μεγᾰρᾰ, *the city Megara*; Τεμπεσ-, n. N. pl. Τεμπη, *the vale of Tempe*.

140. Of some nouns collateral forms exist, sometimes with a slight difference of meaning, sometimes with a difference of usage—one being found in prose, the other in poetry; or one being of a later period than the other. Thus we find

ἁλω-, ἁλων-, ἁλωσ-, and ἁλωα-, f. *threshing-floor*.
διψα-, f. und διψεσ-, n. *thirst*.
Θεμιστ- and Θεμῐτ- or Θεμῐδ-, f. *justice, law, the goddess Justice*.
νᾰπα-, f. and νᾰπεσ-, n. *glen*.
οχθο-, m. and οχθα-, f. *bank*.
οχο-, m. and (in plur.) οχεσ-, n. *chariot*.
πλευρα-, f. and (in plur.) πλευρο-, n. *rib, side*.
σκοτο-, m. and σκοτεσ-, n. *darkness*.
ταω- and ταων-, m. *peacock*.
φαεσ- and φωτ-,[*] n. *light*.
φθογγο-, m. and φθογγα-, f. *voice, sound*.
χωρο-, m. and χωρα-, f. *place*.

[*] The late and anomalous form φωτ- was evidently suggested, in false analogy, by the contracted nom. sing. φως (=φαος): it must not be confounded with the old word φωτ-, m. *man, hero*, which is declined regularly, N. φως; A. φωτᾰ; etc. Compare χρωτ-, m. *skin*, by the side of χροσ-, N. χρως; § 86.

141. Some nouns in ο have one gender in the singular, another in the plural. Thus,

δεσμο-, *chain*,	is m.	in the sing.,	m. & n. in the pl.
ζῠγο-, *yoke*,	is m. & n.	„	n. „
κελευθο-, *way*,	is f.	„	f. & n. „
λυχνο-, *a light*,	is m.	„	m. & n. „
νωτο-, *back*,	is m. & n.	„	n. „
σῖτο-, *corn*,	is m.	„	n. „
στᾰδιο-, *a measure of length*,	is n.	„	m. & n. „
σταθμο-, *stall, station*,	is m.	„	m. & n. „
Ταρτᾰρο-, *Tartarus*,	is m. & f.	„	n. „

142. Many irregularities arise from the coexistence of two crude forms, one or both of which are declined only in part. Some of the most important of these anomalous nouns have been already given in the remarks on the several declensions; others are declined here:—

γονυ- and γονᾰτ-, n. *knee*. N. V. A. γονῠ; G. γονᾰτος; D. γονᾰτῐ; Pl. N. V. A. γονᾰτᾰ; G. γονᾰτων; D. γονᾰσῐ(ν). Similarly is declined

δορυ-, δορᾰτ-, and δορεσ-, n. *beam, spear*. N. V. A. δορῠ; G. δορᾰτος (or δορος); D. δορᾰτῐ (or δορῐ) and δορει; Pl. N. V. A. δορᾰτᾰ and δορη; G. δορᾰτων; D. δορᾰσῐ(ν).*

γῠνα- and γῠναικ-, f. *woman*. N. γῠνη; V. γῠναι; A. γῠναικᾰ; G. γῠναικος; etc.†

δακρυ- and δακρυο-, n. *tear*. N. V. A. δακρῠ and δακρυον; Pl. N. V. A. δακρυᾰ; G. δακρυων; D. δακρῠσῐ(ν) and δακρυοις.

δενδρο- and δενδρεσ- n. *tree*. N. V. A. δενδρον; G. δενδρου; D. δενδρῳ and δενδρει; Pl. N. V. A. δενδρᾰ and δενδρη; G. δενδρων; D. δενδροις and δενδρεσῐ(ν).

Δῐϝ- and Ζεϝ- (ΔιεϝS-), m. *Jupiter*. N. Ζευς; V. Ζευ; A. Διᾰ; G. Διος; D. Διῐ. Also a poetical form—A. Ζηνᾰ, etc.—is found, as from a C. F. Ζην-.

---

* In addition are found such forms as γουνος and γουνᾰτος, δουρος and δουρᾰτος, etc. The inserted υ is perhaps to be referred to the υ of γονυ- and δορυ-. With the lengthened forms γονᾰτος, δορᾰτος, etc., compare προσωπᾰτᾰ, ονειρᾰτᾰ, δεσμᾰτᾰ, poetical neut. pl. from προσωπο-, *face*; ονειρο-, *dream*; δεσμο-, *bond*.

† Compare the diminutive γῠνα-ιο-, n. *a little woman*, and the adjectives γῠνα-ιο- and γῠναικ-ειο-, *womanish*.

PECULIARITIES OF DECLENSION.

Θαλητ- and Θαλη-, m. *Thales.* N. V. Θάλης; A. Θάλητα and Θάλην; G. Θάλητος, Θάλεω, and Θάλου; D. Θάλητι and Θάλῃ.

θεράποντ- and θεράπ-, m. *servant.* θεράποντ- is declined regularly throughout; and from θεράπ- are found A. sing. θεράπα and N. pl. θεράπες.

κάρᾱτ-, n. and κρᾱτ-, m. and f. *head.* N. V. κάρᾱ and κράτα (neut.); A. κάρᾱ and κράτα (m. and n.); G. κράτος; D. κάρᾳ and κράτι; Pl. A. κράτας; G. κράτων; D. κράσι(ν).

κοινωνο- and κοινων-, m. *partner.* κοινωνο- is declined regularly; and in Pl. are also found N. κοινωνες; A. κοινωνας.

κρίνο- and κρίνεσ-, n. *lily.* κρίνο- is declined regularly; and in Pl. are found N. A. κρίνεα(-η), and D. κρίνεσι(ν).

κυον- and κυν-, m. and f. *dog.* N. κυων; V. κυον; A. κύνα; G. κύνος; etc. D. pl. κυσί(ν).

λαϝ- and λᾱο- (?), m. *stone.* N. V. λᾶς; A. λᾶν and λᾶα; G. λᾶος and λᾶου; D. λᾶι; etc. D. pl. λᾶεσι(ν).

ναϝ-, νεϝ-, and νηϝ-, f. *ship.* N. ναυς; A. ναυν; G. νεως; D. νηι; Pl. N. νηες; A. ναυς; G. νεων; D. ναυσί(ν).

Οιδιποδ- and Οιδιπου-, m. *Œdipus.* N. Οἰδίπους; V. Οἰδί-πους and -που; A. Οἰδί-ποδα and -πουν; G. Οἰδί-ποδος and -που; D. Οἰδίποδι: also from a C. F. Οἰδιποδα- are found V. Οἰδίποδα; A. Οἰδιποδᾱν; G. Οἰδιποδᾱ (for -δαο), in lyrical passages.

ονειρο-, m. and n. ονειρᾱτ-, n. *dream.* N. ονειρον and ονειρος; V. ονειρε; A. ονειρον; G. ονειρου; D. ονειρῳ (rarely ονειρᾱτος, ονειρᾱτι); Pl. N. V. A. ονειρᾱτα (rarely ονειρα); G. ονειρᾱτων and ονειρων; D. ονειρᾱσι(ν) and ονειροις. In N. and A. sing. οναρ is found.

ορνιθ- and ορνι-, m. and f. *bird.* N.V. ορνῑς; A. ορνῑθα and ορνῑν; G. ορνῑθος; D. ορνῑθι; Pl. N.V. ορνῑθες and ορνεις; A. ορνῑθας, ορνεις, and ορνῑς; G. ορνῑθων; D. ορνῑσι(ν).

Πυκν-, f. *the Pnyx.* N. Πνυξ; A. Πυκνα; G. Πυκνος; D. Πυκνι: also in later writers Πνυκα, etc.

πυρ- and πυρο-, n. *fire.* N. V. A. πῦρ; G. πῦρος; D. πῦρι; Pl. N. V. A. πῦρα; G. πῦρων; D. πῦροις.

υιο- and υιεϝ-, m. *son.* υιο- is declined regularly throughout; of υιεϝ- are found in the sing. G. υἱεος; D. υἱει; in the plur. N. V. A. υἱεις; G. υἱεων; D. υἱεσι(ν); (υἱευσιν is late).

χερ- and χειρ-, f. *hand*. N. V. χειρ ; Du. N. A. χειρε ; G. D. χεροιν (rarely χειροιν) ; D. pl. χερσῐ(ν) : the other cases are declined from both crude forms ; but in Attic prose the forms from χειρ- are used.

ωτ- (οϝᾰτ-), n. *ear*. N. V. A. ους ; G. ωτος ; D. ωτῐ, etc.

For the dialectic varieties see below, *Of the Dialects*.

143. The following tabular view of the various terminations of the N. S. in the separable (third) declension, and of the crude forms to which they may correspond, is given, partly for the use of those who, having begun the study of Greek on the ordinary system, may wish to engraft on it the crude-form system ; partly to facilitate the consultation of the dictionary.

Ending of Nom. Sing.	Ending of Crude Form.	Examples.		
		Nom.	Gen.	Crude Form.
-μᾰ	-μᾰτ, n.	σωμᾰ,	σωμᾰτος, n. *body*.	σωμᾰτ-
-αις	-αιτ -αιδ	δαις, παις,	δαιτος, f. *meal*. παιδος, m. and f. *child*.	δαιτ- παιδ-
-ᾱν	-ᾱν	παιᾱν,	παιᾱνος, m. *pœan*.	παιᾱν-
-ᾰν	-ᾰν, n. -αντ, n.	μελᾰν, τυψᾰν,	μελᾰνος, n. (adj.) *black*. τυψαντος, n. (part.) *having struck*.	μελᾰν- τυψαντ-
-ᾱρ	-ᾱρ	ψᾱρ,	ψᾱρος, m. *starling*.	ψᾱρ-
-ᾰρ	-ᾰρ -ᾰρ, n. -ᾰτ, n.	οᾰρ, εᾰρ, ημᾰρ,	οᾰρος, f. *wife*. εᾰρος (ηρος), n. *spring*. ημᾰτος, n. *day*.	οᾰρ- ϝεᾰρ- ημᾰτ-
-ᾱς	-ᾰν -αντ	μελᾱς, τυψᾱς,	μελᾰνος, m. (adj.) *black*. τυψαντος, m. (part.) *having struck*.	μελᾰν- τυψαντ-
-ᾰς	-ᾰδ -ᾰσ, n. -ᾰτ, n.	λαμπᾰς, κρεᾰς, τερᾰς,	λαμπᾰδος, f. *lamp*. κρεως, n. *flesh*. τερᾰτος, n. *portent*.	λαμπᾰδ- κρεᾰσ- τερᾰτ-
-αυς	-αϝ	γραυς,	γρᾱυς, f. *old woman*.	γρᾱϝ-
-ειμ	-ερ (-ειρ)	χειρ,	χερος & χειρος, f. *hand*.	χερ- & χειρ-

PECULIARITIES OF DECLENSION.

Ending of Nom. Sing.	Ending of Crude Form.	Examples.		
		Nom.	Gen.	Crude Form.
-εις	-ειδ -εν -εντ	κλεις, εις, λŭθεις,	κλειδος, f. *key.* ἑνος, m. *one.* λŭθεντος, m. (part.) *having been loosened.*	κλειδ- ἑν- λŭθεντ-
-εν	-εν, n. -εντ, n.	τερεν, λŭθεν,	τερενος, n. (adj.) *tender.* λŭθεντος, n. *having been loosened.*	τερεν- λŭθεντ-
-ες	-εσ, n.	σăφες,	σăφους, n. (adj.) *clear.*	σăφεσ-
-ευς	-εϝ	φονευς,	φονεως, m. *murderer.*	φονεϝ-
-ην	-εν -ην	λĭμην, Ἑλλην,	λĭμενος, m. *harbour.* Ἑλληνος, m. *a Greek.*	λĭμεν- Ἑλλην-
-ηρ	-ερ -ηρ	αιθηρ, θηρ,	αιθερος, m. *ether.* θηρος, m. *wild beast.*	αιθερ- θηρ-
-ης	-εσ -ητ	τριηρης, βăρŭτης,	τριηρους, f. *trireme.* βăρŭτητος, f. *weight.*	τριηρεσ- βăρŭτητ-
-ι	-ι, n. -ιτ, n.	σĭνāπĭ, μελĭ,	σĭνāπεως, n. *mustard.* μελĭτος, n. *honey.*	σĭνāπι- μελĭτ-
-ιν	-ιν	δελφῑν,	δελφῑνος, m. *dolphin.*	δελφῑν-
-ις	-ι -ιτ -ιδ -ιθ -ιν	πολĭς, χăρĭς, ελπĭς, ορνῑς, δελφῑς,	πολεως, f. *city.* χăρĭτος, f. *grace.* ελπĭδος, f. *hope.* ορνῑθος, m. and f. *bird.* δελφῑνος, m. *dolphin.*	πολι- χăρĭτ- ελπĭδ- ορνῑθ- δελφῑν-
-ον	-ον, n. -οντ, n.	ευδαιμον, λυον,	ευδαιμονος, n. (adj.) *happy.* λυοντος, n. (part.) *loosening.*	ευδαιμον- λυοντ-
-ορ	-ορ, n.	ἄορ,	ἄορος, n. *sword.*	ἄορ-
-ος	-οτ, n. -εσ, n.	πεφῠκος, γενος,	πεφῠκοτος, n. (part.) *having been born.* γενους, n. *race.*	πεφῠκοτ- γενεσ-

Ending of Nom.Sing.	Ending of Crude Form.	EXAMPLES		Crude Form.
		Nom.	Gen.	
-ους	-οϝ -οδ -οντ	βους, πους,* οδους,	βοος, m. and f. *ox.* ποδος, m. *foot.* οδοντος, m. *tooth.*	βοϝ- ποδ- οδοντ-
-υ	-υ, n.	αστυ,	αστεος, n. *city.*	αστυ-
-ῡν -ῠν	-ῡν -υντ, n.	μοσῦν, δεικνῦν,	μοσῦνος, m. *wooden house.* δεικνυντος, n. (part.) *shewing.*	μοσῦν- δεικνυντ-
-υρ	-υρ, n.	πῦρ,†	πῠρος, n. *fire.*	πῦρ-
-ῡς -ῠς	-υ -υντ -υ -ῠδ	ιχθῦς, δεικνῦς, πηχῠς, χλᾰμῠς,	ιχθυος, m. *fish.* δεικνυντος, m. (part.) *shewing.* πηχεως, m. *cubit.* χλᾰμῠδος, f. *military cloak.*	ιχθυ- δεικνυντ- πηχυ- χλᾰμῠδ-
-ω	-οι	πειθω,	πειθους, f. *persuasion.*	πειθοι-
-ων	-ον -ων -οντ -ωντ	δαιμων, ἀγων, λεων, Ξενοφων,	δαιμονος, m. *deity.* ἀγωνος, m. *public contest.* λεοντος, m. *lion.* Ξενοφωντος, m. *Xenophon.*	δαιμον- αγων- λεοντ- Ξενοφωντ-
-ωρ	-ορ -ωρ, n.	ῥητωρ, ἑλωρ,	ῥητορος, m. *orator.* ἑλωρος, n. *booty.*	ῥητορ- ἑλωρ-
-ως	-ος -ως -οτ -ωτ	αιδως, ἡρως, πεφῠκως, ερως,	αιδους, f. *shame.* ἡρωος, m. *hero.* πεφῠκοτος, m. (part.) *having been born.* ερωτος, m. *love.*	αιδοσ- ἡρωσ- πεφῠκοτ- ερωτ-

* The diphthong, however, appears in this nom. πους (i.e. ποδ-ς) only because the word is a monosyllable; in the D. pl. we have ποσί (ποδσί), not πουσί: and although in the compounds τρίπους, τετράπους, etc., the diphthong was retained in the ordinary language, yet in the old poets the more strictly correct forms τρίπος, τετράπος, etc., also occur. See § 40.

† For the long vowel see above, note ².

Ending of Nom. Sing.	Ending of Crude Form.	Examples.		
		Nom.	Gen.	Crude Form.
-ψ	-π -β -φ	γυψ, χᾰλυψ, κᾰτηλιψ,	γῦπος, m. *vulture.* χᾰλῠβος, m. *steel.* κᾰτηλῐφος, f. *upper story.*	γῦπ- χᾰλῠβ- κᾰτηλίφ-
-ξ	-κ -γ -χ -κτ	φῠλαξ, φλοξ, ονυξ, νυξ,	φῠλᾰκος, m. *watchman* φλογος, f. *flame.* ονῠχος, m. *nail, claw.* νυκτος, f. *night.*	φῠλᾰκ- φλογ- ονῠχ- νυκτ-

ADJECTIVES.

144. The most numerous class of adjectives consists of those which in the masculine and neuter are declined from a crude form in *o*, in the feminine from a crude form in *a*. These are declined like substantives in *o* masc. and neut., and substantives fem. in *a*, except that in every case of the sing. fem. the vowel is ᾱ after ε, ι, and ρ, and after ο preceded by ρ, otherwise η.

	σοφο-, m. n.; σοφα-, f. *clever, wise.*			αισχρο-, m. n.; αισχρα-, f. *ugly, hateful.*		
	Masc.	*Fem.*	*Neut.*	*Masc.*	*Fem.*	*Neut.*
Sing. *Nom.* *Voc.* *Acc.* *Gen.* *Dat.*	σοφος σοφε σοφον σοφου σοφῳ	σοφη σοφη σοφην σοφης σοφῃ	σοφον σοφον σοφον σοφου σοφῳ	αισχρος αισχρε αισχρον αισχρου αισχρῳ	αισχρᾱ αισχρᾱ αισχρᾱν αισχρᾱς αισχρᾳ	αισχρον αισχρον αισχρον αισχρου αισχρῳ
Dual. *N.V.A.* *G.D.*	σοφω σοφοιν	σοφᾱ σοφαιν	σοφω σοφοιν	αισχρω αισχροιν	αισχρᾱ αισχραιν	αισχρω αισχροιν
Plural. *Nom.* *Voc.* *Acc.* *Gen.* *Dat.*	σοφοι σοφοι σοφους σοφων σοφοις	σοφαι σοφαι σοφᾱς σοφων σοφαις	σοφᾰ σοφᾰ σοφᾰ σοφων σοφοις	αισχροι αισχροι αισχρους αισχρων αισχροις	αισχραι αισχραι αισχρᾱς αισχρων αισχραις	αισχρᾱ αισχρᾱ αισχρᾱ αισχρων αισχροις

145. So are declined,

δικαιο-, m. n.; δίκαια-, f. *just*;   N. S. δίκαιος, δικαιά, δίκαιον.
αλλο-, m. n.; αλλα-, f. *other*;   αλλος, αλλη, αλλο.*
ἁπλοο-, m. n.; ἁπλοα-, f. *simple*;   ἁπλοος, ἁπλοη, ἁπλοον.
αθροο-, m. n.; αθροα-, f. *collected*;   αθροος, αθροᾱ, αθροον.

146. Many adjectives of this formation, including most compound adjectives and derivatives in ιο, ειο, and ιμο, with some others, have no special form for the feminine (adjectives of two terminations): as,

ἡσυχυ-, *quiet*;   N. m. f. ἡσυχος,   n. ἡσυχον.
ἀτεκνο-, *childless*;   N. m. f. ἀτεκνος,   n. ἀτεκνον.
καρποφορο-, *fruitful*;   N. m. f. καρποφορος,   n. καρποφορον.
σωτηριο-, *saving*;   N. m. f. σωτηριος,   n. σωτηριον.
βᾰσἴλειο-, *kingly*;   N. m. f. βᾰσἴλειος,   n. βᾰσἴλειον.
δοκῐμο-, *tried*;   N. m. f. δοκῐμος,   n. δοκῐμον.

δικαιο-, βασιλειο-, and a few others, are declined sometimes with three, sometimes with two, terminations.

147. Adjectives in εο and οο undergo contraction (§ 33); οη is contracted into η, οᾰ into ᾱ;† the compounds of νοο-, *mind*; ῥοο- *stream*; πλοο-, *voyage*, are not contracted in the N. and A. of the plural neuter.

148.

	χρῡσεο-,‡ m. n.; χρῡσεα-, f. *golden.*			αργῠρεο-, m. n.; αργῠρεα-, f. *of silver.*		
	Masc.	Fem.	Neut.	Masc.	Fem.	Neut.
Sing. Nom. Gen.	χρῡσεος χρῡσους χρῡσεου χρῡσου etc.	χρῡσεᾱ χρῡση χρῡσεᾱς χρῡσης etc.	χρῡσεον χρῡσουν χρῡσεου χρῡσου etc.	αργῠρεος αργῠρους αργῠρεου αργῠρου etc.	αργῠρεᾱ αργῠρᾱ αργῠρεᾱς αργῠρᾱς etc.	αργῠρεον αργῠρουν αργῠρεου αργῠρου etc.
Plural. Nom.	χρῡσεοι χρῡσοι etc.	χρῡσεαι χρῡσαι etc.	χρῡσεᾰ χρῡσᾱ etc.	αργῠρεοι αργῠροι etc.	αργῠρεαι αργῠραι etc.	αργῠρεᾰ αργῠρᾱ etc.

* On αλλο for αλλον, see § 191.

† These contractions should perhaps be referred to sister-forms in εη ἑᾰ, such as the Ionic διπλεη, etc.

‡ Sometimes χρῡσεο-, with ῠ, in lyrical passages.

ADJECTIVES.

	ἁπλοο-, m. n.; ἁπλοα-, f. simple.			ευνοο-, m. f. n. well-affected.		
	Masc.	Fem.	Neut.	Masc. Fem.		Neut.
Sing. Nom.	ἁπλοος ἁπλους etc.	ἁπλοη ἁπλη etc.	ἁπλοον ἁπλουν etc.	ευνοος ευνους etc.		ευνοον ευνουν etc.
Plural. Nom.	ἁπλοοι ἁπλοι etc.	ἁπλοαι ἁπλαι etc.	ἁπλοᾰ ἁπλᾱ etc.	ευνοοι ευνοι etc.		ευνοᾰ etc.

149. So are declined χαλκεο-, *of copper, brasen*; ἀδελφῐδεο-, *brother's* or *sister's* (*son or daughter*); πορφῠρεο-, *purple*; διπλοο-, *double*, etc.: like ευνοο- are declined ἄνοο-, *foolish*; περιρροο-, *surrounded by water*; απλοο-, *unfit for sea*; and some others.

150. A few adjectives in ω are declined after the so-called Attic declension (§ 131): as, Ἴλεω-, m. f. n. *propitious*; πλεω-, m. n.; πλεα-, f. *full*.* Of σωϝ- and σωο-, *safe*, only forms of the N. and A. sing. and plur. are found, and these not complete in all the genders.

	Ἴλεω-, m. f. n. propitious.		πλεω-, m. n.; πλεα-, f. full.		
	Masc. & Fem.	Neut.	Masc.	Fem.	Neut.
Singular. Nom.	ἵλεως	ἵλεων	πλεως	πλεᾱ	πλεων
Voc.	ἵλεως	ἵλεων	πλεως	πλεᾱ	πλεων
Acc.	ἵλεων	ἵλεων	πλεων	πλεᾱν	πλεων
Gen.	ἵλεω	ἵλεω	πλεω	πλεᾱς	πλεω
Dat.	ἵλεῳ	ἵλεῳ	πλεῳ	πλεᾳ	πλεῳ
Dual. N. V. A.	ἵλεω	ἵλεω	πλεω	πλεᾱ	πλεω
G. D.	ἵλεῳν	ἵλεῳν	πλεῳν	πλεαιν	πλεῳν
Plural. Nom.	ἵλεῳ	ἵλεᾱ	πλεῳ	πλεαι†	πλεᾱ
Voc.	ἵλεῳ	ἵλεᾱ	πλεῳ	πλεαι	πλεᾱ
Acc.	ἵλεως	ἵλεᾱ	πλεως	πλεᾱς	πλεᾱ
Gen.	ἵλεων	ἵλεων	πλεων	πλεων	πλεων
Dat.	ἵλεῳς	ἵλεῳς	πλεῳς	πλεαις	πλεῳς

* Also Ἴλᾱο- and πλεο-, Ion. πλειο-. † Or, πλεᾳ.

Some compound adjectives of this declension also make the A. S. masc. in ω.

151. Adjectives in υ are declined like those substantives in υ in which υ passes into ε (§ 100), except that the gen. sing. ends in ος, not ως, and that contraction does not take place in the neut. pl. The feminine of these adjectives is formed by the addition of -ια to the altered crude form ; α is not lengthened in the N. and A. sing. (§ 119, (8)).

	ἡδυ-, m. n.; ἡδεια-, f. sweet, pleasant.		
	Masc.	Fem.	Neut.
Singular.			
Nom.	ἡδύς	ἡδεῖα	ἡδύ
Voc.	ἡδύ	ἡδεῖα	ἡδύ
Acc.	ἡδύν	ἡδεῖαν	ἡδύ
Gen.	ἡδέος	ἡδείας	ἡδέος
Dat.	ἡδεῖ	ἡδείᾳ	ἡδεῖ
Dual.			
N. V. A.	ἡδέε	ἡδεία	ἡδέε
G. D.	ἡδέοιν	ἡδείαιν	ἡδέοιν
Plural.			
Nom.	ἡδεῖς	ἡδεῖαι	ἡδέα
Voc.	ἡδεῖς	ἡδεῖαι	ἡδέα
Acc.	ἡδεῖς	ἡδείας	ἡδέα
Gen.	ἡδέων	ἡδειῶν	ἡδέων
Dat.	ἡδέσι(ν)	ἡδείαις	ἡδέσι(ν)

151.* So are declined βαθυ-, *deep*; βαρυ-, *heavy*; γλυκυ-, *sweet*; ευρυ-, *broad*; ταχυ-, *swift*.

152. Adjectives and participles in αντ, οντ, υντ, and εντ, are declined like substantives in ντ (§ 74*). The feminine is formed by the addition of σα to the masc. crude form ; αντσα-, οντσα-, υντσα-, become ᾱσα-, ουσα-, ῡσα- ; εντσα- becomes εσσα- in adjectives, εισα- in participles. In the N. and A. sing., α of the fem. remains short (§ 119 (2)).

ADJECTIVES.

	παντ-, m. n.; πασα-, f. all.			λυσαντ-, m. n.; λυσασα-, f. having loosened.		
	Masc.	Fem.	Neut.	Masc.	Fem.	Neut.
Sing.						
Nom.	πᾶς	πᾶσᾰ	πᾶν*	λῡ́σᾱς	λῡ́σᾱσᾰ	λῡ́σᾱν
Voc.	πᾶς	πᾶσᾰ	πᾶν	λῡ́σᾱς	λῡ́σᾱσᾰ	λῡ́σᾱν
Acc.	παντᾰ	πᾶσᾰν	πᾶν	λῡ́σαντᾰ	λῡ́σᾱσᾰν	λῡ́σᾱν
Gen.	παντος	πᾱ́σης	παντος	λῡ́σαντος	λῡσᾱ́σης	λῡ́σαντος
Dat.	παντῐ	πᾱ́σῃ	παντῐ	λῡ́σαντῐ	λῡσᾱ́σῃ	λῡ́σαντῐ
Dual.						
N. V. A.	παντε	πᾱ́σᾱ	παντε	λῡ́σαντε	λῡσᾱ́σᾱ	λῡ́σαντε
G. D.	παντοιν	πᾱ́σαιν	παντοιν	λῡσάντοιν	λῡσᾱ́σαιν	λῡσάντοιν
Plural.						
Nom.	παντες	πᾶσαι	παντᾰ	λῡ́σαντες	λῡ́σᾱσαι	λῡ́σαντᾰ
Voc.	παντες	πᾶσαι	παντᾰ	λῡ́σαντες	λῡ́σᾱσαι	λῡ́σαντᾰ
Acc.	παντᾰς	πᾱ́σᾱς	παντᾰ	λῡ́σαντᾰς	λῡσᾱ́σᾱς	λῡ́σαντᾰ
Gen.	παντων	πᾱσῶν	παντων	λῡσάντων	λῡσᾱσῶν	λῡσάντων
Dat.	πᾶσῐ(ν)	πᾱ́σαις	πᾶσῐ(ν)	λῡ́σᾱσῐ(ν)	λῡσᾱ́σαις	λῡ́σᾱσῐ(ν)

	λυοντ-, m. n.; λυουσα-, f. loosening.*			δοντ-, m. n.; δουσα-, f. having given.†		
	Masc.	Fem.	Neut.	Masc.	Fem.	Neut.
Sing.						
Nom.	λυων	λυουσᾰ	λυον	δους	δουσᾰ	δον
Voc.	λυων	λυουσᾰ	λυον	δους	δουσᾰ	δον
Acc.	λυοντᾰ	λυουσᾰν	λυον	δοντᾰ	δουσᾰν	δον
Gen.	λυοντος	λυουσης	λυοντος	δοντος	δουσης	δοντος
Dat.	λυοντῐ	λυουσῃ	λυοντῐ	δοντῐ	δουσῃ	δοντῐ
Dual.						
N. V. A.	λυοντε	λυουσᾱ	λυοντε	δοντε	δουσᾱ	δοντε
G. D.	λυοντοιν	λυουσαιν	λυοντοιν	δοντοιν	δουσαιν	δοντοιν
Plural.						
Nom.	λυοντες	λυουσαι	λυοντᾰ	δοντες	δουσαι	δοντᾰ
Voc.	λυοντες	λυουσαι	λυοντᾰ	δοντες	δουσαι	δοντᾰ
Acc.	λυοντᾰς	λυουσᾱς	λυοντᾰ	δοντᾰς	δουσᾱς	δοντᾰ
Gen.	λυοντων	λυουσων	λυοντων	δοντων	δουσων	δοντων
Dat.	λυουσῐ(ν)	λυουσαις	λυουσῐ(ν)	δουσῐ(ν)	δουσαις	δουσῐ(ν)

* ᾱ in the monosyllable πᾶν: the compounds 'ἅπαντ- and προπαντ- have, regularly, 'ἅπᾶν and προπᾶν in N. and A. neut. sing.

† All participles in οντ are declined like λυ-οντ-; γνο-ντ-, δο-ντ-, διδο-ντ-, and ἁλο-ντ-, participles in ντ from crude forms in ο (γνο-, know; δο-, give, and 'ἁλο-, be captured), are declined like δοντ-, § 76, n.*

ADJECTIVES.

δεικνυντ-, m. n.; δεικνῦσα-, f. *shewing*.

	Masc.	Fem.	Neut.
Singular.			
Nom.	δεικνῦς	δεικνῦσᾰ	δεικνῦν
Voc.	δεικνῦς	δεικνῦσᾰ	δεικνῦν
Acc.	δεικνυντᾰ	δεικνῦσᾰν	δεικνῦν
Gen.	δεικνυντος	δεικνῦσης	δεικνυντος
Dat.	δεικνυντῐ	δεικνῦσῃ	δεικνυντῐ
Dual.			
N. V. A.	δεικνυντε	δεικνῦσᾱ	δεικνυντε
G. D.	δεικνυντοιν	δεικνῦσαιν	δεικνυντοιν
Plural.			
Nom.	δεικνυντες	δεικνῦσαι	δεικνυντᾰ
Voc.	δεικνυντες	δεικνῦσαι	δεικνυντᾰ
Acc.	δεικνυντᾰς	δεικνῦσᾱς	δεικνυντᾰ
Gen.	δεικνυντων	δεικνῦσων	δεικνυντων
Dat.	δεικνῦσῐ(ν)	δεικνῦσαις	δεικνῦσῐ(ν)

χᾰριεντ-, m. n.; χᾰριεσσα-, f. *graceful*.

	Masc.	Fem.	Neut.
Singular.			
Nom.	χᾰριεις	χᾰριεσσᾰ	χᾰριεν
Voc.	χᾰριεν	χᾰριεσσᾰ	χᾰριεν
Acc.	χᾰριεντᾰ	χᾰριεσσᾰν	χᾰριεν
Gen.	χᾰριεντος	χᾰριεσσης	χᾰριεντος
Dat.	χᾰριεντῐ	χᾰριεσσῃ	χᾰριεντῐ
Dual.			
N. V. A.	χᾰριεντε	χᾰριεσσᾱ	χᾰριεντε
G. D.	χᾰριεντοιν	χᾰριεσσαιν	χᾰριεντοιν
Plural.			
Nom.	χᾰριεντες	χᾰριεσσαι	χᾰριεντᾰ
Voc.	χᾰριεντες	χᾰριεσσαι	χᾰριεντᾰ
Acc.	χᾰριεντᾰς	χᾰριεσσᾱς	χᾰριεντᾰ
Gen.	χᾰριεντων	χᾰριεσσων	χᾰριεντων
Dat.	χᾰριεσσῐ(ν)	χᾰριεσσαις	χᾰριεσσῐ(ν)

ADJECTIVES.

	γράφεντ-, m. n. ; γράφεισα-, f. *having been written*.		
	Masc.	*Fem.*	*Neut.*
Singular.			
Nom.	γράφεις	γράφεισᾰ	γράφεν
Voc.	γράφεις	γράφεισᾰ	γράφεν
Acc.	γράφεντᾰ	γράφεισᾰν	γράφεν
Gen.	γράφεντος	γράφεισης	γράφεντος
Dat.	γράφεντῐ	γράφεισῃ	γράφεντῐ
Dual.			
N. V. A.	γράφεντε	γράφεισᾱ	γράφεντε
G. D.	γράφεντοιν	γράφεισαιν	γράφεντοιν
Plural.			
Nom.	γράφεντες	γράφεισαι	γράφεντᾰ
Voc.	γράφεντες	γράφεισαι	γράφεντᾰ
Acc.	γράφεντᾰς	γράφεισᾱς	γράφεντᾰ
Gen.	γράφεντων	γράφεισων	γράφεντων
Dat.	γράφεισῐ(ν)	γράφεισαις	γράφεισῐ(ν)

153. Perfect participles in οτ form the nom. masc. sing. by a change of the short vowel into ω; τ becomes ς, both in the masc. and neut. (§§ 55, 69). The crude form of the feminine ends in υια.

	λελῠκοτ- m. n. ; λελῠκυια-, f. *having loosened*.		
	Masc.	*Fem.*	*Neut.*
Singular.			
Nom.	λελῠκως	λελῠκυιᾰ	λελῠκος
Voc.	λελῠκως	λελῠκυιᾰ	λελῠκος
Acc.	λελῠκοτᾰ	λελῠκυιᾰν	λελῠκος
Gen.	λελῠκοτος	λελῠκυιᾱς	λελῠκοτος
Dat.	λελῠκοτῐ	λελῠκυιᾳ	λελῠκοτῐ
Dual.			
N. V. A.	λελῠκοτε	λελῠκυιᾱ	λελῠκοτε
G. D.	λελῠκοτοιν	λελῠκυιαιν	λελῠκοτοιν
Plural.			
Nom.	λελῠκοτες	λελῠκυιαι	λελῠκοτᾰ
Voc.	λελῠκοτες	λελῠκυιαι	λελῠκοτᾰ
Acc.	λελῠκοτᾰς	λελῠκυιᾱς	λελῠκοτᾰ
Gen.	λελῠκοτων	λελῠκυιων	λελῠκοτων
Dat.	λελῠκοσῐ(ν)	λ λῠκυιαις	λελῠκοσῐ(ν)

ADJECTIVES.

154. Adjectives in αν, εν, are declined regularly: the crude form of the fem. ends in αινα, εινα (for ανια, ενια, § 45).

	μελᾰν-, m. n.; μελαινα-, f. *black.*			τερεν-, m. n.; τερεινα-, f. *tender.*		
	Masc.	*Fem.*	*Neut.*	*Masc.*	*Fem.*	*Neut.*
Sing.						
Nom.	μελᾱς	μελαινᾰ	μελᾰν	τερην	τερεινᾰ	τερεν
Voc.	μελᾰν	μελαινᾰ	μελᾰν	τερεν	τερεινᾰ	τερεν
Acc.	μελᾰνᾰ	μελαινᾰν	μελᾰν	τερενᾰ	τερεινᾰν	τερεν
Gen.	μελᾰνος	μελαινης	μελᾰνος	τερενος	τερεινης	τερενος
Dat.	μελᾰνῐ	μελαινῃ	μελᾰνῐ	τερενῐ	τερεινῃ	τερενῐ
Dual.						
N.V.A.	μελᾰνε	μελαινᾱ	μελᾰνε	τερενε	τερεινᾱ	τερενε
G.D.	μελᾰνοιν	μελαιναιν	μελᾰνοιν	τερενοιν	τερειναιν	τερενοιν
Plural.						
Nom.	μελᾰνες	μελαιναι	μελᾰνᾰ	τερενες	τερειναι	τερενᾰ
Voc.	μελᾰνες	μελαιναι	μελᾰνᾰ	τερενες	τερειναι	τερενᾰ
Acc.	μελᾰνᾰς	μελαινᾱς	μελᾰνᾰ	τερενᾰς	τερεινᾱς	τερενᾰ
Gen.	μελᾰνων	μελαινων	μελᾰνων	τερενων	τερεινων	τερενων
Dat.	μελᾰσῐ(ν)	μελαιναις	μελᾰσῐ(ν)	τερεσῐ(ν)	τερειναις	τερεσῐ(ν)

So is declined τᾰλᾰν-, m. n.; τᾰλαινα-, f. *wretched.* Homer sometimes has ταλᾱς in the vocative.

155. Adjectives in ον have no distinct form for the feminine: they are declined like substantives in ον. In some words ν is omitted, and contraction ensues.

	σωφρον-, m. f. n. *sound-minded.*		μειζον-, m. f. n. *greater.*	
	Masc. & Fem.	*Neut.*	*Masc. & Fem.*	*Neut.*
Sing.				
Nom.	σωφρων	σωφρον	μειζων	μειζον
Voc.	σωφρον	σωφρον	μειζον	μειζον
Acc.	σωφρονᾰ	σωφρον	μειζονᾰ & μειζω	μειζον
Gen.	σωφρονος	σωφρονος	μειζονος	μειζονος
Dat.	σωφρονῐ	σωφρονῐ	μειζονῐ	μειζονῐ
Dual.				
N.V.A.	σωφρονε	σωφρονε	μειζονε	μειζονε
G.D.	σωφρονοιν	σωφρονοιν	μειζονοιν	μειζονοιν
Plural.				
Nom.	σωφρονες	σωφρονᾰ	μειζονες & μειζους	μειζονᾰ & μειζω
Voc.	σωφρονες	σωφρονᾰ	μειζονες & μειζους	μειζονᾰ & μειζω
Acc.	σωφρονᾰς	σωφρονᾰ	μειζονᾰς & μειζους	μειζονᾰ & μειζω
Gen.	σωφρονων	σωφρονων	μειζονων	μειζονων
Dat.	σωφροσῐ(ν)	σωφροσῐ(ν)	μειζοσῐ(ν)	μειζοσῐ(ν)

156. Like σωφρον- are declined αφρον-, *senseless*; ευδαιμον-, *fortunate*; ελεημον-, *merciful*, and many others. Like μειζον- are declined ἀμεινον-, *better*; καλλῑον-, *more beautiful*; ἧττον-, *less*, and some other comparatives.

157. Adjectives in εσ (m. f. n.), a very numerous class, and frequently formed from substantives in εσ (neut.), are declined like those substantives, except that εs is not changed into οs in the N. S. of the neuter (§§ 84, 90).

	ἀληθεσ-, m. f. n. *true.*			
	Masc. & Fem.		*Neut.*	
Singular.				
Nom.	ἀληθης		ἀληθες	
Voc.	ἀληθες		ἀληθες	
Acc.	(ἀληθεᾰ)	ἀληθη	ἀληθες	
Gen.	(ἀληθεος)	ἀληθους	(ἀληθεος)	ἀληθους
Dat.	(ἀληθεϊ)	ἀληθει	(ἀληθεϊ)	ἀληθει
Dual.				
N. V. A.	(ἀληθεε)	ἀληθη	(ἀληθεε)	ἀληθη
G. D.	(ἀληθεοιν)	ἀληθοιν	(ἀληθεοιν)	ἀληθοιν
Plural.				
Nom.	(ἀληθεες)	ἀληθεις	(ἀληθεᾰ)	ἀληθη
Voc.	(ἀληθεες)	ἀληθεις	(ἀληθεᾰ)	ἀληθη
Acc.	(ἀληθεᾰς)	ἀληθεις	(ἀληθεᾰ)	ἀληθη
Gen.	(ἀληθεων)	ἀληθων	(ἀληθεων)	ἀληθων
Dat.	ἀληθεσϊ(ν)		ἀληθεσϊ(ν)	

Adjectives in εεσ contract εᾰ of the A. sing. and N. A. neut. pl. into ᾱ, not η: as, ενδεᾱ for ενδεεᾰ, from ενδεεσ-, *needy*. In words ending in ιεσ or υεσ both contractions are used: as, ὑγιᾱ and ὑγιη, from ὑγιεσ-, *healthy*; ευφυᾱ and ευφυη, from ευφυεσ-, *well-grown, of good parts*.

158. So are declined ἀκρῑβεσ-, *accurate*; ἀμελεσ-, *careless*; ἀσθενεσ-, *weak*; εγκρᾰτεσ-, *strong*; ευγενεσ-, *well-born*; ευσεβεσ-, *pious*; σᾰφεσ-, *clear*; ὑγιεσ-, *healthy*. On the declension of proper names compounded of γενεσ-, *birth*; κρᾰτεσ-, *power*; σθενεσ-, *strength*, etc., see § 85.

159. The above are the principal classes of adjectives. Many single adjectives, chiefly compounds, of various terminations, are declined like nouns of the separable (third) declension: thus,

ἀπατορ- *fatherless*; N. S. m. f. ἀπάτωρ, n. ἀπάτορ.
 A. S. ἀπάτορα ἀπάτορ, etc.
εὐελπῐδ-, *full of hope*; N. S. m. f. εὐελπῐς n. εὐελπῐ, etc.
φῐλοπολῐδ- & φῐλοπολι-, } *patriotic*; N. S. m. f. φῐλοπολῐς, n. φῐλοπολῐ.
 G. S. m. f. n. φῐλοπολῐδος & φῐλοπολεως, etc.
ιδοι-, *skilful*; N. S. m. f. ιδρῐς, n. ιδρῐ.
 G. S. m. f. n. ιδριος & ιδρεως (§ 97).

160. Many adjectives, either from their form or meaning, admit of no special form for the neuter: as, ἡλῐκ-, *in one's prime*; ἁρπᾰγ-, *rapacious*; μωνῠχ-, *solid-hoofed*; αγνωτ-, *unknown*; αδμητ-, *untamed*; ακμητ-, *unwearied*; γυμνητ-, *light-armed*; ἡμιθνητ-, *half-dead*; πενητ-, *poor*; ἀναλκῐδ-, *cowardly*; ἀπαιδ-, *childless*; αιθων-, *flashing*; μακροχειρ-, *long-handed*. These are all declined regularly: thus, N. S. m. f. ἁρπαξ, πενης, μακροχειρ, etc. Some of these words are accompanied by collateral forms which admit of a neuter: as, αδμητο-, N. S. m. f. αδμητος, n. αδμητον. Similarly are found μωνῠχο-, αγνωτο- or αγνωστο-, ακμητο-, and others.*

161. Adjectives compounded of ποδ-, *foot*, take an anomalous neuter nom. and acc. in -ουν: thus, ἀποδ-, *without feet*; τρῐποδ-, *having three feet*; τετρᾰποδ-, *having four feet*, are declined N. S. m. f. ἀπους, n. ἀπουν, etc.

162. Some adjectives ending in a suffix exclusively masculine, are for the most part only of the masc. gender: thus, εθελοντα-, *voluntary*;† ὑβριστα-, *violent*; νεφεληγερετα- (poet.) *cloud-collecting*, have no feminine. Similarly ηρῐγενεια- (poet.), *early-born*, has no masc.

163. The adjectives μεγα- and μεγᾰλο-, *great*; πολυ- and πολλο-, *much, many*; πρᾱυ- and πρᾱο-, *mild*, are declined partly from one crude form, partly from the other.

---

* Yet the consonant-forms are sometimes found as neuter, at all events in the gen. and dat.: as, δι' αμφιτρητος αυλιου, Soph. Phil. 19; εν μεσοις βοτοις σιδηροκμησιν, Aj. 325.

† But εθελοντην αυτην occurs in Herod. ι. 5.

ADJECTIVES.

	μεγα- and μεγάλο-, m. n.; μεγάλα-, f. *great*.			πολυ- and πολλο-, m. n.; πολλα-, f. *much, many*.		
	Masc.	*Fem.*	*Neut.*	*Masc.*	*Fem.*	*Neut.*
Sing.						
Nom.	μέγας	μεγάλη	μέγα	πολύς	πολλή	πολύ
Voc.	μέγα	μεγάλη	μέγα	πολύ	πολλή	πολύ
Acc.	μέγαν	μεγάλην	μέγα	πολύν	πολλήν	πολύ
Gen.	μεγάλου	μεγάλης	μεγάλου	πολλοῦ	πολλῆς	πολλοῦ
Dat.	μεγάλῳ	μεγάλῃ	μεγάλῳ	πολλῷ	πολλῇ	πολλῷ
Dual.						
N. V. A.	μεγάλω	μεγάλα	μεγάλω	πολλώ	πολλά	πολλώ
G. D.	μεγάλοιν	μεγάλαιν	μεγάλοιν	πολλοῖν	πολλαῖν	πολλοῖν
Plural.						
Nom.	μεγάλοι	μεγάλαι	μεγάλα	πολλοί	πολλαί	πολλά
Voc.	μεγάλοι	μεγάλαι	μεγάλα	πολλοί	πολλαί	πολλά
Acc.	μεγάλους	μεγάλας	μεγάλα	πολλούς	πολλάς	πολλά
Gen.	μεγάλων	μεγάλων	μεγάλων	πολλῶν	πολλῶν	πολλῶν
Dat.	μεγάλοις	μεγάλαις	μεγάλοις	πολλοῖς	πολλαῖς	πολλοῖς

	πρᾱο- and πρᾱΰ-, m. n.; πρᾱεια-, f. *mild*.		
	Masc.	*Fem.*	*Neut.*
Sing.			
Nom.	πρᾶος	πρᾱεῖα	πρᾶον or πρᾱΰ
Voc.	πρᾶε	πρᾱεῖα	πρᾶον
Acc.	πρᾶον	πρᾱεῖαν	πρᾶον
Gen.	πρᾱου	πρᾱείας	πρᾱου
Dat.	πρᾴῳ	πρᾱείᾳ	πρᾴῳ
Dual.			
N. V. A.	πρᾴω	πρᾱεῖα	πρᾴω
G. D.	πρᾴοιν	πρᾱείαιν	πρᾴοιν
Plural.			
Nom.	πρᾶεις or πρᾶοι	πρᾶειαι	πρᾶεα
Voc.	πρᾶεις or πρᾶοι	πρᾶειαι	πρᾶεα
Acc.	πρᾶους	πρᾶείας	πρᾶεα
Gen.	πρᾶέων	πρᾶειων	πρᾶέων
Dat.	πρᾶεσί(ν) or πρᾶοις	πρᾶείαις	πρᾶεσί(ν) or πρᾶοις

Comparison of Adjectives.

164. The most frequently used suffix for the comparative degree of adjectives is -τερο (m. n. -τερα, f.), and for the superlative -τᾰτο (m. n. -τᾰτα, f.).

165. These suffixes are added to the crude form of the simple adjective; but crude forms in ο lengthen ο into ω, if the syllable preceding be short.

Positive.	Comparative.	Superlative.
κουφο-, *light*;	κουφοτερο-, *lighter*;	κουφοτᾰτο-, *lightest.*
πικρο-, *bitter*;	πικροτερο-, *bitterer*;	πικροτᾰτο-, *bitterest.*
σοφο-, *wise*;	σοφωτερο-, *wiser*;	σοφωτᾰτο-, *wisest.*
γλῠκυ-, *sweet*;	γλῠκῠτερο-, *sweeter*;	γλῠκῠτᾰτο-, *sweetest.*
μελᾰν-, *black*;	μελαντερο-, *blacker*;	μελαντᾰτο-, *blackest.*
μᾰκᾰρ-, *blessed*;	μᾰκαρτερο-, *more blessed*;	μᾰκαρτᾰτο-, *most blessed.*
σᾰφεσ-, *clear*;	σᾰφεστερο-, *clearer*;	σᾰφεστᾰτο-, *clearest.*
χᾰριεντ-, *graceful*;	χᾰριεστερο-, *more graceful*; (for χᾰριεντ-τερο-, § 37)	χᾰριεστᾰτο-, *most graceful.*
ἀχᾰρῐτ-, *ungraceful.*	ἀχᾰριστερο-, *more ungraceful*; (for ἀχᾰριτ-τερο-)	ἀχᾰριστᾰτο-, *most ungraceful*;

166. Γεραιο-, *aged*; πᾰλαιο-, *ancient*; and σχολαιο-, *leisurely*, omit ο before these endings—γεραιτερο-, πᾰλαιτερο-, σχολαιτᾰτο-; but from πᾰλαιο- and σχολαιο- the fuller forms are sometimes found. On the other hand, μεσο-, *in the midst*; ἴσο-, *equal*; ευδιο-, *calm*; πρωιο-, *early*; οψιο-, *late*; πλησιο-, *near*, substitute αι for ο or ω in the comparative and superlative: as, μεσαιτερο-, πρωϊαιτᾰτο-, etc.;—ἡσῠχο-, *quiet*, has both ἡσῠχαιτερο- and ἡσῠχωτερο-*;—φῐλο-, *dear*, has φῐλωτερο-(-τᾰτο-), φῐλαιτερο-(-τατο-), and φιλτερο-(τᾰτο-): also φῐλιον-, φῐλιστο- (§ 169). From μεσο- was also formed μεσᾰτο-, *in the midst*, originally a superlative: in like manner νεᾰρο-, *youthful*, and νεᾰτο-, *last*, must be regarded as originally comparative and superlative from νεο-, *young, new*.

---

* These forms in αιτερο, αιτᾰτο, were perhaps originally adverbial comparatives and superlatives, made from such adverbs as πᾰλαι, περᾳ, ἡσῠχῃ, σχολῃ, from which, in like manner, the adjectives πᾰλαιο-, περαιο-, ἡσῠχαιο-, σχολαιο-, were derived. Exactly in the same way must μῠχοιτᾰτο-, *in the remotest corner*, be regarded as formed from μῠχοι, *in the corner*, an adverbial dative from μῠχο-. See Ahrens. G. G. §§ 112. 9, 212. 4.

167. In some adjectives the syllable εσ is inserted between these suffixes and the root: this takes place,

  a. With words in ον: as,

  σωφρον-, *sound-minded*; Comp. σωφρονεστερο-; Sup. σωφρο-
  [νεστατο-.
  ευδαιμον-, *prosperous*; ευδαιμονεστερο-; ευδαι-
  [μονεστατο-.

But πῖον-, *fat*, has πῖοτερο-; and πεπον-, *ripe*, πεπαιτερο-.

  b. With the words ακρᾱτο-, *unmixed*; ερρωμενο-, *strong*; and some others, which make ακρᾱτεστερο-, ερρωμενεστερο-, etc.

168. The words λᾰλο-, *talkative*; πτωχο-, *beggarly*; οψοφᾰγο-, *dainty*; and a few others, take -ιστερο, -ιστᾰτο: as, λᾰλιστερο-, πτωχιστᾰτο-, etc.

169. The second, and less frequent, suffix for the comparative of adjectives is -ιον (ῐ for the most part in the older language, ῑ in Attic), and for the superlative -ιστο: the final vowel of the crude form is rejected before ι. These suffixes are chiefly found in connection with adjectives in υ.

Pos.	Comp.	Sup.
ἡδ-υ-, *sweet*;	ἡδῑον-, *sweeter*;	ἡδιστο-, *sweetest*.
τᾰχ-υ-, *swift*;	θασσον-, *swifter*; (for τᾰχιον-, § 45)	τᾰχιστο-, *swiftest*.
μεγ-α-, *great*;	μειζον-, *greater*; (for μεγιον-, § 45)	μεγιστο-, *greatest*.

These comparatives are declined like other adjectives in ον (§ 155).

170. Very frequently comparatives and superlatives in ῑον, ιστο, are found in connection with positives of a somewhat different crude form, or even containing an entirely different root: thus,

Positive.	Comparative.	Superlative.
αισχρο-, *shameful*;	αισχῑον-, (also αισχροτερο-,	αισχιστο-. αισχροτᾰτο-).
εχθρο-, *hostile*;	εχθῑον-, (also εχθροτερο-,	εχθιστο-. εχθροτᾰτο-).
μᾱκρο-, *long*;	μασσον-, (also μᾱκροτερο-,	μηκιστο- (or μᾱκ-) μᾱκροτᾰτο-).
μῑκρο-, *little*;	μειον-, (also μῑκροτερο-,	μῑκροτᾰτο-).
οικτρο-, *pitiable*;	—— (also οικτροτερο-,	οικτιστο-. οικτρ̥οτᾰτο-).

Positive.	Comparative.	Superlative.
ἀλγεινο-, *painful*;	ἀλγῖον-,	ἀλγιστο-.
κᾱλο-, *beautiful*;	καλλῖον-,	καλλιστο-.
ὀλίγο- (ἐλᾱχυ-), *few*;	ἐλασσον-,	ἐλᾱχιστο-.
		(also ὀλίγιστο-).
πολυ-, *much, many*;	πλειον-,	πλειστο-.
ῥᾳδιο-, *easy*;	ῥᾷον-,	ῥᾳστο-.

171. Many of these forms are connected with neuter substantives in εσ: compare αἰσχεσ-, *shame*; ἐχθεσ-, *hatred*; μηκεσ-, *length*; ἀλγεσ-, *pain*; καλλεσ-, *beauty*; τᾰχεσ-, *swiftness*. Again, the verbs αἰσχῠν-, *shame*; μηκῠν-, *lengthen*; ἀλγῠν-, *pain*, etc., render probable the former existence of adjectives in υ.

172. In connection with ἀγᾰθο-, *brave, good*, the following comparatives and superlatives occur :—

Comp.	Sup.
ἄμεινον-,	
ἀρειον- (Epic),	ἀριστο-.
βελτῖον-,	βελτιστο-.
κρεισσον- (κρειττον-),	κρᾰτιστο- (κρᾰτεσ-, *strength*).
λωῖον, λῷον (poet.),	λῷστο-.
φερτερο- (poet.),	φερτᾰτο-, φεριστο- (poet.).

173. In connection with κᾰκο-, *cowardly, bad*, the following comparatives and superlatives are found :—

Comp.	Sup.
κᾰκῖον-,	κᾰκιστο-.
χειρον- (χερειον-, Ep.),	χειριστο-.*
ἡσσον- (for ἡκιον-),	ἡκιστο-.

174. The following words are more or less defective .—

Pos.	Comp.	Sup.
	ὑστερο-, *later*;	ὑστᾰτο-, *latest*.
(ἐξ, *out of*,)		ἐσχᾰτο-, *farthest*.
(ὕπερ, *over*,)	ὑπερτερο-, *higher*;	ὑπερτᾰτο- & ὑπᾰτο-, *highest*.
(προ, *before*,)	προτερο-, *former*;	πρωτο-, *first*.

* Homer has a defective adjective—A. sing. χερηᾰ; D. χερηῖ; Pl. N. χερηες, *inferior* with which these words are doubtless connected.

ADVERBS FROM ADJECTIVES.

175. Adverbs are formed from adjectives by the addition of the suffix -ως to the crude form: as, σωφρον-, *temperate*, σωφρονως, *temperately*; παντ-, *all*, παντως, *in all ways*.

176. The final vowel of adjectives in ο disappears entirely before the adverbial suffix: σοφο-, *wise*, σοφως, *wisely*; ψῡχρο-, *cold*, ψῡχρως, *coldly*.

177. Words in υ and εσ are modified in the same way as in the gen. sing. of the adjective: σᾰφεσ-, *clear*, σᾰφως (σαφεως), *clearly*; but τᾰχυ-, *quick*, τᾰχεως, *quickly*, without contraction.

178. Very frequently the acc. neut. both of the singular and the plural takes the place of the adverbial form: as, τᾰχῠ, *quickly*; ευ (Epic εῠ), *well*, originally the neuter acc. sing. of an adjective εὐ- or ηὐ-, *noble, good*.

179. Another form of the adverb is in ᾰ: as, τᾰχᾰ (from τᾰχ-υ-), *quickly, perhaps*; 'ᾰμᾰ, *at the same time* (from the obsolete 'ᾰμο-, *one, some*, whence 'ἁμως, etc.); μᾰλᾰ, *very*. To μᾰλᾰ belong the comparative μαλλον (*potius*), and the superlative μᾰλιστᾰ (*potissimum*).

180. For the adverb of the comparative the neuter acc. sing. of the adjective is employed, and for the adverb of the superlative the neuter acc. plur. of the adjective: as, σοφωτερον, *more wisely*; καλλῑον, *more beautifully*; σοφωτᾰρᾰ, *most wisely*; καλλιστᾰ, *most beautifully*. Adverbs in ως are, however, sometimes formed from comparative and superlative adjectives: καλλῑονως, *more beautifully*.

181. The adverb οὑτως, *thus* (from τουτο-, *this*), loses the final ς before a consonant. The following adverbs, derived from prepositions, have entirely lost the ς: ἀνω, *upwards*, from ἀνᾰ, *up*; κᾰτω, *downwards*, from κᾰτᾰ, *down*; εσω, *within*, from ες or εις, *into*; εξω, *without*, from εξ, *out of*; also the comparatives ἀνωτερω, κᾰτωτερω, etc. Similarly are found απωτερω (from ἀπο, *from*), *more remotely*; εγγῠτερω (or εγγῠτερον), *more nearly*; and εγγῠτᾰτω (or εγγῠτᾰτᾰ), *most nearly*, from εγγῠ-, *near*; and a few others.*

PRONOUNS.

The personal pronouns are,—

	First Person. *I. me.*	Second Person. *thou, you.*	Third Person. *him, her, it.*
Singular. *Nom.* *Acc.* *Gen.* *Dat.*	ἐγώ ἐμέ, με ἐμοῦ, μου ἐμοί, μοι	σύ σε σου σοι	— ἑ οὗ οἱ
Dual. *N. A.* *G. D.*	(νωΐ) νω (νωΐν) νῷν	(σφωΐ) σφω (σφωΐν) σφῷν	(σφωε) (σφωΐν)
Plural. *Nom.* *Acc.* *Gen.* *Dat.*	ἡμεῖς ἡμᾶς ἡμῶν ἡμῖν	ὑμεῖς ὑμᾶς ὑμῶν ὑμῖν	σφεῖς, n. σφεά σφᾶς, n. σφεά σφων σφίσι(ν)

183. The crude forms in the singular are ἐ-με- (Lat. *me-*), σε- (L. *te-*), and ἐ- (L. *se-*). The nominatives ἐγώ and σύ are anomalous, that of ἐ- is wanting.

The crude forms in the dual are νω- (L. *no-s*), σφω- (L. *vo-s*), and σφω- : the dual of the 3rd person is not used in prose.

The crude forms in the plural are ἡμε-, ὑμε-, and σφε-.* ἐ- is at once the personal pronoun of the 3rd pers. (L. *eo-*), and a reflexive pronoun. It is not of frequent use in Attic prose, the cases of αὐτο- (with the exception of the nominative) being used instead in the former signification, and the compound ἑαυτο- in the latter (§§ 192, 194).

184. If there is no emphasis on the personal pronoun, its forms are enclitic. In this case the shorter forms of the 1st pers. are alone used: δοκεῖ μοι, *it appears to me*; but ἐμοὶ οὐ σοὶ τοῦτο ἀρέσκει, *it is to me, not to thee, that this is pleasing.* When the forms of the plural are enclitic, the final vowel in the acc. and dat. is sometimes shortened: ἡμᾶς, ὑμῖν, etc.

* Or, perhaps, rather ἡμετ-, ὑμετ-, σφετ-. On the primitive forms of the personal pronouns, see a paper by Mr. Key, *Phil. Soc. Trans.* iv. p. 25.

185. The original demonstrative pronoun of the Greek language was το-, *this, that*. In the declension of this word, τ of the C. F. is softened into ‛ in the N. m. f. of the sing. and plur.; and in the N. and A. n. sing. ν is not added.

	\multicolumn{9}{c}{το-, m. n. τα-, f. *this, that*; *the*.}							
	Singular.			Dual.			Plural.		
	Masc.	Fem.	Neut.	Masc.	Fem.	Neut.	Masc.	Fem.	Neut.
Nom.	ὁ	ἡ	το	τω	τᾱ	τω	οἱ	αἱ	τᾰ
Acc.	τον	την	το				τους	τας	τᾰ
Gen.	του	της	του	τοιν	ταιν	τοιν	των	των	των
Dat.	τῳ	τῃ	τῳ				τοις	ταις	τοις

In Homer το- retains its original demonstrative force: in later Greek it was used as the English definite article *the*.

In Attic the feminine forms of the dual are seldom found, τω, τοιν, being used instead.

186. From the simple demonstrative, or article, το-, other stronger demonstratives are formed: (1) το-δε, *this* (Lat. *ho-*), by the addition of the enclitic demonstrative particle δε; and (2) τουτο-, *this, that* (Lat. *ho-* or *eo-*), by reduplication. Το-δε is declined like the article. Τουτο-, in like manner, softens τ into the aspirate in the N. m. f. sing. and plur., and rejects ν in the N. and A. n. sing.; the diphthong of the first syllable is ου when the vowel of the final syllable is ο or ω, αυ when that vowel is α or η.

	το-δε, m.n.; τα-δε, f. *this*.			τουτο-, m.n.; ταυτα-, f. *this, that*.		
	Masc.	Fem.	Neut.	Masc.	Fem.	Neut.
Singular.						
Nom.	ὁδε	ἡδε	τοδε	οὑτος	αὑτη	τουτο
Acc.	τονδε	τηνδε	τοδε	τουτον	ταυτην	τουτο
Gen.	τουδε	τησδε	τουδε	τουτου	ταυτης	τουτου
Dat.	τῳδε	τῃδε	τῳδε	τουτῳ	ταυτῃ	τουτῳ
Dual.						
N. A.	τωδε	τᾱδε	τωδε	τουτω	ταυτᾱ	τουτω
G. D.	τοινδε	ταινδε	τοινδε	τουτοιν	ταυταιν	τουτοιν
Plural.						
Nom.	οἱδε	αἱδε	τᾰδε	οὑτοι	αὑται	ταυτᾰ
Acc.	τουσδε	τασδε	τᾰδε	τουτους	ταυτᾱς	ταυτᾰ
Gen.	τωνδε	τωνδε	τωνδε	τουτων	τουτων	τουτων
Dat.	τοισδε	ταισδε	τοισδε	τουτοις	ταυταις	τουτοις

F

187. From το-, *this*, are derived, further, τοσο-, *so great, so many* (L. *tanto-, tot*); τοιο-, *of such a kind* (L. *tali-*); and τηλἴκο-, *of such an age, so great;* which are declined regularly (N. S. τοσος, τοση, τοσον, etc.). In Attic prose, however, the forms τοσο-δε, τοιο-δε, τηλἴκο-δε, which are declined regularly, and τοσουτο-, τοιουτο-, τηλἴκουτο- (N. τοσουτος, τοσαυτη, τοσουτο and τοσουτον, etc.), are used instead of the simple forms.

188. The adverbs from το-, το-δε, and τουτο-, are ὡς (earlier, τως), ὡδε (for ὡσδε), and οὑτως or οὑτω, *in this manner, so, thus*. The adverb ὡς (for τως), *thus*, must not be confounded with ὡς, *how, as*, the adverb of the relative pronoun: in accentuated Greek these are distinguished (ὥς, ὧς, *thus;* but ὡς, *how, as*).

189. Εκεινο-, *that yonder* (L. *illo-*), is declined regularly, except that it also rejects the final ν in the N. and A. n. sing.:—

Sing. Nom.	εκεινος	εκεινη	εκεινο
Acc.	εκεινον	εκεινην	εκεινο
	etc.	etc.	etc.

From εκεινο- is formed the adverb εκεινως, *in that way*.

190. The forms of the demonstrative pronouns are often strengthened by the addition of ῑ: thus, οὑτοσῑ, ὁδῑ, εκεινωνῑ, αὑτηῑ, τοισδῑ, etc. Compare in Latin, *hosce, hisce*, etc. In Ionic Greek, and in the poets, εκεινο- is also found in the shorter form κεινο-.

191. Αυτο-, *self* (L. *ipso-*), and αλλο-, *other*, are declined regularly, rejecting, however, ν in the neut. sing.

αυτο-, m. n.; αυτα-, f. *self*.   αλλο-, m. n.; αλλα-, f. *other*.

	Masc.	Fem.	Neut.	Masc.	Fem.	Neut.
Sing. Nom.	αυτος	αυτη	αυτο	αλλος	αλλη	αλλο
Acc.	αυτον	αυτην	αυτο	αλλον	αλλην	αλλο
	etc.	etc.	etc.	etc.	etc.	etc.

192. The personal pronouns compounded with αυτο- give the reflective pronouns; they are declined as follows:—

Singular.   Plural.
Acc. εμαυτον, -ην, *myself*   ἡμᾶς αυτους or αυτᾱς, *ourselves*.
Gen. εμαυτου, -ης,   ἡμων αυτων,
          etc.   etc.

PRONOUNS.

Singular.	Plural.
Acc. σεαυτον, -ην, *thyself*,	ὑμᾶς αυτους or αυτᾱς, *yourselves*.
or σαυτον, -ην,	
Gen. σεαυτου, -ης,	ὑμων αυτων.
or σαυτου, -ης,	
etc.	etc.
Acc. ἑαυτον, -ην, -ο, *himself, her-*	σφᾶς αυτους or αυτᾱς, *themselves*.
or αὑτον, -ην, -ο, [*self, itself.*	and ἑαυτους, -ᾱς, ᾰ,
	or αὑτους, -ᾱς, -ᾰ,
Gen. ἑαυτου, -ης, -ου,	σφων αυτων,
or αὑτου, -ης, -ου,	and ἑαυτων or αὑτων,
etc.	etc.

193. Αυτο-, in connection with, and immediately following, the article το-, signifies *the same*; it is thus declined:—

Sing. *Nom.* ὁ αυτος	ἡ αυτη	το αυτο
or αὑτος (ἁὐτος)	αὑτη (ἁὐτη)*	ταὐτο or ταὐτον

Gen. του αυτου or ταὐτου, της αυτης, του αυτου or ταὐτου, etc.

194. Αυτο- in all its cases, except the nominative, is also used for the pronoun of the 3rd person, *him, her, it,* etc. In this sense it is never placed at the beginning of the sentence.

195. From αλλο- is formed the reciprocal pronoun αλληλο-, *each other*; the N., of course, could not occur: it is thus declined:—

Dual.	Plural.
Acc. (αλληλω, -ᾱ, -ω)	αλληλους, -ᾱς. -ᾰ
Gen. αλληλοιν, -αιν, -οιν	αλληλων
Dat. αλληλοιν, -αιν, -οιν	αλληλοις, -αις, -οις.†

196. The possessive pronouns are derived from the personal, and are declined like adjectives in ο with three terminations (§ 144).

* In accentuated Greek αὑτή or ἁὐτή, whereas the nom. sing. fem. of τουτο-, *this*, is αὕτη: so ταὐτά (for τα αὐτά), *the same things*, but ταῦτα, *these things*.

† This form appears to have arisen from a reduplication. Compare the similar, though more extended, use of *altero-, alio-*, repeated, in Latin.

From εμε- is made εμο-, *mine*, N. εμος, εμη, εμον.
σε- σο-, *thine*, N. σος, ση, σον.
[έ- έο- or ό-, *his, her*, N. έος, έη, έον
or ός, ή, όν.]
ημε-τ- ημετερο-, *our*, N. ημετερος, -ρᾱ, -ρον.
ὑμε-τ- ὑμετερο-, *your*, N. ὑμετερος, -ρᾱ, -ρον.
σφε-τ- σφετερο-, *their*, N. σφετερος, -ρᾱ, -ρον.

197. The possessive pronoun of the 3rd pers. (έο-), is not used in Attic prose; for the simple possessive the genitive αυτου (*ejus*) is employed, and εαυτου (αύτου) for the reflexive: thus, τον πᾰτερᾰ αυτου, *patrem ejus*; τον εαυτου πᾰτερᾰ, *suum patrem*. Similarly, μου, σου (enclitic), ημων, ὑμων, and αυτων, are used for the other possessive pronouns if unemphatic: thus, τον εμον πᾰτερᾰ, *meum patrem*; but τον πᾰτερᾰ μου, *patrem meum*.

198. The relative pronoun is ό-, *who, which, what*. In the N. and A. n. sing. ν is dropped.

	ό-, m. n.; ἁ-, f. *who, which, what.**							
	Singular.			Dual.			Plural.		
	Masc.	Fem.	Neut.	Masc.	Fem.	Neut.	Masc.	Fem.	Neut.
Nom.	ός	ή	ό				οί	αί	ἄ
Acc.	όν	ήν	ό	ώ	ἁ̄	ώ	ούς	ἁ̄ς	ἄ
Gen.	ού	ής	ού				ών	ών	ών
Dat.	ᾧ	ᾗ	ᾧ	οίν	αίν	οίν	οίς	αίς	οίς

199. The direct interrogative pronoun is τῐν-; *who? which? what?* The indirect interrogative, compounded of τῐν- and the relative ό-, is ό-τῐν-. The forms of the direct interrogative, which are then enclitic,† are also used for the indefinite pronoun, *any, some*. In the declension of this word, ν is dropped in the N. and A. neut. sing., and disappears before σ in the N. masc. without compensation, contrary to the rule (§ 40). Compare, also, the shorter forms given below.

---

* The forms of the nom. sing. and plur. of the relative are written in accented Greek as follows: ὅς, ἥ, ὅ; οἵ, αἵ, ἅ; they may thus be distinguished from the corresponding cases of the article, ὁ, ἡ, τό; οἱ, αἱ, τά, where it will be observed that the identical forms have no accent.

† Enclitics are little words which are pronounced with, and as it were *lean on* (εγκλιν-, *lean on*) the word preceding. Hence, when written with other words, they take no accent, except that disyllabic enclitics are in certain cases accented on the second syllable. Thus, while the cases of the interrog. pronoun always have an accent and on the root-syllable, those of the indef. generally have none: τίς; τίνα; *who?* but τις, τινα (sometimes τινά), *some one.*

PRONOUNS. 69

	τίν-, m. f. n. *who?* *which? what?*; *any.* Masc. & Fem. Neut.		ὁ-τίν-, m. n.; ἁ-τίν-, f. *who*, etc. (indirect interrog.); *whosoever.* Masc. Fem. Neut.		
Singular. Nom. Acc. Gen. Dat.	τίς τίνα τίνος τίνι	τί τί τίνος τίνι	ὅστις ὅντινα οὗτινος ᾧτινι	ἥτις ἥντινα ἧστινος ᾗτινι	ὅ τι ὅ τι οὗτινος ᾧτινι
Dual. N. A. G. D.	τίνε τίνοιν	τίνε τίνοιν	ὥτινε οἷντινοιν	ἅτινε αἷντινοιν	ὥτινε οἷντινοιν
Plural. Nom. Acc. Gen. Dat.	τίνες τίνας τίνων τίσι(ν)	τίνα τίνα τίνων τίσι(ν)	οἵτινες οὕστινας ὧντινων οἷστισι(ν)	αἵτινες ἅστινας ὧντινων αἷστισι(ν)	ἅτινα ἅτινα ὧντινων οἷστισι(ν)

For τίνος, τίνι (both interrogative and indefinite), τοῦ and τῷ are often used, and ἄττα for the neut. plur. τίνα (indef.) For οὗτινος, ᾧτινι, ὅτου and ὅτῳ are found; and in the plural, less frequently, ὅτων, ὁτοισί(ν), for ὧντινων, οἷστισί(ν): ἅττα occurs for ἅτινα. To distinguish the neuter pronoun from the conjunction ὅτι, *because, that*, the former is usually written ὅ τί, or ὅ,τί.

200. Another indefinite pronoun is δεινά, *quidam*; it is sometimes uninflected, more usually declined as follows, with the article:—

Singular. N. ὁ, ἡ, τὸ δεινά.   Plural. N. οἱ   δεῖνες.
 A. τον, την, το δεινά.   A. τοὺς δεῖνας.
 G. του, της, του δεῖνος.   G. τῶν δείνων.
 D. τῷ, τῃ, τῷ δεινί.

201. From the relative ὁ- are derived ὁσο-, *how great, how many* (L. *quanto-, quot*), and οἷο-, *of what kind* (L. *quali-*). To these correspond the interrogatives ποσο-; and ποιο; which are also used as indefinite, and the indirect interrogatives ὁποσο- and ὁποιο-. For a more complete list of these forms, see § 203.

202. The indirect interrogatives ὁ-τίν, ὁποσο-, etc., are also relatives (*whoever*, etc.), differing from the simple relative ὁ- as the Latin forms made by adding *-cunque* differ from *quo-*.

TABLE OF CORRELATIVE PRONOUNS.

203.

		Demonstrative.	Relative.	Interrogative.	Indefinite. (*Enclitic.*)	Indirect Interrog. (and Relative).
Greek. English. Latin.		το-, το-δε, τουτο-, *this, that.* ho-, i- or eo-.	ὁ-, *who, which, what.* qui- or quo-.	τίν-; *who? which? what?* qui- or quo-?	τίν-,* *a, any, some.* qui- or quo- (encl.), aliqui-.	ὁ-τίν-, *who, etc.; whoever, etc.* qui-; qui-cunque.
	G. E. L	ἑτερο-, *one of two.* altero-.		ποτερο-; *whether of the two?* utero-?	ποτερο-, *either of the two.* utero- (encl.), alter- utero-.	ὁποτερο-, *whether of the two;* *whichever of the two.* utero-, utero- cunque.
	G. E. L	τοσο-, τοσο-δε, τοσουτο-, *of such a size, or* *number.* tanto-, tot.	ὁσο-, (*as great, as many*) *as.* quanto-, quot.	ποσο-; *how great? how* *many?* quanto-? quot?	ποσο-, *of any size, or num-* *ber.* aliquanto-, etc.; aliquot.	ὁποσο-, *how great, etc.; how* *great soever.* quanto-, etc.; quan- to-cunque, etc.
	G. E. L	τοιο-, τοιο-δε, τοιουτο-, *of such a sort, such.* tali-.	οἱο-, (*such*) *as.* quali-.	ποιο-; *of what sort?* quali-?	ποιο-, *of any sort.* (quali- libet.)	ὁποιο-, *of what sort; of* *what sort soever.* quali-; quali-cunque.
	G. E.	τηλικο-, τηλικο-δε, τηλικουτο-, *of such an age, etc.*	ἡλικο-, (*as old*) *as, etc.*	πηλίκο-; *how old?* etc.	πηλίκο-, *of any age, etc.*	ὁπηλίκο-, *how old, etc.; how old* *soever.*

* In accentuated Greek the interrogative and indefinite pronouns are generally distinguishable, the former having an

204. TABLE OF CORRELATIVE PRONOMINAL ADVERBS.*

	where.	whither.	whence.	road by which.	time.	manner.
το-, *this, that*	τοθί, ενθά	ενθά	ενθεν	τῇ	τοτε	τως, ως
το-δε, *this*	ενθάδε	ενθάδε	ενθενδε	τῇδε		ωδε
τουτο-, *this, that*	ενταυθά	ενταυθά	εντευθεν	ταυτῃ		ουτως
εκεινο-, *that yonder*	εκει	εκεισε	εκειθεν	εκεινῃ		εκεινως
αυτο-, *self,* etc.	αυτοθί, αυτου†	αυτοσε	αυτοθεν			αυτως
ὁ-, *which*	ὁθί, οὑ	οἱ	ὁθεν	ᾗ	ὁτε	ως
[πο-;] *which?*	ποθί; που;	ποι;	ποθεν;	πῇ;	ποτε;	πως; ‡
[πο-,] encl.] *any*	ποθί, που	ποι	ποθεν	πῇ	ποτε	πως
[ὁπο-], *whichever*	ὁποθί, ὁπου	ὁποι	ὁποθεν	ὁπῃ	ὁποτε	ὁπως
ἑτερο-, *other of two*	ἑτερωθί	ἑτερωσε	ἑτερωθεν	ἑτερᾳ		ἑτερως
ποτερο-; *which of two?*	ποτερωθί;	ποτερωσε;				ποτερως;
ὁποτερο-, *whichever of two*	ὁποτερωθί	ὁποτερωσε	ὁποτερωθεν			ὁποτερως
ἑκάτερο-, *each of two*	ἑκατερωθί	ἑκατερωσε	ἑκατερωθεν			ἑκάτερως
ἑκαστο-, *each*	ἑκαστοθί		ἑκαστοθεν		ἑκαστοτε	
ὁμο-, *one and the same*	ὁμου	ὁμοσε	ὁμοθεν	ὁμῇ		ὁμως
αλλο-, *other*	αλλοθί	αλλοσε	αλλοθεν	αλλῃ	αλλοτε	αλλως
παντ-, *all*	παντοθί	παντοσε	παντοθεν	παντῃ	παντοτε	παντως
[αμο-] *one, some*	αμου		αμοθεν	αμῇ		αμως
ουδ-αμο- (ουτιν-), } *not one*	ουδαμοθί (& -μου)	ουδαμοσε	ουδαμοθεν	ουδαμῇ	ουποτε	ουδάμως
μηδ-αμο- (μητιν-), }	μηδαμοθί (& -μου)	μηδαμοσε (-μοι)	μηδάμοθεν	μηδαμῇ	μηποτε	μηδάμως
αμφοτερο-, *both*	αμφοτερωθί	αμφοτερωσε	αμφοτερωθεν	αμφοτερῃ		αμφοτερως
ουδετερο-, } *neither of the two*		ουδετερωσε	ουδετερωθεν			ουδετερως
μηδετερο-, }		μηδετερωσε	μηδετερωθεν			μηδετερως

* Some of the forms included in this table are of rare occurrence; others are only found in the poets, or in Ionic Greek, etc.

† These seeming genitives, αυτου, οὑ, που, etc., are perhaps contractions of the older forms αυτοθι, ὁθι, ποθι, etc.

‡ The *interrogative* pronominal adverbs take an accent in accentuated Greek, ποῖ; πότε; πῶς; and are thus distinguished from the *indefinite* adverbs, which are enclitic, ποι, ποτε (sometimes ποτέ), πως. See § 199.

205. From τιν-, *any*, are derived the negative pronouns ουτιν- (*nēmŏn-, nullo-*), μητιν- (*ne qui-*) *no one, none*; and from ἑτερο-, *one of two*, the negatives ουδετερο-, μηδετερο-, *neither of the two*

206. As from το-, *this*, and ὁ-, *what*, are derived τοιο-, *of this sort*, and οἰο-, *of what sort*; so from αλλο-, *other*, is formed αλλοιο-, *of another sort*; from ἑτερο-, *the other*, ἑτεροιο-, *of the other sort*; from ὁμο-, *one and the same*, ὁμοιο-, *of the same sort*; and from παντ-, *all*, παντοιο-, *of all sorts*.

207. In addition to the adverbial forms from αλλο-, ἑκαστο-, and παντ-, given in the table, the following are found:—

αλλᾰχοθῐ and αλλᾰχου, αλλᾰχοσε, αλλᾰχοθεν, αλλᾰχη.
ἑκαστᾰχοθῐ and ἑκαστᾰχου, ἑκαστᾰχοσε, ἑκαστᾰχοθεν.
παντᾰχοθῐ and παντᾰχου, παντᾰχοσε (-χοι), παντᾰχοθεν, παντᾰχη.

And in like manner from πολλο-, *many*, are derived—

πολλᾰχοθῐ and πολλαχου, πολλᾰχοσε, πολλᾰχοθεν, πολλᾰχη.

208. Other correlatives are τεως and τοφρᾰ, *so long* (L. *tamdiu*); ἑως and οφρᾰ (for ὁφρᾰ), *while* (L. *quamdiu*); ποστος; *which in a series?* and ὁποστος; τηνῐκᾰ (τηνῐκᾰδε, τηνῐκαυτᾰ), *then*; ἡνῐκᾰ, *when*; πηνῐκᾰ; *when?* and ὁπηνῐκᾰ.

209. To relative pronouns and adverbs may be joined the particles δη, δηποτε, and ουν, with the meaning of—*ever* (L. *-cunque*), and the enclitic περ, by which the idea of *precision* is added: ὁστις δηποτε, *quicunque*; ὁπως ουν, *utcunque*; ὡσπερ, *just as*.

NUMERALS.

210. The cardinal, ordinal, and adverbial numbers are as follows:—

NUMERALS.

Arabic Symbols.	Greek Symbols.	Cardinal.	Ordinal.	Adverbs.
1	α'	ἑν-(ϝεν-), m.n.; μια-, f.	πρωτο-	ἅπαξ *
2	β'	δυο-	δευτερο-	δῐ́ς
3	γ'	τρι-	τρῐ́το-	τρῐ́ς
4	δ'	τεσσᾰρ-	τεταρτο-	τετρᾰκῐ́ς
5	ε'	πεντε	πεμπτο-	πεντᾰκῐ́ς
6	ϛ'	ἑξ	ἑκτο-	ἑξᾰκῐ́ς
7	ζ'	ἑπτᾰ	ἑβδομο-	ἑπτᾰκῐ́ς
8	η'	οκτω	ογδοο-	οκτᾰκῐ́ς
9	θ'	εννεᾰ	ενᾰτο- (εννᾰτο-)	ενᾰκῐ́ς
10	ι'	δεκᾰ	δεκᾰτο-	δεκᾰκῐ́ς
11	ια'	ἑνδεκᾰ	ἑνδεκᾰτο-	ἑνδεκᾰκῐ́ς
12	ιβ'	δωδεκᾰ	δωδεκᾰτο-	δωδεκᾰκῐ́ς
13	ιγ'	τρισκαιδεκᾰ	τρισκαιδεκᾰτο-	
14	ιδ'	τεσσᾰρεσκαιδεκα	τεσσᾰρᾰκαιδεκᾰτο-	
15	ιε'	πεντεκαιδεκᾰ	πεντεκαιδεκᾰτο-	
16	ιϛ'	ἑκκαιδεκᾰ	ἑκκαιδεκᾰτο-	
17	ιζ'	ἑπτᾰκαιδεκᾰ	ἑπτᾰκαιδεκᾰτο-	
18	ιη'	οκτωκαιδεκᾰ	οκτωκαιδεκᾰτο-	
19	ιθ'	εννεᾰκαιδεκᾰ	εννεᾰκαιδεκᾰτο-	
20	κ'	εικοσῐ(ν)	εικοστο-	εικοσᾰκῐ́ς
21	κα'	ἑν- και εικοσῐ(ν)	ἑν- (or πρωτο-) και εικοστο-	
30	λ'	τριᾰκοντᾰ	τριᾰκοστο-	τριᾰκοντᾰκῐ́ς
40	μ'	τεσσᾰρᾰκοντᾰ	τεσσᾰρᾰκοστο-	τεσσᾰρᾰκοντᾰκῐ́ς
50	ν'	πεντηκοντᾰ	πεντηκοστι-	πεντηκοντᾰκῐ́ς
60	ξ'	ἑξηκοντᾰ	ἑξηκοστο-	ἑξηκοντᾰκῐ́ς
70	ο'	ἑβδομηκοντᾰ	ἑβδομηκοστο-	ἑβδομηκοντᾰκῐ́ς
80	π'	ογδοηκοντᾰ	ογδοηκοστο-	ογδοηκοντᾰκῐ́ς
90	ϟ'	ενενηκοντᾰ	ενενηκοστο-	ενενηκοντᾰκῐ́ς
100	ρ'	ἑκᾰτον	ἑκᾰτοστο-	ἑκατοντᾰκῐ́ς
200	σ'	διᾰκοσιο- (plural)	διᾰκοσιοστο-	διᾰκοσιᾰκῐ́ς
300	τ'	τριᾰκοσιο-	τριᾰκοσιοστο-	
400	υ'	τετρᾰκοσιο-	τετρᾰκοσιοστο-	
500	φ'	πεντᾰκοσιο-	πεντᾰκοσιοστο-	
600	χ'	ἑξᾰκοσιο-	ἑξᾰκοσιοστο-	
700	ψ'	ἑπτᾰκοσιο-	ἑπτᾰκοσιοστο	
800	ω'	οκτᾰκοσιο-	οκτᾰκοσιοστο-	
900	ϡ'	ενᾰκοσιο-	ενᾰκοσιοστο-	
1,000	͵α	χῑλιο-	χῑλιοστο-	χῑλιᾰκῐ́ς
2,000	͵β	δισχῑλιο-	δισχῑλιοστο-	
10,000	͵ι	μῡριο-	μῡριοστο-	μῡριᾰκῐ́ς

* Probably contracted from 'ἁμᾰκῐ́ς, which would be the regularly made adverb from the old 'ἁμο-, *one, some.* If 'ἁμο- and ὁμο-, *one and the same,* are connected, 'ἅπαξ and ὁμου would be represented both in root and meaning by the Latin *semel, simul.* Compare, further, 'ἁμᾰ, *sim-plex, sim-ilis,* the German *samm-lung,* and English *same.*

211. The letters of the alphabet, in uninterrupted order, are sometimes used as symbols of the numbers. In the notation given above, which is that in most frequent use, ϝ (*vau*), or ϛ (*stigma*), is inserted after ε as the sign for 6 ; ϙ (*koppa*) after π, for 90 ; and ϡ (*sampi*) after ω, for 900. With 1,000 the alphabet begins again ; but a dash is now made *under* the letters: thus, ͵βτμδ´=2344 ; ͵αων ζ´=1857.

212. The cardinal numbers from 1 to 4 are declined as follows :—

ἑν-, m. n. ; μια-, f. *one*.
    Masc. Fem. Neut.
N. εἷς μιᾰ ἕν
A. ἕνᾰ μιᾰν ἕν
G. ἑνός μιᾶς ἑνός
D. ἑνί̆ μιᾳ ἑνί̆

δυο-, m. f. n. *two*.
    M. F. N.
N. A. δυο
G. δυοιν and δυειν
D. δυοιν (rarely δὔσῐ(ν))

τρι-, m. f. n. *three*.
    M. F. N.
N. τρεις τριᾰ
A. τρεις τριᾰ
G.   τριων
D.   τρῐσῐ(ν)

τεσσαρ- (τεττᾰρ-) m. f. n. *four*.
    M. F. N.
N. τεσσᾰρες τεσσᾰρᾰ
A. τεσσᾰρᾰς τεσσᾰρᾰ
G.   τεσσᾰρων
D.   τεσσαρσῐ(ν)

213. Like ἑν- are declined ουδεν-, m. n. ; ουδεμια-, f., and μηδεν-, m. n. ; μηδεμια-, f. *not even one, no one*, compounded of ἑν- and ουδε, μηδε. Δυο is also found undeclined. Αμφο-, *both*, N. A. αμφω G. D. αμφοιν, is interchanged with the plural form αμφοτερ-οι, -αι, -ᾰ ; the neut. sing. αμφοτερον is also frequent.

214. The cardinal numbers from 5 to 199, both included, are undeclined : for 13 and 14, however, are also found τρεις και δεκᾰ and τεσσᾰρες και δεκᾰ, τρεις and τεσσᾰρες being declined. In expressing the composite numbers above 20, the smaller number is generally placed first, και being used ; πεντε και εικοσῐ, 25 : the order is, however, sometimes reversed, and then και may be omitted ; εικοσῐ και πεντε, or εικοσῐ πεντε. In the combination of three numbers, the larger numbers usually precede ; ἑκᾰτον και εικοσῐ και ἑπτᾰ, 127.

215. For the ordinal numbers from 13 to 19, τρῐτο- και δεκᾰτο-, etc., also occur. Above 20, either πεμπτο- και εικοστο-, or εικοστο- πεμπτο-, or πεντε και εικοστο-, may be used.

216. The higher cardinal numbers from 200 upwards, and all the ordinals, are declined regularly as adjectives in ο with three terminations.

217. Distributive numerals are formed by compounding the cardinals with the preposition σύν, *with:* as, σύνδυο, *two by two* (L. *bini*); σύντρεις, *three by three* (*trini*), etc.

218. Multiplicatives are formed by composition with the syllable πλοο-, πλου-: as, ἁπλοο-, ἁπλου-, *simple*; διπλου-, τριπλου-, *twofold, threefold*, etc. Compare the Latin words *simplo-, duplo-,* etc. A series, of similar meaning, is formed in πλάσιο-, διπλάσιο-, *twice as many*; τριπλάσιο-, πολλαπλάσιο-, etc.

219. Numeral adverbs in -ἄχη or -χη are formed (§ 207): as, μοναχῃ, *in one way only* (from μονο-, *single*); δίχη (and δίχα), *in two ways*; τρίχῃ, τετράχῃ, etc.

220. Feminine substantives in -αδ are formed: as, μονάδ-, *the number one, unity*; δυάδ-, *the number two*; τριάδ-, πεμπάδ-, ἑκατοντάδ-, χῑλιάδ-, μυριάδ-: μυριάδ- is used to express multiples of 10,000; τρεις μυριάδες, 30,000, etc.

221. Adjectives in -αιο are formed from many of the ordinal numerals, signifying *on what day an event happened:* thus, δευτεραιο-, τρίταιο-, δεκάταιο-, etc., *on the second, third, tenth day,* etc.: so are made προτεραιο-, ὑστεραιο-, *on the day before, on the day after*; but these are chiefly used in the dat. fem., as τῃ προτεραιᾳ (sc. ἡμερᾳ), *on the day before.*

222. From the most important adjectives of quantity are formed adverbs in -κις: as, ἑκαστάκις, *each time*; πολλάκις, *many times, often*; ὀλιγάκις, *few times, seldom*; ὀσάκις, πλειστάκις, etc.: δυάκις and τριάκις, for δίς and τρίς, are quoted by a grammarian from Aristophanes.

VERBS.

223. In the conjugation of the Greek verb are distinguished—
   a. Three numbers: *singular, dual,* and *plural;* and three persons in each number.

224. *b.* Three voices: *active* (or simple), ετράπον, *I turned;* ελῡσα, *I loosened: middle* or *reflective,* ετραπομην, *I turned myself:* ελῡσάμην, *I loosened for myself:* * and *passive,* ετράπην, *I was turned;* ελύθην, *I was let loose.*

   * E. g. ἐλύσαντο τους φίλους, they set *their* friends free.

225. There are special forms for the passive voice only in the indefinite tenses; in the other tenses, the middle forms have at the same time a passive signification.

226. Verbs which are only found in the middle or passive are called *deponents*.

227. *c.* Two main classes of tenses:—

A. Principal Tenses: viz.

Present-Imperfect,	λύω, *I am loosening.*
Present-Perfect,	λελῠκᾰ, *I have loosened.*
Future (simple),	λύσω, *I shall loosen.*
Future-Perfect (pass.),	λελύσομαι, *I shall have been let loose.*

B. Historical Tenses: viz.

Past-Imperfect,	ἔλυον, *I was loosening.*
Past-Perfect,	ἐλελύκη, *I had loosened.*
Aorist, or *Past-Indefinite** (of two forms),	ἔλυσᾰ (1 aor.), *I loosened.* ἔτρᾰπον (2 aor.), *I turned.*

228. The imperfect tenses, present and past, signify (1) an action, etc., going on at the time specified: as, τύπτω, *I am striking;* ἐτυπτον, *I was striking:* and (2) an action, etc., repeated or habitual: as, τύπτω, *I* (habitually) *strike;* ἐτυπτον, *I used to strike.*

229. The perfect tenses of the Greek verb signify not only that the action, etc., is completed, but that its consequences survive: τέθνηκᾰ, *I have died, am dead;* ἐκεκλήμην, *I had been called, my name was;* λελύσομαι, *I shall have been let loose, I shall be free.* No separate form exists for the future-perfect in the active voice: when such a tense is required, it is expressed by a periphrasis of the perf. participle and the future of ἐσ-, *be:* λελυκὼς ἔσομαι, *I shall have loosened.*

230. By *indefinite* or *aorist* (αοριστο-, *undefined*), is meant that the action, etc., simply, is signified, no regard being had to its duration or completeness: ἔτυψᾰ, *I struck.* An indefinite tense, therefore, may either signify a single and momentary action, or an action of some duration contemplated as momentary.

231. The simple future active is, according to the nature of the verb, either imperfect (a future *state*), σιγήσω, *I shall be silent,* or, more frequently, indefinite (a future *action*), τύψω, *I shall strike.* In the passive the future of this form, τύψομαι, is

---

* See, however, § 310.

only imperfect (*I shall receive blows*, not, *I shall be struck*), a distinct form existing for the indefinite future.

232. *d.* Five moods, viz.

Indicative,	λυομεν, *we are loosening.*
	ελυομεν, *we were loosening.*
Subjunctive,	λυωμεν, *we are to loosen* (solvamus).
	λυοιμεν, *we were to loosen* (solveremus).
Imperative,	λυετε, *loosen ye!*
Infinitive,	λυειν, *to loosen,* or *loosening* (subst.).
Participle,	λυοντ-, *loosening* (adj.).

233. The past tenses of the subjunctive and the future subj. are commonly treated as constituting a distinct mood, called the *optative*: thus, for example, λυωμεν (pres.-imperfect subj.) is called the present subjunctive, and λυοιμεν (past-imperfect subj.), the present optative. These tenses, however, are as closely connected in use and signification as the present and past tenses of the subjunctive in Latin.

234. The infinitive and participle, as partaking partly of the nature of the verb, and partly of the nature of the substantive or adjective, are sometimes comprehended under the name of the *participial* mood.

235. In addition to these forms verbal adjectives are derived with the endings -το and -τεο: as, λῠτο-, *solubili-*; λῠτεο-, *solvendo-*.

236. The original person-endings were, probably, as follows:—

		ACTIVE.			MIDDLE AND PASSIVE.		
		Principal Tenses.	*Historical Tenses.*	*Imperative.*	*Principal Tenses.*	*Historical Tenses.*	*Imperative.*
Singular,	1.	-μῐ	-ν (for μ)		-μαι	-μην	
	2.	-σῐ	-s	-θῐ	-σαι	-σο	-σο
	3.	-τῐ	-ν (for τ)	-τω	-ται	-το	-σθω
Dual,	1.	-μεν	-μεν		-μεθον	-μεθον	
	2.	-τον	-τον	-τον	-σθον	-σθον	-σθον
	3.	-τον	-την	-των	-σθον	-σθην	-σθων
Plural,	1.	-μεν	-μεν		-μεθᾰ	-μεθᾰ	
	2.	-τε	-τε	-τε	-σθε	-σθε	-σθε
	3.	-νσῐ* (for -ντι)	-ν* (for -ντ)	-ντων	-νται	-ντο	-σθων

* Older forms were, -ᾱσῐ, -σᾰν (for (σ)αντι, σαντ). See § 337, and *n.*

237. The person-endings of the principal tenses of the active voice are best seen in the pres.-imperf. indicative of ἐσ-, *be*:

Singular.	Dual.	Plural.
1. εἰ-μί (for ἐσ-μί)	ἐσ-μεν	ἐσ-μεν (Ion. εἰ-μεν)
2. ἐσ-σί (Att. εἰ or εἰς)	ἐσ-τον	ἐσ-τε
3. ἐσ-τί(ν)	ἐσ-τον	εἰ-σί(ν)

238. The endings of the three persons in the singular are, properly, affixed pronouns, *I, thou, he*; and may be compared with the crude forms of the personal pronouns, -μί with με-, -σί with σε-, and -τί with the C. F. of the article το-.

239. The 1st person of the dual always coincides, in the active voice, with the 1st person plural.

240. According to the manner in which these suffixes are added to the tense-forms two principal conjugations may be distinguished:

The *first* conjugation connects the personal suffixes with the tense-forms of the present and past imperfect, and of the 2 aorist (active and middle), by means of a vowel called the *connecting vowel*, or *vowel of inflexion*: as, λυ-ο-μεν.

The connecting vowel is sometimes ε(η), sometimes ο(ω). In the indicative it is ο before μ or ν, ε before σ or τ; in the present tenses of the subjunctive it is ω before μ, η before σ or τ; in the past tenses of the subjunctive (optative) it is always ο, forming the diphthong οι with the vowel ι, which is characteristic of those tenses; in the infinitive it is always ε, and in the participle ο.

As the 1 pers. sing. of the present-imperfect indic. active in this conjugation ends in -ω, the verbs which belong to it are often called *verbs in* Ω.

241. The *second*, and much less frequent but older, conjugation connects the personal suffixes with the tense-forms of the present and past imperfect and 2 aorist without any connecting vowel: as, ἐσ-μεν, *we are*.

As the 1 person sing. of the present-imperfect indic. active in this conjugation retains the original ending -μί, the verbs belonging to it are often called *verbs in* MI.

The forms of the other tenses are common to both conjugations.

242. The characteristic of the subjunctive mood in the present

tenses consists in the lengthened connecting vowel: pres.-imperf. of the indic. λυομεν, *we are loosening*; of the subj. λυωμεν, *we are to loosen*.

243. The characteristic of the subjunctive in the past and future tenses consists in an ι inserted before the person-endings, which usually combines with the preceding vowel to form a diphthong, οι, αι, or ει; past-imperfect of the indic. ἐλυομεν, *we were loosening*; of the subj. λυοιμεν, *we were to loosen*.

244. The present tenses of the subj. have the personal suffixes of the principal tenses.

245. The past and future tenses of the subj. (opt.) have the personal suffixes of the historical tenses, except that in the 1 pers. sing. -μῐ is used, and that in the 3 pers. sing. ν is always dropped, as it is frequently in the indic. (§ 272, etc.). The forms of these tenses are, however, sometimes found with η prefixed to the person-endings; the 1 pers. sing. then ends in ν. The suffixes thus become with the mood-vowel—

ι-ην, ι-ης, ι-η; ι-ητον, ι-ητον; ι-ημεν, ι-ητε, ι-ησᾰν or ι-εν.

These forms are, in Attic, preferred, *for the singular*, in the imperfect of contract verbs and of verbs in μῐ, in the 2 aor. of verbs ending in vowels, and in the future of liquid verbs; also in the rarely used past-perf. subj. The forms without η are, however, sometimes found in the singular, and those with η occur in the plural, at all events in the 1 and 2 persons.

246. The original ending of the infinitive mood was, in the active, -μεναι, or, with the connecting vowel, -ε-μεναι; and in the middle, -σθαι, or, with the connecting vowel, -ε-σθαι.

247. The original ending of the participle was, in the active, -ντ (ο-ντ), and in the middle, -μενο (-ο-μενο).

Of the Augment.

248. All the historical tenses of the indicative mood take, in addition to the person-endings, a further sign of past time, called the *augment*. The augment is either *syllabic* or *temporal*.

249. The syllabic augment consists in the vowel ε prefixed to the root, and is admitted by all verbs which begin with a consonant: as, λυ-, *loosen*, ἐλυον, *I was loosening*; τυπ-, *beat*, ἐτυπην, *I was beaten*. An initial ρ is doubled after the augment:*

* See § 286. n.

ῥιπτ-(ῥιφ-), *throw,* ερριπτον, *I was throwing.* In three verbs, βουλ- (m.),* *wish;* δυνα- (m.), *be able;* μελλ-, *be going to —,* the syllabic augment sometimes appears in the form η: ηβουλομην, *I was desirous;* ηδυνάμην, *I was able;* ημελλον, *I was going to —,* as well as εβουλομην, etc.

250. The temporal augment consists in a lengthening of the initial vowel of the root, and is admitted by all verbs which begin with a vowel. Thus,

α becomes η:	ἀγ-,	*lead,*	ηγον, *I was leading.*
ε	η	ελα-, *drive,*	ηλᾰσᾰ, *I drove.*
ο	ω	ορυχ-, *dig,*	ωρυξᾰ, *I dug.*
ῐ	ῑ	ἱκ- (m.), *come,*	ἱκομην, *I came.*
ῠ	ῡ	ὑφᾰν-, *weave,*	ὑφαινον, *I was weaving.*
αι	η	αισθ- (m.), *perceive,*	ησθομην, *I perceived.*
αυ	ηυ	αυδα-, *speak,*	ηυδων, *I was speaking.*
οι	ῳ	οικτερ-, *pity,*	ῳκτειρᾰ, *I pitied.*

The long vowels η, ω, ῑ, ῡ, and, for the most part, the diphthongs ει, ευ, ου, do not take the augment.

251. The following verbs beginning with ε take ει instead of η in the augmented tenses: εα-, *suffer;* εθῐδ-, *accustom;* ελῐκ-, *roll;* ελκ- or ελκυ-, *draw;* ἑπ- (m.), *follow;* εργαδ- (m.), *labour;* ἑρπ- or ἑρπῠδ-, *creep;* ἑστια-, *feast;* ἑχ-, *hold;* also (in the 2 aor., and the 1 aor. pass.), ἑ-, *let go, send;* and the aorist roots ἑλ-, *seize,* and ἑδ-, *seat.* The reason of this peculiarity appears to be that the roots in question originally began with a consonant, either F or σ, and therefore took the syllabic augment: when F or σ was dropped, ε of the augment combined with ε of the root to form ει.†

252. For the same reason the verbs ἁδ-, *please;* ἁγ-, *break;* ἁλο-, *be captured;* ωθε-, *push;* ωνε- (m.), *buy,* take the syllabic augment in some or all of the augmented tenses: as, εᾰδον (for εFᾰδον, Hom. ευᾰδον), *I pleased,* etc. Similarly from ἰδ-, *see* (ori-

---

* The symbol (m.) inserted after the crude form of a verb signifies that that verb is inflected only in the *middle* or reflexive voice (deponents). Many of these verbs, however, have aorists of the passive form with the deponent meaning.

† Compare ἑπ-, ἑρπ-, and ἑδ- with the Latin roots sĕc- or sequ-, serp-, and sĕd-; εργαδ- and the subst. εργο- n. *work,* with the English *work,* and German *Werk;* and εχ- with its 2 aor. εσχ-ον (for ε-σεχ-ον), the bye-form ισχ-ω, and the future σχησ-ω.

ginally Ϝιδ-, Latin vĭd-), the 2 aor. is ειδον (i.e. εἶδον from ἐϜιδον), *I saw*, not ἴδον.

253. 'Εορτᾰδ-, *keep holiday*, takes the augment on the second syllable: ἑωρταζον, *I was keeping holiday*. The compound verb ἄν-οιγ-, *open;* ὁρα-, *see;* and ἀνδᾰν- ('ᾰδ-), *please*, take both the syllabic and temporal augment: ἑωρων, *I beheld;* ἀνεῴγον, *I was opening;* ἑηνδανον (Hom.), *I was pleasing*.

254. Verbs compounded with a preposition have the augment between the preposition and the root: as, εἰσ-φερ-, *bring in*, εἰσεφερον, *I was bringing in;* προσ-ἀγ-, *lead up*, προσηγον, *I was leading up*. Ἐκ has the form ἐξ before the vowel ε: ἐκ-βᾰλ-, *throw out*, ἐξεβᾰλον, *I threw out*. Σὺν and ἐν, if they have undergone any change before the initial consonant of the verbal root, resume their original form: συλ-λεγ-, *gather together*, σὺνελεξᾰ, *I gathered together;* ἐμ-βᾰλ-, *throw in*, ἐνεβᾰλον, *I threw in*. The final vowel of prepositions ending in a vowel is elided before the augment: ἀπο-φερ-, *bear away*, ἀπεφερον, *I was bearing away:* but περῐ, *round* and προ *before*, never suffer elision: περῐεβᾰλον, προυβᾰλον, for προεβᾰλον.

255. Verbs which are not compounded with prepositions, but derived from compound nouns, regularly take the augment at the beginning: as, ἐναντιο- (m.), *oppose oneself* (from ἐναντιο-, *opposite*), ἠναντιουμην, *I was opposing myself;* παρρησιᾰδ- (m.), *speak boldly* (from παρρησια-, *boldness of speech*), ἐπαρρησιᾰσᾰμην, *I spoke boldly*. Yet in the Attic dialect many follow the rule of compound verbs: as, ἐκκλησιᾰδ-, *hold an assembly* (from ἐκκλησια-, *assembly*), ἐξεκλησιαζον, *I was holding an assembly;* 'ὑποπτευ-*suspect* (from 'ὑποπτο-, *suspicious*), 'ὑπωπτευσᾰ, *I suspected*.

256. Some compound verbs had so entirely lost this character that they were treated as simples: as, κᾰθευδ-, *sleep*, ἐκᾰθευδον, *I was sleeping;* κᾰθῐδ-, *make sit down*, ἐκᾰθῐσᾰ, *I seated:* but κᾰθηνδον is also found. Some of these verbs take a double augment: as, ἀνεχ- (m.), *uphold;* ἀνορθο-, *set upright;* past-imperf. 1 pers. ἠνειχομην, ἠνωρθουν, and a few others.

Other irregularities and exceptions to the general rules will be found in dictionaries.

Of the Crude Form of the Verb, ana the Tense-Forms.

257. By the *crude form* of a verb is meant that form from the union of which with the endings of persons, tenses, and

moods, in obedience to the laws of letter-change, all the various forms of that verb may be explained. Thus, from an inspection of the forms λυω, *I am loosening*; λύσω, *I shall loosen*; λελύκα, *I have loosened*: τῑμαω, *I honour, value*; τῑμησομεν, *we shall honour*; τετῑμηκεν, *he has honoured*, it is seen that λυ- and τῑμα- are the crude forms of those verbs. Again, from the same crude forms, by the addition of certain other suffixes, nouns are derived: e. g. λῠσι-, *the act of loosening*; λῠτηρ-, *one who loosens*; λυτοο-. *ransom*: τῑμησι-, *valuation*; τῑμητα-, *one who values, censor*; τῑμημᾱτ-, *estimate*.

258. If the C. F. of a verb cannot be further analysed it is called a *root*, and the verb made from it a *root-verb*. But if the C. F. be itself the C. F. of a noun formed by some noun-suffix, or if it be formed by the addition of some verbal suffix, the verb is called a *derived verb*. Thus, τῑμα- is at the same time the C. F. of a feminine substantive signifying *honour*, derived from the root τι-, *pay* (honour), by addition of the fem. suffix -μα, and the C. F. of a derived verb signifying *render honour*.

259. By a *tense-form* is meant that form from which, by addition of the personal suffixes, the several persons of the tense are made: thus, τῑμησ- is the future tense-form of τῑμα-, whence are made τῑμησω, *I shall honour*, τῑμησεις, *you will honour*, etc.

260. *Imperfect Tense-Form.*—From the imperfect tense-form are conjugated the present and past imperfect tenses, active and middle.*

The imperfect tense-form is not always the same as the crude form of the verb: it is much more frequently the C. F. strengthened by some addition or modification. Thus, λειπω is *I am leaving*, and λειπ- is the imperfect T. F., but the C. F. of the verb is λῐπ-, as seen in the 2 aor. ελῐπον, *I left*. This strengthened form is sometimes called the *increased form*.

261. There are many different ways of making the increased form, and according to the relation existing between the crude form of the verb and the increased form of the imperfect tenses, verbs may be divided into several classes.

262. I. Verbs in which the C. F. is not increased. To this class belong most verbs whose C. F. ends in a vowel (sometimes called *pure verbs*), and many verbs ending in some consonant:

* That is, middle and passive, so far as these voices coincide, § 225.

as, λυ-, *loosen*; παυ-, *make to cease*; νῖκα-, *conquer*; φιλε-, *love*; δουλο-, *enslave*; τρεπ-, *turn*; ἀγ-, *lead*; μεν-, *remain*. In all these the imperfect tense-form coincides with the crude form.

263. II. Verbs in which the C. F. is increased by strengthening the root-vowel.

a. When the final letter is a mute consonant: as, C. F. τᾰκ-, *melt*; λᾰβ-, *take*; φῠγ-, *flee*; πῐθ-, *persuade*; τρῐβ-, *rub*: I. F. (increased forms) τηκ-, ληβ-,* φευγ-, πειθ-, τρῑβ-.

b. When the final letter is a liquid (ν or ρ): as, C. F. φθερ-, *destroy*; φᾰν-, *shew*; ἀμῠν-, *drive off*: I. F. φθειρ-, φαιν-, ἀμῡν-. But these words should perhaps be referred to the next class (see § 45, *d.*).

264. III. Verbs in which the C. F. is increased by adding ι cons. (§ 45).

a. If the final consonant be any k-sound, it generally passes into σσ (later Attic ττ): thus, C. F. φῠλᾰκ-, *watch*; τᾰγ-, *arrange*; ὀρῠχ-, *dig*: I. F. φῠλασσ-, τασσ-, ορυσσ-. But many words ending in γ, including several signifying sound, have their increased form in ζ: as, C. F. κρᾰγ-, *scream*; οιμωγ-, *cry* οιμοι; σφᾰγ-, *butcher*: I. F. κραζ-, οιμωζ-, σφαζ- (and σφαττ-).

b. If the final consonant be δ, it passes generally into ζ: thus, C. F. φρᾰδ-, *tell*: I. F. φραζ-. Some verbs ending in τ have their increased-form ending in σσ (ττ): C. F. πλᾰτ-, *mould*; ερετ-, *row*; ἁρμοτ-, *fit*: I. F. πλασσ-, ερεσσ-, ἁρμοττ- (and ἁρμοζ-).

c. A few words ending in a p-sound have increased forms ending in σσ or ζ: thus, from πεπ-, *cook*; νῐβ-, *wash*, the increased forms are πεσσ-, νιζ- (later νιπτ-).

d. Final λ passes into λλ: thus, C. F. βᾰλ-, *throw*; αγγελ-, *announce*: I. F. βαλλ-, αγγελλ-.

265. IV. Verbs in which the crude form is increased by some consonantal affix.

a. ἀν or ν is added.

When ἀν is added, if the root-syllable be short, either it is strengthened by prefixing to the final mute its cognate nasal (§ 26), or, less commonly, the added syllable is lengthened: thus, C. F. αισθ- (m.), *perceive*; τῠχ-, *hit*; μᾰθ-, *learn*; λᾰβ-, *take*: I. F. αισθ-ἀν-, τυγχ-ἀν-, μανθ-ἀν-, λαμβ-ἀν-: C. F. ἱκ-, *come*; ἁλῐτ-, *sin*: I. F. ἱκ-ἀν-, ἁλῐτ-αιν-.

* See below, IV, *a.*

When ν is added, the root-vowel is often lengthened: C. F. τεμ-, *cut*; δακ-, *bite*; βα-, *go*; ελα-, *drive*: I. F. τεμν-, δακν-, βαιν-, ελαυν-. But in some of these verbs the ν may have claims to be regarded as originally part of the root.

b. νε is added: C. F. ἱκ- (m.) *come*; I. F. ἰκ-νε-.

c. νυ is added. Some verbs of this formation have roots ending in σ, which passes into ν before νυ (§ 48). Thus, C. F. δεικ- (δἰκ-), *shew*; ζευγ- (ζὕγ-), *join*; ἐσ-, *clothe*: I. F. δεικ-νυ-, ζευγ-νυ-, ἑν-νυ-.

d. τ is added to many roots ending in a p-sound: C. F. τυπ-, *strike*; βλᾰβ-, *thwart*; βᾰφ-, *dip*: I. F. τυπτ-, βλαπτ-, βαπτ-.

e. εθ or θ is added: C. F. φλεγ-, *scorch*; εδ-, *eat*; πλα-, *fill*: I. F. φλεγ-εθ-, εσθ- (for εδ-θ-), πληθ- (*be full*). The verbs of this class are chiefly poetical, and coexist with forms made from the simple root; e. g. φλεγ-ω, εδ-ω, πιμπλημι (*I fill*). The 2 aor. is also found strengthened by addition of εθ or ᾰθ.

266. V. Verbs in which the C. F. is increased by adding ισκ or σκ: C. F. ἁλ-ο-, *be captured*; γηρα-, *grow old*; εὑρ-, *find*; πᾰθ-, *suffer*; χᾰν-, *yawn, gape*: I. F. ἁλισκ-, γηρασκ-, εὑρισκ-, πασχ- (for παθσκ-), χασκ-. Verbs of this class usually signify, in those tenses which contain the element σκ, the beginning or progress of an action, etc., and are hence called *inceptives*.

267. VI. Verbs in which the C. F. is increased by reduplication, that is, by prefixing to the root a syllable consisting of its initial consonant and the vowel ῐ; the short vowel of the root is then often elided: C. F. δο-, *give*; γεν-, *become*; πετ-, *fall*: I. F. διδο-, γιγν-, πιπτ- (for γῐγεν-, πῐπετ-). This mode of formation is often combined with the preceding: thus, from γνω-, *be of opinion*; δρα-, *run away*, the increased forms are γιγνωσκ-, διδρασκ-.

268. VII. Verbs in which the C. F. is increased by the addition of ε:* C. F. δοκ-, *seem*; κᾰλ-, *call*; ὠθ-, *push*: I. F. δοκε-, κᾰλε-, ωθε-. On the other hand, in many words the short form is used in the imperfect tenses, while the longer form in ε appears in the other tenses: thus, βουλ- (m.), *wish*, is the imperfect T. F.; while the future, perfect, and aorist are made from βουλε-.

---

* This ε is perhaps a modification of ι cons., and may be compared with *i* in such Latin verbs as *căpi-*, *răpi-*, *făci-*, which also only appears in the imperfect (and future) tenses.

269. By the side of a few simple verbs the root-vowel of which is ε, collateral forms exist, made by adding ε or a to the C. F., and changing the root-vowel into ο in the former case, into ω in the latter: thus, φοβε- (m.) is found by the side of φεβ- (m.), *take to flight, fear*; φορε- (with a slight change of meaning), by the side of φερ-, *carry*; τρωπα-, by the side of τρεπ-, *turn*. Sometimes a substantive seems to connect the earlier and later forms: thus, φεβ-, *flee*; φοβο-, m. *flight, terror*; derived verb φοβε-, *put to flight, frighten*, and (mid.) *conceive terror, fear*.

270. VIII. Verbs ending in ϝ or σ properly fall under classes I. and II.; but as they have certain peculiarities in common, it is convenient to class them by themselves.

ϝ is dropped in the increased form; a before ϝ becomes αι (in later Attic ā), ε generally remains unchanged; in those tenses in which a consonant follows the C. F., αϝ and εϝ for the most part become αυ and ευ. Roots in εϝ often retain traces of a primitive root in υ. Thus from καϝ-, *burn*; χεϝ- (originally χυ-), *pour*, the imperfect T. F. are και- (Att. κā-), χε- (poet. χει-).

Σ is dropped in the imperfect T. F., sometimes with, more frequently without, compensation: in the other tenses it is dropped before σ,* but generally reappears before μ, τ, or θ. It is not always easy to determine with certainty what was the final consonant of verbs ranged under this class; many exhibit traces of a lost dental mute, which of course appears as σ before μ, τ, or θ. Thus from κλασ- (κλαδ-?), *break*; σπασ- (σπαδ-?), *draw*; νασ-, *dwell*; τελεσ-, *complete* (compare the subst. τελεσ-, n. *end*); κλειδ-, *shut* (κλειδ-, f. *key*), the imperfect tense-forms are κλα-, σπα-, ναι-, τελε- (poet. τελει-), κλει-.

271. The imperfect tenses, present and past, are made from the imperfect tense-form (increased form), by the addition of the person-endings, with the connecting vowels proper to the several moods and persons (§§ 236, 240).

272. In the First Conjugation (verbs in Ω) the personal suffixes of the singular are much disguised, coalescing with the connecting vowel. It is to be observed that,

(1.) In the 1 p. sing. pres.-imperf. indic. act., -μι is dropped, and ο lengthened into ω: λυω for λυομι.

In the 2 and 3 pp. sing. -εσι and -ετι become -εις and -ει. In the present subj. the ι becomes subscript, -ης and -η.

* But see § 40, n.

In the 3 p. plur. -ονσι (for -οντι) becomes -ουσι: λυουσι for λυοντι. The original form in οντι was retained in Doric. With λυοντι compare the Latin *solvunt*.

(2.) In the 2 p. sing. of the pres. indic. mid. -ῃ or -ει results from -ε(σ)αι : λυῃ or λυει for λυεσαι (§ 48) : ει is the pure Attic form, and the only existing form in the three words οιει, *thou thinkest;* βουλει, *thou wishest;* and οψει, *thou wilt see.* In like manner σ is dropped in the subj., λυῃ (never λυει) for λυησαι.

(3.) In the 3 p. sing. past-imperf. indic. act. the suffix ν (for τ, § 55) was only retained before vowels and the longer pauses (§ 56).

(4.) In the 2 p. sing. of the past-imperf. indic., and of the imperf. imperat., in the middle voice, -ου arises from ε(σ)ο : ελυου for ελυεσο, λυου for λυεσο. In the 2 p. sing. past subj. mid. -οιο arises from -οισο.

(5.) In the 2 p. sing. imperf. imperat. act. the ending -θι is dropped : λυ-ε, *loosen!* for λυ-ε-θι.

(6.) In the infin. act. -αι of the ending -ε-μεναι was thrown away ; μ was then dropped, and ε-εν contracted to ειν : λυ-ειν for λυ-ε-μεν, from λυ-ε-μεναι.*

(7.) The C. F. of the participle in the active ends in -οντ (m. and n.; -ουσα, f.); in the middle and passive in -ομενο (f. -υμενα). For the declension see §§ 152, 144.

273. Verbs whose crude forms end in α, ε, or ο, regularly contract those vowels with the connecting vowels of the endings according to the rules laid down in § 33.† Hence they are called *Contract Verbs.* Verbs ending in the weak vowels ι or υ do not suffer contraction (§ 32).

274. The past-imperfect indic., active and middle, will of course have the augment prefixed.

* Such forms as λυεμεν and λυεμεναι are found, however, in the older poets.

† The four verbs ζα-, *live;* πεινα-, *be hungry;* διψα-, *be thirsty;* χρα- (m.), *use;* and a few others, contract into η (ῃ) instead of ᾱ (ᾳ): thus we find in the infin. ζην, πεινην, διψην, χρησθαι, for ζᾶν, πεινᾶν, etc.; and in the indic. ζῃς, ζῃ, ζητε, etc., for ζᾳς, etc. Similarly ρῑγο-, *freeze,* contracts into ω and ῳ, as well as into ου and οι: infin. ρῑγων and ρῑγουν; subj. ρῑγῳ and ρῑγοι, etc. Monosyllable roots ending in ε- only take those contractions which issue in ει: thus, from πλε-, *sail,* is found πλεω, *I sail,* not πλω; but the 2 p. is regularly πλεις for πλεεις.

275. *Future Tense-Form.* — From the future tense-form is deduced the future tense, active and middle. It is regularly made by the addition of -(ε)σ to the crude form of the verb; the ε is usually dropped: as, λυ-, *loosen*; λῡσ-, *shall loosen*. The future is thus formed in all words ending in vowels or mute consonants. The gutturals combine with σ to make ξ; the labials to make ψ; the dentals and σ are rejected before it (§§ 39, 40): as, ἀγ-, *lead*; γραφ-, *write*; ᾀδ-, *sing*; σπενδ-, *pour*; τελεσ-, *complete*: future T. F. ἀξ-, γραψ-, ᾀσ-, σπεισ- (§ 41), τελεσ-.

276. The σ of the future is generally added to the crude form of the verb: thus, τῠπ-, *beat*; φῠλᾰκ-, *watch*; φρᾰδ-, *tell*, the increased forms of which are τυπτ-, φῠλασσ-, φραζ-, have in the future τυψ-, φῠλαξ-, φρᾱσ-. But in those verbs (Class II.) which end in mutes, and make their increased forms by lengthening the radical vowel, and in some others, the future is made from the increased form: thus, λῐπ-, *leave*, I. F. λειπ-, future T. F. λειψ-, not λιψ-; λᾰβ-, *take*, I. F. ληβ- and λαμβ-αν-, future T. F. ληψ- (Ion. λαμψ-).

277. Verbs ending in a vowel have the vowel lengthened before σ of the future; α becomes ᾱ if ε, ι, or ρ precede, otherwise η: thus C. F. δρα-, *do*; ἐα-, *allow*; τῑμα-, *honour*; ποιε-, *make*; δουλο-, *enslave*; λυ-, *loosen*: future T. F. δρᾱσ-, ἐᾱσ-, τῑμησ-, ποιησ-, δουλωσ-, λῡσ-. There are some exceptions to this rule; but of these the greater number are apparent only, a final consonant (σ or δ) having been lost between the vowel of the root and the future σ: thus, τελε(σ)-, *complete*, future τελεσ- (§ 279).

278. Verbs ending in λ, μ, ν, ρ, originally retained the old form of the future, εσ: as, βᾰλ-, *throw*, future T. F. βαλεσ-, not βαλσ-; σ was then omitted (§ 48), and, in Attic, contraction ensued of ε with the vowels of the person-endings: ἀμῡν-, *ward off*; ἀγγελ-, *announce*; νεμ-, *distribute*; φθερ-, *destroy*: future T. F. ἀμῠνε-, ἀγγελε-, νεμε-, φθερε-, for ἀμῠνεσ-, etc. Three verbs, κελ-, *drive to land*; κῠρ-, *meet*; ὀρ-, *rouse*, form the future in σ without ε —κελσ-, κυρσ-, ορσ-.

279. *Attic Future.* — Many verbs ending in ᾰδ and ῐδ, whose futures end in ᾰσ and ῐσ, and others which exhibit in the future σ preceded by a short vowel, frequently throw out σ (§ 48); contraction then ensues of ᾰ or ε with the person-endings, according to the usual rules: thus, ἐλᾰ-, *drive;* τελε(σ)-, *complete:* future T. F. ἐλᾰσ-, τελεσ-; 1 p. pl. ἐλᾰσομεν (ελαομεν), ελωμεν, τελέσομεν (τελεομεν), τελουμεν. Between ι and the person-endings the original ε was retained, and then contracted: κομῐδ-, *convey,* fut. 1 p. pl. κομῐσομεν, or κομιουμεν (not κομιομεν). This form is called the *Attic future.*

Other irregularities, affecting individual verbs, will be noticed in the tables, or found in dictionaries.

280. The person-endings of the future tense are, in the indicative, the same as those of the present-imperfect; in the subjunctive (opt.), as those of the past-imperfect. There is no future of the imperative. In the infinitive and participle the endings are those of the imperfect.

281. In the active and middle there exist no special forms for the future-indefinite, the simple future in σ being indefinite in verbs of an *active,* imperfect only in verbs of a *static* signification (§ 231). Thus, λῡσω, *I shall loosen,* is indefinite; σῑγησω, *I shall be silent,* is imperfect: αρξω is either indefinite, *I shall obtain the command,* or imperfect, *I shall exercise rule.* But the passive voice possesses a distinct future-indefinite (§ 331), and the simple future in σ is used only as a future-imperfect: this future is, consequently, much more frequently found with the middle, than with the passive signification; and hence it is usually called the *future middle.* It is, however, no less a tense of the passive voice than the corresponding forms of the present and past imperfect, and is always employed when its peculiar shade of meaning is required.*

282. The future middle is often found with an active signification, especially in verbs expressing some act of the body ending in oneself, so that a reflective form is reasonable: as, ἀκου-, *hear;* ᾳδ-, *sing;* βᾰδιδ-, *walk:* futures, ἀκουσομαι, *I shall hear;* ᾳσομαι, *I shall sing;* βᾰδιουμαι, *I shall walk.*

283. For the future perfect, see §§ 308, 309.

284. *Perfect Tenses.*—From the perfect tense-form are made the present and past perfect tenses of the active middle and passive, and the future perfect (sometimes called the third future), which is for the most part confined to the middle and passive.

---

* As in Soph. Phil. 48, και φυλαξεται στιβος, which Schneidewin interprets by εν φυλακῃ εσται.

VERBS.

285. The leading characteristic of the perfect tenses is the reduplication, which consists in prefixing to the root its initial consonant followed by the vowel ε. In verbs compounded with prepositions the reduplication is inserted between the preposition and the root: as, λυ-, *loosen*, perfect T. F. λελυ-; but εκλυ-, perfect T. F. εκλελυ-.

The reduplication is retained through all the moods, and in the participles.

286. In forming the reduplication the following rules are to be observed:—

a. If the C. F. of the verb begin with an aspirated consonant, the corresponding *tenuis* is substituted in the reduplication (§ 44): as, χωρε-, *give place*; θυ-, *sacrifice*; φραδ-, *tell*: perfect T. F. κεχωρη-, τεθυ-, πεφραδ-.

b. If the C. F. of the verb begin with two consonants (not a mute and liquid), or with a double consonant, or with ρ, the syllabic augment (ε) is prefixed instead of the reduplication (ρ being at the same time doubled*): ῥαγ-, *break*; στελ-, *send*; ζητε-, *seek*; perfect T. F. ερρωγ-, εσταλ-, εζητη-. But κτα- (m.), *acquire*; μνα- (m.), *remember*; and στα-, *stand*, make κεκτη-, μεμνη-, εστη- for (σεστη-).

c. If the C. F. of the verb begin with a mute followed by a liquid, the mute only appears in the reduplication: as, γραφ-, *write*; πλαγ-, *strike*; πνεϜ-, *breathe:* perfect T. F. γεγραφ-, πεπληγ-, πεπνευ-. But verbs beginning with γν take the augment only; verbs beginning with βλ, γλ, have both formations (§ 60, *b.*).

287. Words beginning with a vowel have the initial vowel lengthened, as in the case of the temporal augment: as, ορθο-, *straighten*, perfect T. F. ωρθω-.

288. Some verbs beginning with *a, ε,* or *o,* take, however, instead of this augmented vowel, what is termed the Attic reduplication, which consists in a repetition of the first syllable of the root, the original initial vowel being lengthened: as,

---

* The ground of this peculiarity appears to be that initial ρ had been, in the old language, almost always preceded by Ϝ; hence the perfects of verbs beginning with ρ were only entitled to the augment, and when Ϝ was removed ρ was doubled. Compare ῥαγ-, with Latin *frag-*; ῥιφ-, *throw*; ῥιζο-, *make to strike root*; ῥεγ-, *work*, with the German *werfen, Wurzel, Werk*: Ϝρηξι-, for ρηξι-, *breaking*, is cited by a grammarian from Alcæus. (Ahrens.)

ἀκου- (ἀκοϝ-), *hear*; ἐλυθ-, *come*; ὀρυχ-, *dig*: perfect T. F. ἀκηκο-, ἐληλυθ-, ὀρωρυχ-.

289. The verbs ʽἁλο-, *be taken*; ἀγ-, *break*; ἰκ-, *seem*; ἐθ- (or ηθ-), *be accustomed*; ἀν-οιγ-, *open*, which originally began with ϝ, have in their perfect, ἑᾱλω-, ἑᾱγ-, ἐοικ-, ἐιωθ- (and ἐωθ-), ἀν-εῳγ- (from ϝεϝᾱλω-, etc.).

Other irregularities will be noticed in the *Tables of Principal Parts*.

290. *Perfect Active Tense-Form.*—In the older stage of the language a perfect active was seldom formed from any other than root-verbs. If the root ended in a vowel, κ was inserted between that vowel and the person-endings. In Attic Greek, however, the formation of a perfect active was extended to all classes of verbs, and the insertion of κ became a leading feature of the tense, the older and simpler form of the tense being retained only in root-verbs. Thus of the perfect active two forms are to be distinguished, the older, or (so called) 2nd perfect, and the more recent, or 1st perfect. The 2 perf., again, is sometimes called the *strong*, and the 1 perf. the *weak* form of the tense.

291. *Older, or Second, Perfect.*—The 2 perf. is much the less frequent form of the tense. It is formed immediately from the C. F. of the verb, but the following vowel-changes must be attended to: ἀ is lengthened into ᾱ after ρ, otherwise into η; as, κρᾰγ-, *cry out*; πλᾰγ-, *strike*; perfect T. F. κεκρᾱγ-, πεπληγ-; but ῥᾰγ-, *break*, has ἐρρωγ-: ε becomes ο; as, γεν-, *become*, perf. T. F. γεγον-. Verbs of class II. *a.* generally use the increased form in the perfect, as in the future, ει becoming οι; as, λῐπ- (λειπ-), *leave*; φῠγ- (φευγ-), *flee*: perf. T. F. λελοιπ-, πεφευγ-.

292. *First Perfect.*—The 1 perf. tense-form is made by adding κ to the reduplicated root: as, λυ-, *loosen*, perf. T. F. λελῠκ-. The final vowel of pure verbs is regularly lengthened before κ, as before σ of the future.

293. In words ending in any of the guttural or labial mutes κ is not added, but the final mute is aspirated instead: as, βλᾰβ-, *thwart, hurt*; κοπ-, *cut*; ἀγ-, *lead*; φῠλᾰκ-, *watch*: 1 perf. T. F. βεβλᾰφ-, κεκοφ-, ηχ-, πεφῠλᾰχ-: φ and χ, of course, undergo no change,—γρᾰφ-, *write*, 1 perf. T. F. γεγρᾰφ-. Three verbs, πεμπ-, *send*; τρεπ-, *turn*; κλεπ-, *steal*, change ε into ο in the 1 perf., πεποιφ-. τετροφ- (also τετρᾰφ-), κεκλοφ-.

294. The dental mutes go out before κ: as, φρᾰδ-, *tell*: πῐθ- (πειθ-) *persuade*: 1 perf. T. F. πεφρᾱκ-, πεπεικ-.

295. Monosyllabic words ending in λ, ν, or ρ, and having ε as their radical vowel, change this ε into α in the 1 perf.: as, στελ-, *send*; φθερ-, *destroy*: 1 perf. T. F. εσταλκ-, εφθαρκ-: final ν is often thrown out:* τεν-, *stretch*; κρῐν-, *judge*: perf. T. F. τετᾰκ-, κεκρῐκ-. The perfects of βᾰλ-, *throw*; κᾰμ-, *toil*; τεμ-, *cut*; θᾰν-, *die*, suffer transposition of the vowel, which is then lengthened, βεβληκ-, κεκμηκ-, τετμηκ-, τεθνηκ- (*metathesis*).†

296. From some verbs both forms of the perfect are made. The 1 perf. is then usually transitive, the 2 perf. intransitive: the 2 perf. of some verbs is intransitive even when no 1 perf. is found.

297. The person-endings of the present perfect of the indic. active are attached by means of a connecting vowel α: the 1 p. sing. takes no suffix, the final ῐ is dropped in the 2 and 3 pp. sing., and in the 3 p. ᾰ becomes ε, ν (for τ) being retained before vowels and the longer stops: in the 3 p. plur. -αντῐ becomes -ᾱσῐ.

298. The person-endings of the past-perfect indic. active are those of the historical tenses, but these are attached to the tense-form by means of the diphthong ει.‡ In the 3 p. plur. the ending is -σᾰν, and the connecting vowel ε, not ει. In the older Attic the forms of the singular end in -η, -ης, -ει(ν), contracted from the earlier Ionic -εᾰ, -εᾰς, -εε(ν); and ε seems to have been used rather than ει in the 1 and 2 pp. plur.

299. In the past-perf. indic. the augment is prefixed to the

---

* Final ν of these roots disappears also in other forms, and should rather be regarded as foreign to the root.

† It has also been proposed to explain these forms as derived, by syncope, from βεβᾰληκ-, etc. (§ 46, *n.*).

‡ Such is the usual explanation of the syllables ᾰ and ει in the perfect tenses of the active. It has been argued, however, with much probability that these vowels are rather integral elements of the tenses in question, corresponding to that element which in the Latin stands between the sibilated (or other) perfect tense-form and the person-endings, and perhaps representing the verb *be*. Thus, ἑστηκ-η or ἑστηκ-εα (i. e. ἑστηκ-εσ-α?), *I had stationed myself*, will answer to stet-ĕra-m, ἑστηκ-ης or ἑστηκ-εα-ς to stet-ĕra-s, ἑστηκ-εσα-ν to stet-ĕra-nt, etc. The 1 person suffix, which is wanting to the form in -η, is seen in the common ἑστηκειν This view will be found consistent with that presented in § 337, *n*.; ἱστᾰ-σᾰν, *they were placing*, ἑστηκ-εσᾰ-ν, *they were from placing* (themselves). Key, *Lat. Gr.* § 475, *n.*

reduplicated root; it is, however, very frequently omitted in Attic Greek.

300. In the subjunctive the perfect (present and past) has the same endings as the imperfect. In the past-perfect the endings -οιην, -οιης, -οιη, are preferred for the singular, as in contract verbs.

301 The imperative of the perf. act. is only found in a few isolated forms, almost exclusively of verbs whose perf. is used as a new present; the old ending of the 2 sing. in θί is preferred: as, ἑστᾰθί, *stand!* τεθνᾰθί, *die!* τεθνᾰτω, *let him die;* κεκραχθί, *shout!* γέγωνε, *speak!*

302. The ending of the infinitive is -εναι (for -μεναι*); the C. F. of the participle ends in -οτ (m. and n.; -υια, f.). For the declension see § 153.

303. *Perfect Middle and Passive.*—The present and past perfect tenses of the mid. and pass. are formed by adding to the reduplicated T. F. the same person-endings as in the imperfect tenses, but without any connecting vowel: thus, λυ-, *loosen,* perfect T. F. λελυ-, 1 p. perf. indic. mid. λέλυμαι, 2 p. λέλυσαι, etc.: past perf. indic. ἐλελύμην, etc.: infin. λελύσθαι, partic. λελυμενο-.

304. The perfect tenses of the subjunctive are formed by means of the perf. partic. passive and the corresponding mood of ἐσ-, *be.*†

305. The same rules apply on the lengthening of the final vowel of contract verbs as in the 1 perf. active. In like manner ε of monosyllabic roots ending in λ, ν, ρ, passes into α: τρεφ- (θρεφ-), *nourish;* τρεπ-, *turn;* and στρεφ-, *twist,* also change ε into α in the perf. passive: as, τέθραμμαι, *I have been nourished,* τέτραμμαι, ἐστραμμαι.

306. As the person-endings begin with consonants, in annexing these to roots ending in a consonant various changes become necessary:—

    a. Before μ (§ 38),

	C. F.	1 p. perf. pas.
any guttural becomes γ:	πλεκ-, *plait,*	πέπλεγμαι.
dental	σ: πιθ- (πειθ-), *persuade,*	πέπεισμαι.
labial	μ: γραφ-, *write,*	γέγραμμαι.

* The fuller suffix is seen in the Epic forms ἑστᾰμεναι and ἑστᾰμεν. ἰδμεναι and ἰδμεν.

† From κτα- (in.), *acquire,* and a very few other verbs, are formed εκτωμαι, κεκτημην (also -ψμην), etc.

Roots ending in γγ, γχ, μπ, lose γ and μ before those endings which begin with μ: as, σφιγγ-, *squeeze*; καμπ-, *bend*; 1 p. perf. pas. εσφιγμαι, not εσφιγγμαι; κεκαμμαι, not κεκαμμμαι. N before μ generally becomes σ, sometimes μ. Those verbs which drop final ν in the perfect active (§ 295), drop it in the passive also.

  b. Before σ (§§ 39, 40),

	C. F.	2 p. perf. pas.
any guttural becomes κ:	τᾰγ-, *array*,	τεταξαι (κσ).
dental is dropped:	πῐθ-,	πεπεισαι.
labial becomes π:	γρᾰφ-,	γεγραψαι (πσ).

  c. Before τ (§§ 36, 37),

		C. F.	3 p. perf. pas.
any guttural becomes κ:		τᾰγ-,	τετακται.
dental	σ:	πῐθ-,	πεπεισται.
labial	π:	γρᾰφ-,	γεγραπται.

  d. σ of σθ is dropped when a consonant immediately precedes, the preceding consonant being subjected to the usual laws (§ 48): as, τεταχθε, βεβλαφθαι, for τεταγσθε, βεβλαβσθαι.

  e. The endings of the 3 p. plur., -νται and -ντο, cannot be pronounced after roots ending in a consonant. Sometimes the Ionic endings, -ᾰται, -ᾰτο, are substituted, before which γ, κ, β, π, are aspirated: as, C. F. τᾰγ-, τετᾰχαται, *they have been arrayed*. More frequently a circumlocution is employed of the perf. part. with the 3 p. plur. of the pres. and past tenses of εσ-, *be*: as, πεπεισμενοι (or -μεναι) εισι, *they have been persuaded*; π. ησᾰν, *they had been persuaded*.

  307. In many verbs ending with a vowel, σ appears to be inserted before μ and τ in the perfect passive: as, C. F. τελε-, *complete*; σπα-, *draw*; ἀκου-, *hear*: perf. pass. τετελεσμαι, εσπασται, ηκουσμεθᾰ. In most of these cases, especially when the preceding vowel is short, it will be found that the σ is rather part of the root, and has disappeared from it in other forms of the verb, or represents some other consonant which has so disappeared (§ 270).

  308. *Future Perfect* (3rd Future), *Mid. and Pass.*—This tense adds σ to the perfect T. F., and takes the person-endings of the principal tenses (-ομαι, etc.): as, C. F. λυ-, *loosen*; πρᾱγ-, *do*: 1 p. fut. perf. λελῡσομαι, πεπραξομαι. This tense is not formed from verbs whose C. F. ends in a liquid.

309. Two instances only occur of a future-perfect in the active and these are from verbs whose perfects have acquired the force of a new present: ἑστηξ-, *shall stand*; τεθνηξ-, *shall be dead*. In other cases, when a fut.-perf. is required in the active, it is formed by means of the perf. part. and the future of ἐσ-, *be*: λελυκώς (-κυιᾰ) ἔσομαι, *I shall have loosened*.

310. *Aorist* (or *Indefinite*) *Tenses*.—The indicative mood possesses no special form for the present-indefinite, *I strike*: in the few instances in which this tense is required the past-indefinite is generally employed. Hence by the term *aorist* the *past-indefinite* is usually meant, unless the contrary is specified: yet the subjunctive contains distinct forms for the present and past indef.; the aorist imperative is, of course, present; and the infinitive of the aorist, as of the other tenses, is either present or past: the aorist participle, like the aorist indicative, is almost exclusively a past-indefinite. The passive voice has a future-indefinite throughout.

310.* Of the Aorist Tense, as of the Perfect, there are two distinct forms: the older form, commonly called the *Second Aorist;* and the more recent, commonly called the *First Aorist:* the 2 aor. is sometimes termed the *strong* form of the tense, and the 1 aor. the *weak* form. These tenses are identical in meaning, and are seldom both formed from the same verb, or (if formed from the same verb) both in use at the same period. See, however, § 323.

311. The middle aorists have not, like the imperfect tenses of the middle, the signification of the passive as well: thus, ἐτυψά-μην (1 aor. mid.) is only *I struck myself*, not *I was struck*. The passive voice possesses a distinct form for the aorist, as it does for the future-indefinite.

312. The aorists, first and second, take the augment in the indicative.

313. *Older*, or *Second Aorist Tense-Form.*—From the 2 aor. tense-form is deduced the 2 aor. tense, active and middle. The tense-form is the pure crude form of the verb.

314. In many verbs having ε for their radical vowel, this ε passes into α in the 2 aor.: as, τρεπ-, *turn*, 2 aor. T. F. τρᾰπ-, or, with the augment, ἐτρᾰπ-. The 2 aor. of ἄγ-, *lead*, ἀγᾰγ-, and a few other 2 aorists which are only used in poetry, are formed by reduplication.

315. The inflexion of the 2 aor., active and middle, is the same as that of the imperfect in all the moods.

316. The 2 aor. is for the most part only found in verbs which have an increased form different from the pure crude form. Hence it is (with a few exceptions, § 332) not found in vowel-verbs.

317. *First Aorist Tense-Form.*—From the 1 aor. tense-form is deduced the 1 aor. tense, active and middle. The tense-form is made by the addition of the syllable σα to the crude form of the verb: C.F. λυ-, γράφ-, τελε(σ)-, 1 aor. T.F. ελῡσα-, εγραψα-, ετελεσα-. The remarks in § 275, etc., on the modification of consonants and vowels before σ of the future, apply equally to this tense.

318. Words ending in λ, μ, ν, or ρ, which form the future without σ, also reject σ in the 1 aor. The radical vowel is lengthened in compensation: ᾰ becomes ᾱ after ε, ι, or ρ, otherwise η; ε becomes ει; ῐ and ῠ become ῑ and ῡ. Observe, however, that ᾱρ-, *raise*, and 'ἁλ- (m.), *leap*, though presenting η in the 1 aor. indic. by virtue of the augment, have ᾱ, not η, in the other moods. A few other verbs have ᾱ for η even in Attic, as κερδᾰν-, *gain*; κοιλᾰν-, *make hollow*; λευκᾰν-, *whiten*; οργᾰν-, *make angry*: 1 aor. T. F. (with the augment) ελευκᾱνα-, εκερδᾱνα-, εκοιλᾱνα-, ωργᾱνα-. Some verbs, as σημᾰν-, *shew*; κᾰθᾰρ-, *cleanse*; τετρᾰν-, *bore*; and μιᾰν-, *pollute*, vary between ᾱ and η, εσημηνα- and εσημᾱνα-, etc. The four verbs ᾰρ-, *fit*, κελ-, κῠρ-, ορ- (§ 278), and κεντ-ε-*goad*, make the 1 aor. regularly in σα, ηρσα-, εκελσα-, εκερσα-, ωρσα-, εκενσα-: μᾰχ- (m.), *fight*, and a few other words insert ε before σ εμᾰχεσᾰμην, *I fought*, etc.

319. In affixing the person-endings, observe that

In the 1 p. sing. indic. act. ν is not added: in the 3 p. α passes into ε, and ν is retained before vowels and the longer pauses, ετυψεν or ετυψε.

In the 2 p. sing. indic. mid. α(σ)ο becomes ω.

In the present tense of the subj. act. and mid. α of the tense-form is absorbed in ω and η of the endings; and in the past tense it combines with the mood-vowel ι to form αι.

In the 2 and 3 p. sing. and the 3 p. plural of the past subj. act. the forms of the Æolic aorist, -ειᾰς, -ειε(ν), -ειᾰν, are preferred even in Attic.

The 2 p. sing. imperat. act. has a suffix ν, and α passes into ο: in the 2 p. sing. imperat. mid. ι is added for the person-ending.

320. In the infin. act. the mood-ending, the syllable μεν being dropped, coalesces with α of the tense-form into the diphthong αι. The infin. mid. ends, without change, in -ασθαι.

The C. F. of the particip. in the active ends in -αντ (m. and n.; -ᾱσα, f.); in the middle in -ἄμενο (m. and n.; -ἄμενα, f.) For the declension see §§ 152, 144.

321. Three forms of the 1 aor. will be found to coincide exactly, the 3 p. sing. past subj. act., the infin. act., and the 2 p. sing. imper. mid. In accented Greek these forms are often distinguishable by a difference of accent.*

322. The 1 aor. is the form of the aorist tense for all verbs which cannot, (and for many which can), form the 2 aor. Hence it is found in all contract verbs, in most verbs ending in a liquid, and in all derived verbs.

323. From some verbs both forms of the aorist are made, the 1 aor. having a transitive, the 2 aor. an intransitive signification (§ 333).

324. *Aorists Passive.*—The aorist of the passive is made from a different tense-form from that employed in the active and middle. There are two forms of the tense, as in the other voices.

325. *Older,* or *Second Aorist.*—The tense-form of the 2 aor. is made by adding ε to the pure C. F. of the verb. As in the 2 aor. active, ε in monosyllabic roots is sometimes changed into ᾰ: C. F. τῠπ-, *strike;* τρεφ-, *nourish:* 2 aor. T. F. τῠπε-, τρᾰφε-; whence ἐτύπην, *I was struck;* ἐτράφην, *I was nourished.*

326. *First Aorist.*—The tense-form of the 1 aor. is made by adding θε to the pure C. F. of the verb. On the necessary changes of final consonants before θ, see §§ 36, 37. The final vowels of vowel-verbs are, with few exceptions, lengthened, as

---

* The 3 p. sing. of the aor. past subj. act. always has the acute accent on the penult., the inf. act. is always accented on the penult., with the circumflex *if the vowel be long,* the imper. mid. is accented (with the acute) on the antepenult. in a word of more than two syllables, but in a disyllable it will be identical with the inf. act.: thus, from the roots βουλευ-, *advise;* τῠπ-, *strike;* πρᾱγ-, *do;* καλ-ε-, *call,* we shall have

Past subj. act.	Inf. act.	Imper. mid.
βουλεύσαι (or βουλεύσειε(ν), etc.)	βουλεῦσαι	βούλευσαι
τύψαι	τύψαι	τύψαι
πρᾶξαι	πρᾶξαι	πρᾶξαι
καλέσαι	καλέσαι	κάλεσαι

IMPERFECT

Greek C. F. Increased Forms. English.			λυ- loosen.	λιπ-, τυπ-, πρᾰγ-, φρᾰδ-, αγγελ- λειπ-, τυπτ-, πρασσ-, φραζ-, αγγελλ- leave, strike, do, tell, announce.	
INDICATIVE		Present-Imperfect.	S. λυ-ω λυ-εις λυ-ει D.2. λυ-ε-τον λυ-ε-τον P. λυ-ο-μεν λυ-ε-τε λυ-ουσι(ν)	λειπ-ω, τυπτ-ω, πρασσ-ω, φραζ-ω, αγγελλ-ω,	-εις, -ει, etc.
		Past-Imperfect.	S. ε-λυ-ο-ν ε-λυ-ε-ς ε-λυ-ε-(ν) D.2. ε-λυ-ε-τον ε-λυ-ε-την P. ε-λυ-ο-μεν ε-λυ-ε-τε ε-λυ-ο-ν	ελειπ-ον, ετυπτ-ον, επρασσ-ον, εφραζ-ον, ηγγελλ-ον,	-ες, -ε(ν), etc.
SUBJUNCTIVE		Present. (SUBJUNCTIVE.)	S. λυ-ω λυ-ῃς λυ-ῃ D.2. λυ-η-τον λυ-η-τον P. λυ-ω-μεν λυ-η-τε λυ-ω-σι(ν)	λειπ-ω, τυπτ-ω, πρασσ-ω, φραζ-ω, αγγελλ-ω,	-ῃς, -ῃ, etc.
		Past. (OPTATIVE.)	S. λυ-οι-μῐ λυ-οι-ς λυ-οι D.2. λυ-οι-τον λυ-οι-την P. λυ-οι-μεν λυ-οι-τε λυ-οι-εν	λειπ-οιμῐ, τυπτ-οιμῐ, πρασσ-οιμῐ, φραζ-οιμῐ, αγγελλ-οιμῐ,	-οις, -οι, etc.
IMPERATIVE			S.2. λυ-ε λυ-ε-τω D.2. λυ-ε-τον λυ-ε-των P.2. λυ-ε-τε λυ-ο-ντων or λυ-ε-τωσᾰν	λειπ-ε, τυπτ-ε, πρασσ-ε, φραζ-ε, αγγελλ-ε,	-ετω, etc.
INFINITIVE			λυ-ειν	λειπειν, τυπτειν, πρασσειν, φραζειν, αγγελλειν	
PARTICIPLE			λυ-ο-ντ-	λειπο-ντ-, τυπτο-ντ-, πρασσο-ντ-, φραζο-ντ-, αγγελλοντ-	

TABLE I. — ACTIVE.

	τῑμα- honour.	αιτε- ask.		δουλο- enslave.	
	τῑμῶ	αιτε-ω	αιτῶ	δουλο-ω	δουλῶ
ς	τῑμᾷς	αιτε-εις	αιτεῖς	δουλο-εις	δουλοῖς
	τῑμᾷ	αιτε-ει	αιτεῖ	δουλο-ει	δουλοῖ
ον	τῑμᾶτον	αιτε-ετον	αιτεῖτον	δουλο-ετον	δουλοῦτον
ον	τῑμᾶτον	αιτε-ετον	αιτεῖτον	δουλο-ετον	δουλοῦτον
μεν	τῑμῶμεν	αιτε-ομεν	αιτοῦμεν	δουλο-ομεν	δουλοῦμεν
ε	τῑμᾶτε	αιτε-ετε	αιτεῖτε	δουλο-ετε	δουλοῦτε
οσῐ(ν)	τῑμῶσῐ(ν)	αιτε-ουσῐ(ν)	αιτοῦσῐ(ν)	δουλο-ουσῐ(ν)	δουλοῦσῐ(ν)
ν	ετῑμων	ῃτε-ον	ῃτουν	εδουλο-ον	εδουλουν
ς	ετῑμᾱς	ῃτε-ες	ῃτεις	εδουλο-ες	εδουλους
(ν)	ετῑμᾱ	ῃτε-ε(ν)	ῃτει	εδουλο-ε(ν)	εδουλου
τον	ετῑμᾶτον	ῃτε-ετον	ῃτειτον	εδουλο-ετον	εδουλουτον
την	ετῑμᾶτην	ῃτε-ετην	ῃτειτην	εδουλο-ετην	εδουλουτην
μεν	ετῑμωμεν	ῃτε-ομεν	ῃτουμεν	εδουλο-ομεν	εδουλουμεν
τε	ετῑμᾶτε	ῃτε-ετε	ῃτειτε	εδουλο-ετε	εδουλουτε
ν	ετῑμων	ῃτε-ον	ῃτουν	εδουλο-ον	εδουλουν
	τῑμῶ	αιτε-ω	αιτῶ	δουλο-ω	δουλῶ
ς	τῑμᾷς	αιτε-ῃς	αιτῇς	δουλο-ῃς	δουλοῖς
	τῑμᾷ	αιτε-ῃ	αιτῇ	δουλο-ῃ	δουλοῖ
ον	τῑμᾶτον	αιτε-ητον	αιτητον	δουλο-ητον	δουλῶτον
ον	τῑμᾶτον	αιτε-ητον	αιτητον	δουλο-ητον	δουλῶτον
μεν	τῑμῶμεν	αιτε-ωμεν	αιτωμεν	δουλο-ωμεν	δουλῶμεν
ε	τῑμᾶτε	αιτε-ητε	αιτητε	δουλο-ητε	δουλῶτε
σῐ(ν)	τῑμῶσῐ(ν)	αιτε-ωσῐ(ν)	αιτωσῐ(ν)	δουλο-ωσῐ(ν)	δουλῶσῐ(ν)
ην	τῑμῴην	αιτε-οιην	αιτοιην	δουλο-οιην	δουλοίην
ης	τῑμῴης	αιτε-οιης	αιτοιης	δουλο-οιης	δουλοίης
η	τῑμῴη	αιτε-οιη	αιτοιη	δουλο-οιη	δουλοίη
τον	τῑμῷτον	αιτε-οιτον	αιτοιτον	δουλο-οιτον	δουλοίτον
την	τῑμῷτην	αιτε-οιτην	αιτοιτην	δουλο-οιτην	δουλοίτην
μεν	τῑμῷμεν	αιτε-οιμεν	αιτοιμεν	δουλο-οιμεν	δουλοίμεν
τε	τῑμῷτε	αιτε-οιτε	αιτοιτε	δουλο-οιτε	δουλοίτε
εν	τῑμῷεν	αιτε-οιεν	αιτοιεν	δουλο-οιεν	δουλοίεν
	τῑμᾱ	αιτε-ε	αιτει	δουλο-ε	δουλου
ω	τῑμᾱτω	αιτε-ετω	αιτειτω	δουλο-ετω	δουλουτω
ον	τῑμᾶτον	αιτε-ετον	αιτειτον	δουλο-ετον	δουλουτον
ων	τῑμᾶτων	αιτε-ετων	αιτειτων	δουλο-ετων	δουλουτων
ε	τῑμᾶτε	αιτε-ετε	αιτειτε	δουλο-ετε	δουλουτε
των or	τῑμωντων or	αιτε-οντων or	αιτουντων or	δουλο-οντων or	δουλουντων or
ωσᾰν	τῑμᾱτωσᾰν	αιτε-ετωσᾰν	αιτειτωσᾰν	δουλο-ετωσᾰν	δουλουτωσᾰν
-εν)	τῑμᾶν	(αιτε-ε-εν)	αιτειν	(δουλο-ε-εν)	δουλουν
τ-	τῑμωντ-	αιτε-οντ-	αιτουντ-	δουλο-οντ-	δουλουντ-

IMPERFECT TENSES.

Greek C. F. Increased Forms. English.			λυ- loosen.	λῐπ-, τῠπ-, πρᾱγ-, φρᾰδ-, αγγελ- λειπ-, τυπτ-, πρασσ-, φραζ-, ἀγγελλ- leave, strike, do, tell, announce.	
INDICATIVE.	*Present-Imperfect.*	S. D. P.	λυ-ο-μαι λυ-ῃ, or λυ-ει λυ-ε-ται λυ-ο-μεθον λυ-ε-σθον λυ-ε-σθον λυ-ο-μεθᾰ λυ-ε-σ?- λυ-ο-νται	λειπ-ομαι, τυπτ-ομαι, πρασσ-ομαι, φραζ-ομαι, αγγελλ-ομαι, } -ῃ (ει), -εται, etc.	
	Past-Imperfect.	S. D. P.	ε-λυ-ο-μην ε-λυ-ου ε-λυ-ε-το ε-λυ-ο-μεθον ε-λυ-ε-σθον ε-λυ-ε-σθην ε-λυ-ο-μεθᾰ ε-λυ-ε-σθε ε-λυ-ο-ντο	ελειπ-ομην, ετυπτ-ομην, επρασσ-ομην, εφραζ-ομην, ηγγελλ-ομην, } -ου, -ετο, etc.	
SUBJUNCTIVE.	*Present.* (SUBJUNCTIVE.)	S. D. P.	λυ-ω-μαι λυ-ῃ λυ-η-ται λυ-ω-μεθον λυ-η-σθον λυ-η-σθον λυ-ω-μεθᾰ λυ-η-σθε λυ-ω-νται	λειπ-ωμαι, τυπτ-ωμαι, πρασσ-ωμαι, φραζ-ωμαι, αγγελλ-ωμαι, } -ῃ, -ηται, etc.	
	Past. (OPTATIVE.)	S. D. P.	λυ-οι-μην λυ-οι-ο λυ-οι-το λυ-οι-μεθον λυ-οι-σθον λυ-οι-σθην λυ-οι-μεθᾰ λυ-οι-σθε λυ-οι-ντο	λειπ-οιμην, τυπτ-οιμην, πρασσ-οιμην, φραζ-οιμην, αγγελλ-οιμην, } -οιο, -οιτο, etc.	
IMPERATIVE.		S. 2. D. 2. P. 2. 	λυ-ου λυ-ε-σθω λυ-ε-σθον λυ-ε-σθων λυ-ε-σθε λυ-ε-σθων or λυ-ε-σθωσᾰν	λειπ-ου, τυπτ-ου, πρασσ-ου, φραζ-ου, αγγελλ-ου, } -εσθω, etc.	
INFIN-ITIVE.			λυ-ε-σθαι	λειπεσθαι, τυπτεσθαι, πρασσεσθαι, φραζεσθαι, αγγελλεσθαι	
PARTI-CIPLE.			λυ-ο-μενο-	λειπομενο-, τυπτομενο-, ποασσομενο-, φραζομενο-, αγγελλομενο-	

MIDDLE AND PASSIVE. TABLE II.

τῑμα- honour.		αιτε- ask.		δουλο enslave.	
μαι	τῑμωμαι	αιτε-ομαι	αιτουμαι	δουλο-ομαι	δουλουμαι
(ει)	τῑμᾷ	αιτε-ῃ (ει)	αιτῃ (ει)	δουλο-ῃ (ει)	δουλοι
ται	τῑμᾶται	αιτε-εται	αιτειται	δουλο-εται	δουλουται
μεθον	τῑμωμεθον	αιτε-ομεθον	αιτουμεθον	δουλο-ομεθον	δουλουμεθον
σθον	τῑμασθον	αιτε-εσθον	αιτεισθον	δουλο-εσθον	δουλουσθον
σθον	τῑμασθον	αιτε-εσθον	αιτεισθον	δουλο-εσθον	δουλουσθον
μεθᾰ	τῑμωμεθᾰ	αιτε-ομεθᾰ	αιτουμεθᾰ	δουλο-ομεθᾰ	δουλουμεθᾰ
σθε	τῑμασθε	αιτε-εσθε	αιτεισθε	δουλο-εσθε	δουλουσθε
νται	τῑμωνται	αιτε-ονται	αιτουνται	δουλο-ονται	δουλουνται
ομην	ετῑμωμην	ῃτε-ομην	ῃτουμην	εδουλο-ομην	εδουλουμην
ου	ετῑμω	ῃτε-ου	ῃτου	εδουλο-ου	εδουλου
ιτο	ετῑμᾶτο	ῃτε-ετο	ῃτειτο	εδουλο-ετο	εδουλουτο
ομεθον	ετῑμωμεθον	ῃτε-ομεθον	ῃτουμεθον	εδουλο-ομεθον	εδουλουμεθον
εσθον	ετῑμασθον	ῃτε-εσθον	ῃτεισθον	εδουλο-εσθον	εδουλουσθον
εσθην	ετῑμασθην	ῃτε-εσθην	ῃτεισθην	εδουλο-εσθην	εδουλουσθην
ομεθᾰ	ετῑμωμεθᾰ	ῃτε-ομεθᾰ	ῃτουμεθᾰ	εδουλο-ομεθᾰ	εδουλουμεθᾰ
εσθε	ετῑμασθε	ῃτε-εσθε	ῃτεισθε	εδουλο-εσθε	εδουλουσθε
οντο	ετῑμωντο	ῃτε-οντο	ῃτουντο	εδουλο-οντο	εδουλουντο
μαι	τῑμωμαι	αιτε-ωμαι	αιτωμαι	δουλο-ωμαι	δουλωμαι
	τῑμᾷ	αιτε-ῃ	αιτῃ	δουλο-ῃ	δουλοι
ται	τῑμᾶται	αιτε-ηται	αιτηται	δουλο-ηται	δουλωται
μεθον	τῑμωμεθον	αιτε-ωμεθον	αιτωμεθον	δουλο-ωμεθον	δουλωμεθον
σθον	τῑμασθον	αιτε-ησθον	αιτησθον	δουλο-ησθον	δουλωσθον
σθον	τῑμασθον	αιτε-ησθον	αιτησθον	δουλο-ησθον	δουλωσθον
μεθᾰ	τῑμωμεθᾰ	αιτε-ωμεθᾰ	αιτωμεθᾰ	δουλο-ωμεθᾰ	δουλωμεθᾰ
σθε	τῑμασθε	αιτε-ησθε	αιτησθε	δουλο-ησθε	δουλωσθε
νται	τῑμωνται	αιτε-ωνται	αιτωνται	δουλο-ωνται	δουλωνται
ιμην	τῑμῳμην	αιτε-οιμην	αιτοιμην	δουλο-οιμην	δουλοιμην
ιο	τῑμῳο	αιτε-οιο	αιτοιο	δουλο-οιο	δουλοιο
ιτο	τῑμῳτο	αιτε-οιτο	αιτοιτο	δουλο-οιτο	δουλοιτο
ιμεθον	τῑμῳμεθον	αιτε-οιμεθον	αιτοιμεθον	δουλο-οιμεθον	δουλοιμεθον
ισθον	τῑμῳσθον	αιτε-οισθον	αιτοισθον	δουλο-οισθον	δουλοισθον
ισθην	τῑμῳσθην	αιτε-οισθην	αιτοισθην	δουλο-οισθην	δουλοισθην
ιμεθᾰ	τῑμῳμεθᾰ	αιτε-οιμεθᾰ	αιτοιμεθᾰ	δουλο-οιμεθᾰ	δουλοιμεθᾰ
ισθε	τῑμῳσθε	αιτε-οισθε	αιτοισθε	δουλο-οισθε	δουλοισθε
ιντο	τῑμῳντο	αιτε-οιντο	αιτοιντο	δουλο-οιντο	δουλοιντο
υ	τῑμω	αιτε-ου	αιτου	δουλο-ου	δουλου
σθω	τῑμασθω	αιτε-εσθω	αιτεισθω	δουλο-εσθω	δουλουσθω
σθον	τῑμασθον	αιτε-εσθον	αιτεισθον	δουλο-εσθον	δουλουσθον
σθων	τῑμασθων	αιτε-εσθων	αιτεισθων	δουλο-εσθων	δουλουσθων
σθε	τῑμασθε	αιτε-εσθε	αιτεισθε	δουλο-εσθε	δουλουσθε
σθων or	τῑμασθων or	αιτε-εσθων or	αιτεισθων or	δουλο-εσθων or	δουλουσθων or
σθωσᾰν	τῑμασθωσᾰν	αιτε-εσθωσᾰν	αιτεισθωσᾰν	δουλο-εσθωσᾰν	δουλουσθωσᾰν
σθαι	τῑμασθαι	αιτε-εσθαι	αιτεισθαι	δουλο-εσθαι	δουλουσθαι
μενο-	τῑμωμενο-	αιτε-ομενο-	αιτουμενο-	δουλο-ομενο-	δουλουμενο-

FUTURE TE[NSE]

Greek C. F. Increased Forms. English.		λυ- loosen.	λῐπ-, τῠπ-, πρᾱγ-, φρᾱ[δ-] λειπ-, τυπτ-, πρασσ-, φρα[ζ-] leave, strike, do, tell.
INDICATIVE		S. λῡ-σ-ω λῡ-σ-εις λῡ-σ-ει D.2. λῡ-σ-ε-τον λῡ-σ-ε-τον P. λῡ-σ-ο-μεν λῡ-σ-ε-τε λῡ-σ-ουσῐ(ν)	λειψ-ω, τυψ-ω, πραξ-ω, φρᾱσ-ω, } -εις, -ει. etc.
SUBJUNCTIVE (OPTATIVE)		S. λῡ-σ-οι-μῐ λῡ-σ-οι-ς λῡ-σ-οι D.2. λῡ-σ-οι-τον λῡ-σ-οι-την P. λῡ-σ-οι-μεν λῡ-σ-οι-τε λῡ-σ-οι-εν	λειψ-οιμῐ, τυψ-οιμῐ, πραξ-οιμῐ, φρᾱσ-οιμῐ, } -οις, -οι, etc.
INFIN- ITIVE		λῡ-σ-ειν	λειψειν, τυψειν, πραξειν, φρᾱ[σειν]
PARTI- CIPLE		λῡ-σ-οντ-	λειψοντ-, τυψοντ-, πραξοντ- φρᾱσοντ-

FUTURE TENSE.—M[IDDLE]

INDICATIVE		S. λῡ-σ-ο-μαι λῡ-σ-ῃ (ει) λῡ-σ-ε-ται D. λῡ-σ-ο-μεθον λῡ-σ-ε-σθον λῡ-σ-ε-σθον P. λῡ-σ-ο-μεθᾰ λῡ-σ-ε-σθε λῡ-σ-ο-νται	λειψ-ομαι, τυψ-ομαι, πραξ-ομαι, φρᾱσ-ομαι, } -ῃ (ει), -εται, etc
SUBJUNCTIVE (OPTATIVE)		S. λῡ-σ-οι-μην λῡ-σ-οι-ο λῡ-σ-οι-το D. λῡ-σ-οι-μεθον λῡ-σ-οι-σθον λῡ-σ-οι-σθην P. λῡ-σ-οι-μεθᾰ λῡ-σ-οι-σθε λῡ-σ-οι-ντο	λειψ-οιμην, τυψ-οιμην, πραξ-οιμην, φρᾱσ-οιμην, } -οιο, -οιτο, etc.
INFIN- ITIVE		λῡ-σ-ε-σθαι	λειψεσθαι, τυψεσθαι, πραξε[σθαι] φρᾱσεσθαι
PARTI- CIPLE		λῡ-σ-ο-μενο-	λειψομενο-, τυψομενο-, πραξομ[ενο-] φρᾱσομενο-

.—ACTIVE.   TABLE III.

αγγελ-, αγγελλ-, (Liquid Future) announce.		τῑμα-, honour,	αιτε-, ask,	δουλο- enslave.
αγγελε-ω	αγγελω			
αγγελε-εις	αγγελεις			
αγγελε-ει	αγγελει			
αγγελε-ετον	αγγελειτον	τῑμησ-ω,	}	
αγγελε-ετον	αγγελειτον	αιτησ-ω,	} -εις, -ει, etc.	
αγγελε-ομεν	αγγελουμεν	δουλωσ-ω,	}	
αγγελε-ετε	αγγελειτε			
αγγελε-ουσῐ(ν)	αγγελουσῐ(ν)			
αγγελε-οιην	αγγελοιην			
αγγελε-οιης	αγγελοιης			
αγγελε-οιη	αγγελοιη			
αγγελε-οιτον	αγγελοιτον	τῑμησ-οιμῐ,	}	
αγγελε-οιτην	αγγελοιτην	αιτησ-οιμῐ,	} -οις, -οι, etc.	
αγγελε-οιμεν	αγγελοιμεν	δουλωσ-οιμῐ,	}	
αγγελε-οιτε	αγγελοιτε			
αγγελε-οιεν	αγγελοιεν			
αγγελε-ειν	αγγελειν	τῑμησειν,	αιτησειν,	δουλωσειν
αγγελε-οντ-	αγγελουντ-	τῑμησοντ-,	αιτησοντ-,	δουλωσοντ-

LE AND PASSIVE.   TABLE IV.

αγγελε-ομαι	αγγελουμαι			
αγγελε-ῃ (ει)	αγγελῃ (ει)			
αγγελε-εται	αγγελειται			
αγγελε-ομεθον	αγγελουμεθον	τῑμησ-ομαι,	}	
αγγελε-εσθον	αγγελεισθον	αιτησ-ομαι,	} -ῃ (ει), -εται, etc.	
αγγελε-εσθον	αγγελεισθον	δουλωσ-ομαι,	}	
αγγελε-ομεθᾰ	αγγελουμεθᾰ			
αγγελε-εσθε	αγγελεισθε			
αγγελε-ονται	αγγελουνται			
αγγελε-οιμην	αγγελοιμην			
αγγελε-οιο	αγγελοιο			
αγγελε-οιτο	αγγελοιτο			
αγγελε-οιμεθον	αγγελοιμεθον	τῑμησ-οιμην,	}	
αγγελε-οισθον	αγγελοισθον	αιτησ-οιμην,	} -ῳο, -οιτο, etc.	
αγγελε-οισθην	αγγελοισθην	δουλωσ-οιμην,	}	
αγγελε-οιμεθᾰ	αγγελοιμεθᾰ			
αγγελε-οισθε	αγγελοισθε			
αγγελε-οιντο	αγγελοιντο			
αγγελε-εσθαι	αγγελεισθαι	τῑμησεσθαι, αιτησεσθαι, δουλωσεσθαι		
αγγελε-ομενο-	αγγελουμενο-	τῑμησομενο-, αιτησομενο-, δουλωσομενο-		

PERFECT TE[NSE]

				First Perfect	
Greek C. F. Increased Forms. English.			λυ- loosen.	τῠπ-, πρᾱγ-, φρᾰδ-, τυπτ-, πρασσ-, φραζ-, strike, do, tell,	
Indicative.		Present-Perfect.	S. λε-λῠ-κᾰ́ λε-λῠ-κᾰ́-ς λε-λῠ-κε-(ν) D.2. λε-λῠ-κᾰ́-τον λε-λῠ-κᾰ́-τον P. λε-λῠ-κᾰ́-μεν λε-λῠ-κᾰ́-τε λε-λῠ-κᾱ́σῐ(ν)	τετῠ́φ-ᾰ, πεπρᾱ́χ-ᾰ, πεφρᾰ́κ-ᾰ, ηγγελκ-ᾰ,	} -ᾰς, -ε(ν
		Past-Perfect.	S. ε-λε-λῠ́-κη or -κειν ε-λε-λῠ́-κης or -κεις ε-λε-λῠ́-κει D.2. ε-λε-λῠ́-κει-τον ε-λε-λῠ́-κει-την P. ε-λε-λῠ́-κει-μεν ε-λε-λῠ́-κει-τε ε-λε-λῠ́-κε-σᾰν	ετετῠ́φ-η, -ειν, επεπρᾱ́χ-η, -ειν, επεφρᾰ́κ-η, -ειν, ηγγελκ-η, -ειν,	} -ης or -ει
Subjunctive.		Present. (Subjunct.)	λε-λῠ́-κω λε-λῠ́-κῃς etc. as in the Imperfect.	Th[e] Subjunctive Te[nse]	
		Past. (Optative).	S. λε-λῠ́-κ-οι-ην ⎫ λε-λῠ́-κ-οι-ης ⎬ or ⎧ -κ-οι-μῐ λε-λῠ́-κ-οι-η ⎭ ⎨ -κ-οι-ς D.2. λε-λῠ́-κ-οι-τον ⎩ -κ-οι λε-λῠ́-κ-οι-την P. λε-λῠ́-κ-οι-μεν λε-λῠ́-κ-οι-τε λε-λῠ́-κ-οι-εν		
Imperative.			(λε-λῠ́-κ-ε λε-λῠ́-κ-ετω) etc.	The Imperativ[e]	
Infinitive.			λε-λῠ́-κ-εναι	τετῠφεναι, πεφρᾰκεναι,	πεπρᾱ[χεναι,] ηγγελκ[εναι]

			SECOND PERFECT.	
'ελ- 'ελλ- ounce.	τῑμα-, αιτε-, δουλο- honour, ask, enslave.		λῐπ-, πρᾱγ- λειπ-, πρασσ- leave, do.	
c.	τετῑμηκ-ᾰ, ῃτηκ-ᾰ, δεδουλωκ-ᾰ, } -ᾰς, -ε(ν), etc.		λε-λοιπ-ᾰ, πε-πρᾱγ-ᾰ, } -ᾰς, -ε(ν), etc.	
ι, etc.	ετετῑμηκ-η, -ειν, ῃτηκ-η, -ειν, εδεδουλωκ-η, -ειν, } -ης or -εις, -ει, etc.		ε-λε-λοιπ-η, -ειν, ε-πε-πρᾱγ-η, -ειν, } -ης or -εις, -ει, etc.	

of the Perfect are also often made by combining the Perfect Participle
ith the corresponding forms of εσ-, *be*: thus—

Pres.-Perf. λελῠκως ω, ῃς, ῃ
λελῠκοτες ωμεν, ητε, ωσῐ(ν)
Past-Perf. λελῠκως ειην, ειης, ειη
λελῠκοτες ειημεν, ειητε, ειεν

---

the Perfect is very seldom used in the Active Voice; see § 301.

	τετῑμηκεναι, ῃτηκεναι, δεδουλωκεναι		λε-λοιπ-εναι, πε-πρᾱγ-εναι
,	τετῑμηκοτ-, ῃτηκοτ-, δεδουλωκοτ-		λε-λοιπ-οτ-, πι-πρᾱγ-οτ-

PERFECT TENSES.—

Greek C. F. Increased Forms. English.			λυ- loosen.	τύπ- τυπτ- strike.	π(π(π(
INDICATIVE.	Present-Perfect.	S.	λε-λύ-μαι	τετυμ-μαι	πεπραγ-/
			λε-λύ-σαι	τετυψαι	πεπραξα:
			λε-λύ-ται	τετυπ-ται	πεπρακ-τ
		D.	λε-λύ-μεθον	τετυμ-μεθον	πεπραγ-/
			λε-λυ-σθον	τετυφ-θον	πεπραχ-(
			λε-λυ-σθον	τετυφ-θον	πεπραχ-(
		P.	λε-λύ-μεθᾰ	τετυμ-μεθᾰ	πεπραγ-/
			λε-λυ-σθε	τετυφ-θε	πεπραχ-(
			λε-λυ-νται	τετυμ-μενοι εισῐ(ν)	πεπραγ-/
	Past-Perfect.	S.	ε-λε-λύ-μην	ετετυμ-μην	επεπραγ-
			ε-λε-λύ-σο	ετετυψο	επεπραξο
			ε-λε-λύ-το	ετετυπ-το	επεπρακ-
		D.	ε-λε-λύ-μεθον	ετετυμ-μεθον	επεπραγ-
			ε-λε-λυ-σθον	ετετυφ-θον	επεπραχ-
			ε-λε-λυ-σθην	ετετυφ-θην	επεπραχ-
		P.	ε-λε-λύ-μεθᾰ	ετετυμ-μεθᾰ	επεπραγ-
			ε-λε-λυ-σθε	ετετυφ-θε	επεπραχ-
			ε-λε-λυ-ντο	τετυμ-μενοι ησαν	πεπραγ-/
	Fut. Perf.		λε-λύ-σ-ο-μαι, etc. like Future Imperfect.	τετυψομαι, etc.	πεπραξομ
SUBJUNCTIVE.	Pres. (SUBJ.)	S.	λε-λύ-μενος ω, ῃς, ῃ	τετυμ-μενος ω, etc.	πεπραγ-/
		P.	λε-λύ-μενοι ωμεν, ητε, ωσῐ(ν)		
	Past. (OPTATIVE.)	S.	λε-λύ-μενος ειην, ειης, ειη	τετυμ-μενος ειην, etc.	πεπραγ-μ
		P.	λε-λύ-μενοι ειημεν, ειητε, ειεν		
	Fut.		λε-λύ-σ-οι-μην, etc. like Future Imperfect.	τετυψοιμην, etc.	πεπραξοι
IMPERATIVE.		S. 2.	λε-λύ-σο	τετυψο	πεπραξο
			λε-λυ-σθω	τετυφ-θω	πεπραχ-θ
		D.2.	λε-λυ-σθον	τετυφ-θον	πεπραχ-θ
			λε-λυ-σθων	τετυφ-θων	πεπραχ-θ
		P.2.	λε-λυ-σθε	τετυφ-θε	πεπραχ-θ
			λε-λυ-σθων or	τετυφ-θων or	πεπραχ-θ
			λε-λυ-σθωσᾰν	τετυφ-θωσᾰν	πεπραχ-θ
INFINITIVE.			λε-λυ-σθαι	τετυφ-θαι	πεπραχ-θ
			λε-λύ-σ-ε-σθαι	τετυψεσθαι	πεπραξεσ
PARTICIPLE.			λε-λύ-μενο-	τετυμ-μενο-	πεπραγ-μ
			λε-λύ-σ-ο-μενο-	τετυψομενο-	πεπραξομ

TABLE VI.

	φράδ- φραζ- tell.	αγγελ- αγγελλ- announce.	τῑμα-, honour,	αιτε-, ask,	δουλο- enslave.
	πεφρασ-μαι πεφρά-σαι πεφρασ-ται πεφρασ-μεθον πεφρα-σθον πεφρα-σθον πεφρασ-μεθᾰ πεφρα-σθε πεφρασ-μενοι εισῐ(ν)	ηγγελ-μαι ηγγελ-σαι ηγγελ-ται ηγγελ-μεθον ηγγελ-θον ηγγελ-θον ηγγελ-μεθᾰ ηγγελ-θε ηγγελ-μενοι εισῐ(ν)	τετῑμη-μαι, ῃτη-μαι, δεδουλω-μαι,	} -σαι, -ται, etc. (like λυ-).	
	επεφρασ-μην επεφρά-σο επεφρασ-το επεφρασ-μεθον επεφρα-σθον επεφρα-σθην επεφρασ-μεθᾰ επεφρα-σθε πεφρασ-μενοι ησᾰν	ηγγελ-μην ηγγελ-σο ηγγελ-το ηγγελ-μεθον ηγγελ-θον ηγγελ-θην ηγγελ-μεθᾰ ηγγελ-θε ηγγελ-μενοι ησᾰν	ετετῑμη-μην, ῃτη-μην, εδεδουλω-μην,	} -σο, -το, etc. (like λυ-).	
			τετῑμησομαι, ῃτησομαι, δεδουλωσομαι, etc.		
	πεφρασ-μενος ω, etc.	ηγγελ-μενος ω, etc.	τετῑμημενος ῃτημενος δεδουλωμενος	} ω, ῃς, ῃ, etc.	
	πεφρασ-μενος ειην, etc.	ηγγελ-μενος ειην, etc.	τετῑμημενος ῃτημενος δεδουλωμενος	} ειην, ειης, ειη, etc.	
			τετῑμησοιμην, ῃτησοιμην, δεδουλωσοιμην, etc.		
	πεφρά-σο πεφρα-σθω πεφρα-σθον πεφρα-σθων πεφρα-σθε πεφρα-σθων or πεφρα-σθωσᾰν	ηγγελ-σο ηγγελ-θω ηγγελ-θον ηγγελ-θων ηγγελ-θε ηγγελ-θων or ηγγελ-θωσᾰν	τετῑμη-σο, ῃτη-σο, δεδουλω-σο,	} -σθω, etc. (like λυ-).	
	πεφρα-σθαι	ηγγελ-θαι	τετῑμησθαι, ῃτησθαι, δεδουλωσθαι τετῑμησεσθαι, etc.		
	πεφρασ-μενο-	ηγγελ-μενο-	τετῑμημενο-, ῃτημενο-, δεδουλω- τετῑμησομενο-, etc. [μενο-		

AORIST TE[N]

FIRST AORIST.

Greek C. F. Increased Forms. English.	λυ- *loosen.*	τὔπ-, πρᾱγ-, φράδ- τυπτ-, πρασσ-, φραζ- *strike, do, tell.*	φ φ s[ ]
INDICATIVE.	S. ε-λῦ-σᾰ ε-λῦ-σᾰ-ς ε-λῦ-σε(ν) D.2. ε-λῦ-σᾰ-τον ε-λῦ-σᾰ-την P. ε-λῦ-σᾰ-μεν ε-λῦ-σᾰ-τε ε-λῦ-σᾰ-ν	ετυψ-ᾰ, επραξ-ᾰ, } -ᾰς, -ε(ν), etc. εφρᾰσ-ᾰ,	εφτ[ηγ[ημ[
SUBJUNCTIVE. *Pres.-Indef.* (SUBJUNCTIVE.)	S. λῡ-σ-ω λῡ-σ-ῃς λῡ-σ-ῃ D.2. λῡ-σ-η-τον λῡ-σ-η-τον P. λῡ-σ-ω-μεν λῡ-σ-η-τε λῡ-σ-ω-σῐ(ν)	τυψ-ω, πραξ-ω, } -ῃς, -ῃ, etc. φρᾰσ-ω,	φη[αγγ ἄμ[
SUBJUNCTIVE. *Past-Indef.* (OPTATIVE.)	S. λῡ-σαι-μῐ λῡ-σαι-ς or λῡσειᾰς λῡ-σαι or λῡσειε(ν) D.2. λῡ-σαι-τον λῡ-σαι-την P. λῡ-σαι-μεν λῡ-σαι-τε λῡ-σαι-εν or λῡσεῖαν	τυψ-αιμῐ, -αις, -αι, πραξ-αιμῐ, } or or etc. φρᾰσ-αιμῐ, -ειᾰς, -ειε(ν),	φη[αγγ ἄμ[
IMPERATIVE.	S.2. λῡ-σον λῡ-σᾰ-τω D.2. λῡ-σᾰ-τον λῡ-σᾰ-των P.2. λῡ-σᾰ-τε λῡ-σᾰ-ντων or λῡ-σᾰ-τωσᾰν	τυψ-ον, πρᾱξ-ον, } -ᾰτω, etc. φρᾰσ-ον,	φην αγγ ἄμ[
INFIN- ITIVE.	λῡ-σα-ι	τυψαι, πραξαι, φρᾰσαι	
PARTI- CIPLE.	λῡ-σα-ντ-	τυψαντ-, πραξαντ-, φρᾰσαντ-	φην

| αγγελ-, ἄμῡν- | τῑμα-, αιτε-, δουλο- | λῐπ- |
| αγγελλ-, ἄμῡν- | | λειπ- |
announce, ward off.	honour, ask, enslave.	leave.
} -ᾰς, -ε(ν), etc.	ετῑμησ-ᾰ, ῃτησ-ᾰ, } -ᾰς, -ε(ν), etc. εδουλωσ-ᾰ,	ε-λῐπ-ο-ν ε-λῐπ-ε-ς ε-λῐπ-ε(ν) ε-λῐπ-ε-τον ε-λῐπ-ε-την ε-λῐπ-ο-μεν ε-λῐπ-ε-τε ε-λῐπ-ο-ν
} -ῃς, -ῃ, etc.	τῑμησ-ω, αιτησ-ω, } -ῃς, -ῃ, etc. δουλωσ-ω,	λῐπ-ω λῐπ-ῃς λῐπ-ῃ λῐπ-η-τον λῐπ-η-τον λῐπ-ω-μεν λῐπ-η-τε λῐπ-ω-σῐ(ν)
μῐ, } -αις, -αι, ῐ, } or or etc. -ειᾰς, -ειε(ν),	τῑμησ-αιμῐ, -αις, -αι, αιτησ-αιμῐ, } or or etc. δουλωσ-αιμῐ, } -ειᾰς, -ειε(ν),	λῐπ-οι-μῐ λῐπ-οι-ς λῐπ-οι λῐπ-οι-τον λῐπ-οι-την λῐπ-οι-μεν λῐπ-οι-τε λῐπ-οι-εν
', } -ᾰτω, etc.	τῑμησ-ον, αιτησ-ον, } -ᾰτω, etc. δουλωσ-ον,	λῐπ-ε λῐπ-ε-τω λῐπ-ε-τον λῐπ-ε-των λῐπ-ε-τε λῐπ-ο-ντων or λῐπ-ε-τωσᾰν
, αγγειλαι, ἄμῡναι	τῑμησαι, αιτησαι, δουλωσαι	λῐπ-ειν
αγγειλαντ-, ἄμῡναντ-	τῑμησαντ-, αιτησαντ-, δουλωσαντ-	λῐπ-οντ-

AORIST TE[N]

FIRST AORIST.

		Greek C. F. Increased Forms. English.	λυ- loosen.	τύπ-, τυπτ-, strike,	πρᾱγ-, πρασσ-, do,	φρᾰδ-, φραζ-, tell.	
INDICATIVE.			S. ε-λῡ-σᾰ-μην ε-λῡ-σω (σα-ο) ε-λῡ-σᾰ-το D. ε-λῡ-σᾰ-μεθον ε-λῡ-σα-σθον ε-λῡ-σα-σθην P. ε-λῡ-σᾰ-μεθᾰ ε-λῡ-σα-σθε ε-λῡ-σα-ντο	ετυψ-ᾰμην, επραξ-ᾰμην, εφρᾱσ-ᾰμην,	} -ω, -ᾰτο, etc.	εφ[ηγ ημ
SUBJUNCTIVE.	Pres.-Indef. (SUBJUNCTIVE.)		S. λῡ-σ-ω-μαι λῡ-σ-ῃ λῡ-σ-η-ται D. λῡ-σ-ω-μεθον λῡ-σ-η-σθον λῡ-σ-η-σθον P. λῡ-σ-ω-μεθᾰ λῡ-σ-η-σθε λῡ-σ-ω-νται	τυψ-ωμαι, πραξ-ωμαι, φρᾱσ-ωμαι,	} -ῃ, -ηται, etc.	φη αγ ᾰμ
	Past-Indef. (OPTATIVE.)		S. λῡ-σαι-μην λῡ-σαι-ο λῡ-σαι-το D. λῡ-σαι-μεθον λῡ-σαι-σθον λῡ-σαι-σθην P. λῡ-σαι-μεθᾰ λῡ-σαι-σθε λῡ-σαι-ντο	τυψ-αιμην, πραξ-αιμην, φρᾱσ-αιμην,	} -αιο, -αιτο, etc.	φη αγ ᾰμ
IMPERATIVE.			S.2. λῡ-σαι λῡ-σα-σθω D.2. λῡ-σα-σθον λῡ-σα-σθων P.2. λῡ-σα-σθε λῡ-σα-σθων or λῡ-σα-σθωσᾰν	τυψ-αι, πραξ-αι, φρᾱσ-αι,	} -ασθω, etc.	φη αγ ᾰμ
INFINITIVE			λῡ-σα-σθαι	τυψασθαι, πραξασθαι, φρᾱσασθαι		
PARTICIPLE.			λῡ-σᾰ-μενο-	τυψαμενο-, πραξαμενο-, φρᾰσαμενο-		

S.—MIDDLE.   TABLE VIII.

					SECOND AORIST.
αγγελ-, αγγελλ-, announce,	ἀμῡν-, ἀμῡν- ward off.	τῑμα-, honour,	αιτε-, ask,	δουλο-, enslave.	λῐπ-, λειπ-, leave.
μην, ἄμην, μην, } -ω, -ᾰτο, etc.		ετῑμησ-ἄμην, ῃτησ-ἄμην, εδουλωσ-ἄμην, } -ω, -ᾰτο, etc.			ε-λῐπ-ο-μην ε-λῐπ-ου (εο) ε-λῐπ-ε-το ε-λῐπ-ο-μεθον ε-λῐπ-ε-σθον ε-λῐπ-ε-σθην ε-λῐπ-ο-μεθᾰ ε-λῐπ-ε-σθε ε-λῐπ-ο-ντο
αι, ωμαι, μαι, } -ῃ, -ηται, etc.		τῑμησ-ωμαι, αιτησ-ωμαι, δουλωσ-ωμαι, } -ῃ, -ηται, etc.			λῐπ-ω-μαι λῐπ-ῃ λῐπ-η-ται λῐπ-ω-μεθον λῐπ-η-σθον λῐπ-η-σθον λῐπ-ω-μεθᾰ λῐπ-η-σθε λῐπ-ω-νται
ιην, αιμην, ιμην, } -αιο, -αιτο, etc.		τῑμησ-αιμην, αιτησ-αιμην, δουλωσ-αιμην, } -αιο, -αιτο, etc.			λῐπ-οι-μην λῐπ-οι-ο λῐπ-οι-το λῐπ-οι-μεθον λῐπ-οι-σθον λῐπ-οι-σθην λῐπ-οι-μεθᾰ λῐπ-οι-σθε λῐπ-οι-ντο
αι, ι, } -ασθω, etc.		τῑμησ-αι, αιτησ-αι, δουλωσ-αι, } -ασθω, etc.			λῐπ-ου (εο) λῐπ-ε-σθω λῐπ-ε-σθον λῐπ-ε-σθων λῐπ-ε-σθε λῐπ-ε-σθων or λῐπ-ε-σθωσᾰν
ασθαι,	αγγειλασθαι, ἀμῡνασθαι	τῑμησασθαι, αιτησασθαι, δουλωσασθαι			λῐπ-ε-σθαι
μενο-,	αγγειλᾰμενο-, ἀμῡνᾰμενο-	τῑμησᾰμενο-, αιτησᾰμενο-, δουλωσᾰμενο-			λῐπ-ο-μενο-

FIRST AO

Greek C. F. Increased Forms. English.		λυ- loosen.		λῐπ-, πρ λειπ-, πρ leave, do
INDICATIVE.		S. ε-λῠ-θη-ν ε-λῠ-θη-ς ε-λῠ-θη D.2. ε-λῠ-θη-τον ε-λῠ-θη-την P. ε-λῠ-θη-μεν ε-λῠ-θη-τε ε-λῠ-θη-σᾰν		ελειφ-θην, επραχ-θην, εφρασ-θην, ηγγελ-θην,
SUBJUNCTIVE.	Pres.-Indef. (SUBJUNCTIVE.)	S. λῠ-θω λῠ-θῃς λῠ-θῃ D.2. λῠ-θη-τον λῠ-θη-τον P. λῠ-θω-μεν λῠ-θη-τε λῠ-θω-σῐ(ν)		λειφ-θω, πραχ-θω, φρασ-θω, αγγελ-θω,
	Past-Indef. (OPTATIVE.)	S. λῠ-θειη-ν λῠ-θειη-ς λῠ-θειη D 2. λῠ-θειη-τον λῠ-θειη-την P. λῠ-θειη-μεν λῠ-θειη-τε λῠ-θειη-σᾰν	or λῠ-θει-τον λῠ-θει-την λῠ-θει-μεν λῠ-θει-τε λῠ-θει-εν	λειφ-θειην, πραχ-θειην, φρασ-θειην, αγγελ-θειην
IMPERATIVE.		S. 2. λῠ-θη-τῐ λῠ-θη-τω D.2. λῠ-θη-τον λῠ-θη-των P.2. λῠ-θη-τε λῠ-θε-ντων or λῠ-θη-τωσᾰν		λειφ-θητῐ, πραχ-θητῐ, φρασ-θητῐ, αγγελ-θητῐ,
INFINITIVE.		λῠ-θη-ναι		λειφθην φρασθη
PARTICIPLE.		λῠ-θε-ντ-		λειφθεν φρασθει

FIRST FUTURE PASSIVE.

INDIC.	S. λῠ-θη-σ-ο-μαι λῠ-θη-σ-ῃ (ει) λῠ-θη-σ-ε-ται etc.	λειφθησ-ομ πραχθησ-ο φρασθησ-ο αγγελθησ-ο
SUBJ. (OPTAT.)	S. λῠ-θη-σ-οι-μην λῠ-θη-σ-οι-ο λῠ-θη-σ-οι-το etc.	λειφθησ-οιμ πραχθησ-οι φρασθησ-οι αγγελθησ-ο
INFINITIVE.	λῠ-θη-σ-ε-σθαι	λειφθησεσ φρασθησεα
PARTICIPLE.	λῠ-θη-σ-ο-μενο-	λειφθησομ φρασθησο

			SECOND AORIST.	2 AOR. ACT. VOW. VERB	
τῑμα-, honour,	αιτε-, ask,	δουλο- enslave.	τῠπ- τυπτ- strike.	βα- βαιν- go.	
ῑμη-θην, τη-θην, ουλω-θην,	} -θης, -θη, etc.		ε-τῠπ-η-ν ε-τῠπ-η-ς ε-τῠπ-η ε-τῠπ-η-τον ε-τῠπ-η-την ε-τῠπ-η-μεν ε-τῠπ-η-τε ε-τῠπ-η-σᾰν	ε-βη-ν ε-βη-ς ε-βη ε-βη-τον ε-βη-την ε-βη-μεν ε-βη-τε ε-βη-σᾰν	AORIST TENSES.—PASSIVE.
μη-θω, τη-θω, υλω-θω,	} -θῃς, -θῃ, etc.		τῠπ-ω τῠπ-ῃς τῠπ-ῃ τῠπ-η-τον τῠπ-η-τον τῠπ-ω-μεν τῠπ-η-τε τῠ--ω-σῐ(ν)	βω βῃς βῃ βη-τον βη-τον βω-μεν βη-τε βω-σῐ(ν)	
μη-θειην, τη-θειην, υλω-θειην,	} -θειης, -θειη, etc.		τῠπ-ειη-ν τῠπ-ειη-ς τῠπ-ειη τῠπ-ειη-τον } or { τῠπ-ει-τον τῠπ-ειη-την τῠπ-ει-την τῠπ-ειη-μεν τῠπ-ει-μεν τῠπ-ειη-τε τῠπ-ει-τε τῠπ-ειη-σᾰν τῠπ-ει-εν	βα-ιη-ν βα-ιη-ς βα-ιη βα-ιη-τον } or { βα-ι-τον βα-ιη-την βα-ι-την βα-ιη-μεν βα-ι-μεν βα-ιη-τε βα-ι-τε βα-ιη-σᾰν βα-ι-εν	
μη-θητῐ, τη-θητῐ, υλω-θητῐ,	} -θητω, etc.		τῠπ-η-θῐ τῠπ-η-τω τῠπ-η-τον τῠπ-η-των τῠπ-η-τε τῠπ-ε-ντων or τῠπ-η-τωσᾰν	βη-θῐ βη-τω βη-τον βη-των βη-τε βα-ντων or βη-τωσᾰν	
τῑμηθηναι,	αιτηθηναι, δουλωθηναι		τῠπ-η-ναι	βη-ναι	TABLE IX.
τῑμηθεντ-,	αιτηθεντ-, δουλωθεντ-		τῠπ-ε-ντ-	βα-ντ-	
ITE PASSIVE.			SECOND FUTURE PASSIVE.		TABLE X.
ιηθησ-ομαι, τηθησ-ομαι, υλωθησ-ομαι,	} -ῃ (ει), -εται, etc.		τῠπ-η-σ-ομαι τῠπ-η-σ-ῃ (ει) τῠπ-η-σ-ε-ται etc.		
ιηθησ-οιμην, τηθησ-οιμην, υλωθησ-οιμην,	} -οιο, -οιτο, etc.		τῠπ-η-σ-οι-μην τῠπ-η-σ-οι-ο τῠπ-η-σ-οι-το etc.		
ῑμηθησεσθαι,	αιτηθησεσθαι, δουλωθησεσθαι		τῠπ-η-σ-ε-σθαι		
ιηθησομενο-,	αιτηθησομενο-, δουλωθησομενο-		τῠπ-η-σ-ο-μενο-		

before other consonant-suffixes: C. F. πρᾱγ-, ἄο; τῑμα-, *honour*: 1 aor. T. F. πραχθε-, τῑμηθε-; whence ἐπράχθη, *it was done*; ἐτῑμήθη, *he was honoured*. As in the perfect passive, σ is sometimes inserted before θ in this tense, most frequently after short vowels, more rarely after long vowels or diphthongs. See, however, § 307.

327. The 2 aor. pass. is of much less frequent occurrence than the 1 aor.; it is not found in derivative verbs, or in vowel-verbs, nor, with very few exceptions, is it found in verbs which have a 2 aor. in the active voice.

328. The person-endings of both passive aorists are the same as those of the 2 aor. active, except that in the 3 p. plur. indic. -σᾰν is used: they are added to the tense-form without any connecting vowel, ε of the T. F. being lengthened into η before those endings which begin with a single consonant: in the 3 p. sing. indic. ε becomes η, and ν is never added. In the indic. the augment is, of course, prefixed. In the 2 p. sing. imperative the old ending, -θῐ, is retained, and in the 1 aor. -θηθῐ becomes -θητι (§ 44).

329. In the present tenses of the subj., ε of the T. F. is contracted with the long vowels of the suffixes. In the past tenses this ε forms a diphthong with the mood-vowel ι: in the sing. of these tenses, and sometimes even in the dual and plur., the endings -ην, -ης, etc., are used instead of -μῐ, -ς, etc. (§ 245).

330. The termination of the infin. is -ναι, from the earlier -μεναι*: of the participle, -ντ: 2 aor. T. F. τῠπε-, infin. τῠπῆναι, part. C. F. τῠπεντ- (m. and n.; τῠπεισα-, f.). (§ 152.)

331. *Futures Indef. Passive* (1st and 2nd).—In addition to the simple future pass. (fut. imperf.) a future indef. is formed by adding σ to the unaugmented T. F. of the aorist; ε of course becomes η. There are two forms of this tense, corresponding to the two forms of the aorist: C. F. τῠπ-, *strike*, 2 fut. pass. T. F. τῠπησ-; C. F. πρᾱγ-, *do*. 1 fut. pass. T. F. πραχθησ-. The person-endings are the same as those of the simple future. The fut.-indef. differs in meaning from the fut.-imperf. as the aorist (past-indef.) differs from the past-imperf.

332. It has been said (§ 316) that verbs ending in a vowel have no 2 aor. active. There are, however, a few verbs of this class, almost all of which are made in the imperfect tenses from

* The fuller form is seen in the Epic φάνημεναι, etc.

II

an increased form ending in a consonant, which have a 2 aor. active formed by addition of the several suffixes without a connecting vowel. The vowel of the root, if short, is lengthened in those forms in which a single consonant follows, but remains unchanged before ι in the past tenses of the subj., and before ντ in the partic. and 3 p. plur. imperat., as in these forms the syllable is already long ; -σᾰν is the ending of the 3 p. pl. indic.; -θῐ of the 2 p. sing. imper.; -ναι of the infin.; and the nom. masc. of the partic. is made by adding s. These aorists, therefore, agree in inflection with the 2 aor. passive, and it will be observed that they are all, with the doubtful exception of ἐγνων, intransitive.

If the C. F. end in o, this vowel becomes ω in the present tenses subj., and absorbs the vowel of the suffix.

333. Some of these verbs have also a 1 aor. of the ordinary formation : in this case the 1 aor. is regularly transitive : e. g. C. F. βα-, *go*; γνω-, *have an opinion*; δυ-, *enter*; στα-, *stand*; φυ-, *be born:* 2 aor. ἐβην, *I went*; ἐγνων, *I had an opinion, knew*; ἐδυν, *I entered*; ἐστην, *I stood*; ἐφυν, *I was born:* 1 aor. ἐβησᾰ, *I caused to go*; ἀν-ἐγνωσᾰ, *I caused change of opinion, persuaded*; κᾰτ-ἐδυσᾰ, *I caused to sink*; ἐστησᾰ, *I caused to stand*; ἐφυσᾰ, *I produced, begat.* Of δυ-, στα-, and φυ-, the imperfect tenses, pres. and past, and the simple future are, like the 1 aor., transitive, the perfect tenses, like the 2 aor., intransitive.

334. In the following tables a type of each of the leading varieties of inflection found under the First Conjugation is presented at one view. The verb λυ-, *loosen*, has been adopted for a standard, as its crude form undergoes no change in the imperfect tenses, and as it, ending in the weak vowel υ (§ 32), everywhere exhibits the various suffixes unaffected by any collision either of consonants or of vowels, so that the suffix and root are always seen distinct and entire. It has not, however, been thought necessary to conjugate every verb with equal fulness in every tense : the contract verbs, for instance, which are given each at full length in the imperfect tenses, are thrown into one column in the future, as their endings are now the same as those of the standard, λυ-; while the liquid verb ἀγγελ-, which in the former tenses was ranged with the mute verbs, receives in the future a column to itself, since its endings are here peculiar.

IMPERFECT

Greek C. F. Increased Forms. English.			σταˑ ἰ-στα- stand		
Indicative	*Present-Imperfect*	S. D.2. P.	ἵ-στη-μῐ ἵ-στη-ς ἵ-στη-σῐ(ν) ἵ-στᾰ-τον ἵ-στᾰ-τον ἵ-στᾰ-μεν ἵ-στᾰ-τε ἵ-στᾰ-σῐ(ν)		τῐ-θη-μῐ τῐ-θη-ς τῐ-θη-σῐ(ν) τῐ-θε-τον τῐ-θε-τον τῐ-θε-μεν τῐ-θε-τε τῐ-θε-ᾱσῐ(ν
	Past-Imperfect	S. D.2. P.	ἵ-στη-ν ἵ-στη-ς ἵ-στη ἵ-στᾰ-τον ἵ-στᾰ-την ἵ-στᾰ-μεν ἵ-στᾰ-τε ἵ-στᾰ-σᾰν		ἐ-τῐ-θη-ν ἐ-τῐ-θη-ς ἐ-τῐ-θη ἐ-τῐ-θε-τον ἐ-τῐ-θε-την ἐ-τῐ-θε-μεν ἐ-τῐ-θε-τε ἐ-τῐ-θε-σᾰν
Subjunctive	*Present.* (Subjunctive).	S. D.2. P.	ἱ-στω ἱ-στῃς ἱ-στῃ ἱ-στη-τον ἱ-στη-τον ἱ-στω-μεν ἱ-στη-τε ἱ-στω-σῐ(ν)		τῐ-θω τῐ-θῃς τῐ-θῃ τῐ-θη-τον τῐ-θη-τον τῐ-θω-μεν τῐ-θη-τε τῐ-θω-σῐ(ν)
	Past. (Optative).	S. D.2. P.	ἱ-στα-ιη-ν ἱ-στα-ιη-ς ἱ-στα-ιη ἱ-στα-ιη-τον ἱ-στα-ιη-την ἱ-στα-ιη-μεν ἱ-στα-ιη-τε ἱ-στα-ιη-σᾰν	or { ἱ-στα-ι-τον ἱ-στα-ι-την ἱ-στα-ι-μεν ἱ-στα-ι-τε ἱ-στα-ι-εν	τῐ-θε-ιη-ν τῐ-θε-ιη-ς τῐ-θε-ιη τῐ-θε-ιη-το τῐ-θε-ιη-τη τῐ-θε-ιη-με τῐ-θε-ιη-τε τῐ-θε-ιη-σᾰ
Imperative		S.2. D.2. P.2.	ἵ-στη ἱ-στᾰ-τω ἱ-στᾰ-τον ἱ-στᾰ-των ἱ-στᾰ-τε ἱ-στα-ντων or ἱ-στᾰ-τωσᾰν		τῐ-θει τῐ-θε-τω τῐ-θε-τον τῐ-θε-των τῐ-θε-τε τῐ-θε-ντων τῐ-θε-τωσᾰ
Infinitive			ἱ-στᾰ-ναι		τῐ-θε-ναι
Participle			ἱ-στα-ντ-		τῐ-θε-ντ-

SES.—ACTIVE. TABLE XI.

		δο- δῐ-δο- give.		δεικ- (δῐκ-) δεικ-νυ- shew.
	τῐθεις	δῐ-δω-μῐ δῐ-δω-ς δῐ-δω-σῐ(ν) δῐ-δο-τον δῐ-δο-τον δῐ-δο-μεν δῐ-δο-τε δῐ-δο-ᾱσῐ(ν)		δεικ-νῡ-μῐ δεικ-νῡ-ς δεικ-νῡ-σῐ(ν) δεικ-νῠ-τον δεικ-νῠ-τον δεικ-νῠ-μεν δεικ-νῠ-τε δεικ-νυ-ᾱσῐ(ν)
or	ε-τῐ-θουν ε-τῐ-θεις ε-τῐ-θει	ε-δῐ-δω-ν ε-δῐ-δω-ς ε-δῐ-δω ε-δῐ-δο-τον ε-δῐ-δο-την ε-δῐ-δο-μεν ε-δῐ-δο-τε ε-δῐ-δο-σᾰν	or { ε-δῐ-δουν ε-δῐ-δους ε-δῐ-δου	ε-δεικ-νῡ-ν ε-δεικ-νῡ-ς ε-δεικ-νῡ ε-δεικ-νῠ-τον ε-δεικ-νῠ-την ε-δεικ-νῠ-μεν ε-δεικ-νῠ-τε ε-δεικ-νῠ-σᾰν
		δῐ-δω δῐ-δῳς δῐ-δῳ δῐ-δω-τον δῐ-δω-τον δῐ-δω-μεν δῐ-δω-τε δῐ-δω-σῐ(ν)		δεικ-νυ-ω δεικ-νυ-ῃς δεικ-νυ-ῃ etc.
or	τῐ-θε-ι-τον τῐ-θε-ι-την τῐ-θε-ι-μεν τῐ-θε-ι-τε τῐ-θε-ι-εν	δῐ-δο-ιη-ν δῐ-δο-ιη-ς δῐ-δο-ιη δῐ-δο-ιη-τον δῐ-δο-ιη-την δῐ-δο-ιη-μεν δῐ-δο-ιη-τε δῐ-δο-ιη-σᾰν	or { δῐ-δο-ι-τον δῐ-δο-ι-την δῐ-δο-ι-μεν δῐ-δο-ι-τε δῐ-δο-ι-εν	δεικ-νυ-οι-μῐ δεικ-νυ-οι-ς δεικ-νυ-οι etc.
		δῐ-δου δῐ-δο-τω δῐ-δο-τον δῐ-δο-των δῐ-δο-τε δῐ-δο-ντων or δῐ-δο-τωσᾰν		δεικ-νῡ δεικ-νῠ-τω δεικ-νῠ-τον δεικ-νῠ-των δεικ-νῠ-τε δεικ-νυ-ντων or δεικ-νῠ-τωσᾰν
		δῐ-δο-ναι		δεικ-νῠ-ναι
		δῐ-δο-ντ-		δεικ-νυ-ντ-

IMPERFECT TENSES.—MIDDLE AND PASSIVE.

TABLE XII.

Greek C. F. Increased Forms. English.		στα- ἱ-στα- stand.	θε- τι-θε- place.	δο- δι-δο- give.	δεικ- (δικ-) δεικ-νυ- shew.
INDICATIVE					
Present-Imperfect.	S.	ἱ-στἄ-μαι ἱ-στἄ-σαι ἱ-στἄ-ται	τί-θε-μαι τί-θε-σαι τί-θε-ται	δί-δο-μαι δί-δο-σαι δί-δο-ται	δεικ-νῠ-μαι δεικ-νῠ-σαι δεικ-νῠ-ται
	D.	ἱ-στἄ-μεθον ἱ-στα-σθον ἱ-στα-σθον	τί-θε-μεθον τί-θε-σθον τί-θε-σθον	δί-δο-μεθον δί-δο-σθον δί-δο-σθον	δεικ-νῠ-μεθον δεικ-νυ-σθον δεικ-νυ-σθον
	P.	ἱ-στἄ-μεθα ἱ-στα-σθε ἱ-στα-νται	τί-θε-μεθα τί-θε-σθε τί-θε-νται	δί-δο-μεθα δί-δο-σθε δί-δο-νται	δεικ-νῠ-μεθα δεικ-νυ-σθε δεικ-νυ-νται
Past-Imperfect.	S.	ἱ-στἄ-μην ἱ-στἄ-σο ἱ-στἄ-το	ἐ-τι-θε-μην ἐ-τι-θε-σο ἐ-τι-θε-το	ἐ-δι-δο-μην ἐ-δι-δο-σο ἐ-δι-δο-το	ἐ-δεικ-νῠ-μην ἐ-δεικ-νῠ-σο ἐ-δεικ-νῠ-το
	D.	ἱ-στἄ-μεθον ἱ-στα-σθον ἱ-στα-σθην	ἐ-τι-θε-μεθον ἐ-τι-θε-σθον ἐ-τι-θε-σθην	ἐ-δι-δο-μεθον ἐ-δι-δο-σθον ἐ-δι-δο-σθην	ἐ-δεικ-νυ-μεθον ἐ-δεικ-νυ-σθον ἐ-δεικ-νυ-σθην
	P.	ἱ-στἄ-μεθα ἱ-στα-σθε ἱ-στα-ντο	ἐ-τι-θε-μεθα ἐ-τι-θε-σθε ἐ-τι-θε-ντο	ἐ-δι-δο-μεθα ἐ-δι-δο-σθε ἐ-δι-δο-ντο	ἐ-δεικ-νυ-μεθα ἐ-δεικ-νυ-σθε ἐ-δεικ-νυ-ντο
(IVE)	S.	ἱ-στω-μαι ἱ-στῃ ἱ-στη-ται	τί-θω-μαι τί-θῃ τί-θη-ται	δί-δω-μαι δί-δῳ δί-δω-ται	δεικ-νυ-ω-μαι δεικ-νυ-ῃ δεικ-νυ-ηται

Subjunctive	*Pres.* (Subj.)	S.	ἱ-στῆ-σθον ἱ-στώ-μεθᾰ ἱ-στῆ-σθε ἱ-στῶ-νται	τι-θῆ-σθον τι-θώ-μεθᾰ τι-θῆ-σθε τι-θῶ-νται	δι-δῶ-σθον δι-δώ-μεθᾰ δι-δῶ-σθε δι-δῶ-νται	δεικ-νύ-ω-μην δεικ-νύ-η-ο δεικ-νύ-οι-το etc.
	Past. (Optative).	S.	ἱ-σταί-μην ἱ-σται-ο ἱ-σται-το	τι-θεί-μην τι-θεῖ-ο τι-θεῖ-το	δι-δοί-μην δι-δοῖ-ο δι-δοῖ-το	
		D.	ἱ-σται-μεθον ἱ-σται-σθον ἱ-σται-σθην	τι-θεί-μεθον τι-θεῖ-σθον τι-θεί-σθην	δι-δοί-μεθον δι-δοῖ-σθον δι-δοί-σθην	
		P.	ἱ-σταί-μεθᾰ ἱ-σται-σθε ἱ-σται-ντο	τι-θεί-μεθᾰ τι-θεῖ-σθε τι-θεῖ-ντο	δι-δοί-μεθᾰ δι-δοῖ-σθε δι-δοῖ-ντο	
Imperative.		S.2.	ἵ-στᾰ-σο ἱ-στά-σθω	τί-θε-σο τι-θέ-σθω	δί-δο-σο δι-δό-σθω	δείκ-νυ-σο δεικ-νύ-σθω
		D.2.	ἵ-στα-σθον ἱ-στά-σθων	τί-θε-σθον τι-θέ-σθων	δί-δο-σθον δι-δό-σθων	δείκ-νυ-σθον δεικ-νύ-σθων
		P.2.	ἵ-στα-σθε ἱ-στά-σθων or ἱ-στά-σθωσᾰν	τί-θε-σθε τι-θέ-σθων or τι-θέ-σθωσᾰν	δί-δο-σθε δι-δό-σθων or δι-δό-σθωσᾰν	δείκ-νυ-σθε δεικ-νύ-σθων or δεικ-νύ-σθωσᾰν
Infinitive.			ἵ-στα-σθαι	τί-θε-σθαι	δί-δο-σθαι	δείκ-νυ-σθαι
Participle.			ἱ-στά-μενο-	τι-θέ-μενο-	δι-δό-μενο-	δεικ-νύ-μενο-

SECOND A

ACTIVE.

Greek C. F. English.	στα- stand.	θε- place.	
INDICATIVE.	S. ε-στη-ν ε-στη-ς ε-στη D.2. ε-στη-τον ε-στη-την P. ε-στη-μεν ε-στη-τε ε-στη-σᾰν	{ singular { not found ε-θε-τον ε-θε-την ε-θε-μεν ε-θε-τε ε-θε-σᾰν	{ si { no ε-δο- ε-δο- ε-δο- ε-δο- ε-δο-
SUBJUNCTIVE. *Pres.* (SUBJ.)	S. στω στῃς etc., as in Imperfect.	θω θῃς etc., as in Imperf.	δω δῳς etc., as
Past. (OPTAT.)	S. στα-ιη-ν στα-ιη-ς etc., as in Imperfect.	θε-ιη-ν θε-ιη-ς etc., as in Imperf.	δο-ιη δο-ιη etc., as
IMPERATIVE.	S. 2. στη-θῐ στη-τω D.2. στη-τον στη-των P. 2. στη-τε στα-ντων or στη-τωσᾰν	θε-ς θε-τω θε-τον θε-των θε-τε θε-ντων or θε-τωσᾰν	δο-ς δο-τ(δο-τ(δο-τ(δο-τ(δο-ν δο-τ(
INFINITIVE	στη ναι	θει-ναι	δου-
PARTICIPLE.	στα-ντ-	θε-ντ-	δο-ν

CONJUGATION OF THESE VERBS IN TI

Future.	στησ-ω, -εις, -ει, etc.	θησ-ω, -εις, -ει, etc.	δωσ-ω,
1 *Aorist.*	εστησ-ᾰ, -ᾰς, -ε(ν), etc.	εθηκ-ᾰ, -ᾰς, -ε(ν) in Indicative Active only; very in the Plural, especially in the	εδωκ-ᾰ,
Perfect INDIC.	S. ἑστηκᾰ ἑστηκᾰς ἑστηκε(ν) D.2. ἑστηκᾰτον } { ἑστᾰτον ἑστηκᾰτον } { ἑστᾰτον P. ἑστηκᾰμεν } or { ἑστᾰμεν ἑστηκᾰτε } { ἑστᾰτε ἑστηκᾰσῐ(ν) } { ἑστᾰσῐ(ν) etc. etc.	τεθεικᾰ τεθεικᾰς etc.	δεδω δεδω ett
IMPER.	S.2. ἑστηκε } { ἑστᾰθῐ ἑστηκετω } or { ἑστᾰτω etc. etc.		
INFIN.	ἑστηκεναι or ἑστᾰναι	τεθεικεναι	δεδω
PART.	ἑστηκοτ- or ἑστωτ-	τεθεικοτ-	δεδω

TABLE XIII.

MIDDLE.

	στα- stand.	θε- place.	δο- give.
ar nd	στα– has no Second Aorist in the Middle Voice.	S. ε-θε-μην ε-θου ε-θε-το D. ε-θε-μεθον ε-θε-σθον ε-θε-σθην P. ε-θε-μεθα ε-θε-σθε ε-θε-ντο	ε-δο-μην ε-δου ε-δο-το ε-δο-μεθον ε-δο-σθον ε-δο-σθην ε-δο-μεθᾰ ε-δυ-σθε ε-δο-ντο
mperf.		S. θω-μαι θῃ etc., as in Imperf.	δω-μαι δῳ etc., as in Imperf.
mperf.		S. θε-ι-μην θε-ι-ο etc., as in Imperf.	δο-ι-μην δο-ι-ο etc., as in Imperf.
r		S. 2. θου θε-σθω D.2. θε-σθον θε-σθων P.2. θε-σθε θε-σθων or θε-σθωσᾰν	δου δο-σθω δο-σθον δο-σθων δο-σθε δο-σθων or δο-σθωσᾰν
		θε-σθαι	δο-σθαι
		θε-μενο-	δο-μενο-

FUTURE, FIRST AORIST, AND PERFECT.

-ει, etc.	στησ-ομαι, -ῃ, etc.	θησ-ομαι, -ῃ, etc.	δωσ-ομαι, -ῃ, etc.
-ε(ν) ly found 2 Pers.	MID. εστησᾰμην εστησω, etc. PAS. εστᾰθ-ην, -ης, etc.	ετεθ-ην, -ης, -η, etc.	εδοθ-ην, -ης, -η, etc.
	ἑστᾰμαι ἑστᾰσαι etc.	τεθειμαι τεθεισαι etc.	δεδομαι δεδοσαι etc.
	ἱστασθαι ἱστᾰμενο-	τεθεισθαι τεθειμενο-	δεδοσθαι δεδομενο-

General View of the Conjugation of λυ-, *loosen*, an[d

		Indicative.		Subjunctive.		
		Act.	Mid. and Pass.	Act.	Mid. and Pass.	
Imperfect	*Present.*	λυω γράφω	λυομαι γράφομαι	λυω γράφω	λυωμαι γράφωμαι	λι γρ
	Past.	ελυον εγράφον	ελυοκ ηι εγμαφομην	λυοιμῐ γράφοιμῐ	λυοιμην γράφοιμην	
	Future.	[λῡσω γραψω]	λῡσομαι (Pass.) γραψομαι (Pass.)		P. λῡσοιμην γραψοιμην	
Perfect	*Present.*	λελῠκᾰ γεγράφᾰ	λελῠμαι γεγραμμαι	λελῠκω γεγράφω	λελῠμενος ω γεγραμμενος ω	[λ. γε]
	Past.	ελελῠκη εγεγράφη	ελελῠμην εγεγραμμην	λελῠκοιην γεγράφοιην	λελῠμενος ειην γεγραμμενος ειην	
	Future.	[λελῠκως εσομαι γεγράφως εσομαι]	λελῡσομαι γεγραψομαι		λελῡσοιμην γεγραψοιμην	
Indefinite	*Present.*			λῡσω γραψω	M. λῡσωμαι γραψωμαι P. λῠθω γράφω	λῠ γρ
	Past.	ελῡσᾰ εγραψᾰ	M. ελῡσᾰμην εγραψᾰμην P. ελῠθην εγράφην	λῡσαιμῐ γραψαιμῐ	M. λῡσαιμην γραψαιμην P. λῠθειην γράφειην	
	Future.	λῡσω γραψω	M. λῡσομαι γραψομαι P. λῠθησομαι γράφησομαι	λῡσοιμῐ γραψοιμῐ	M. λῡσοιμην γραψοιμην P. λῠθησοιμην γράφησοιμην	

φ-, *write*, in the several Voices, Moods and Tenses.   TABLE XIV.

	IMPERATIVE.	INFINITIVE.		PARTICIPLE.	
t.	Mid. and Pass.	Act.	Mid. and Pass.	Act.	Mid. and Pass.
	λυου	λυειν	λυεσθαι	λυων	λυομενος
	γράφου	γράφειν	γράφεσθαι	γράφων	γράφομενος
		λυειν	λυεσθαι	λυων	λυομενος
		γράφειν	γράφεσθαι	γράφων	γράφομενος
			P. λῡσεσθαι		P. λῡσομενος
			γραψεσθαι		γραψομενος
]	λελῠσο	λελῠκεναι	λελυσθαι	λελῠκως	λελῠμενος
	γεγραψο	γεγράφεναι	γεγραφθαι	γεγράφως	γεγραμμενος
		λελῠκεναι	λελυσθαι	λελῠκως	λελιˊμενος
		γεγράφεναι	γεγραφθαι	γεγρᾰφως	γεγραμμενος
			λελῡσεσθαι		λελῡσομενος
			γεγραψεσθαι		γεγραψομενος
	M. λῡσαι	λῡσαι	M. λῡσασθαι		
	γραψαι	γραψαι	γραψασθαι		
	P. λῠθητῐ		P. λῠθηναι		
	γράφηθῐ		γράφηναι		
		λῡσαι	M. λῡσασθαι	λῡσᾱς	M. λῡσᾰμενος
		γραψαι	γραψασθα	γραψᾱς	γραψᾰμενος
			P. λῠθηναι		P. λῠθεις
			γράφηναι		γράφεις
		λῡσειν	M. λῡσεσθαι	λῡσων	M. λῡσομενος
		γραψειν	γραψεσθαι	γραψων	γραψομενος
			P. λῠθησεσθαι		P. λῠθησομενος
			γράφησεσθαι		γράφησομενος

SECOND, OR OLDER, CONJUGATION (VERBS IN ΜΙ).

335. The second conjugation differs from the first in the inflexion of the imperfect tenses, present and past, and of the 2 aorist.

336. All the endings of the imperfect and 2 aor. tenses are added to the C. F. without connecting vowel except in the subj., where the long vowels ω and η, and the vowel ι, must be regarded as the sign of mood.

337. The endings peculiar to this conjugation are as follows. In the Active :—

Indic. Pres. imperf. 1 p. sing. -μῐ ; 3 p. sing. -σῐ(ν), for -τῐ(ν); 3 p. pl. -ᾱσῐ(ν) for -αντῐ(ν).*

Past-imperf. and 2 aor. ; 3 p. pl. -σᾰν (but see § 332).

Those verbs of this conjugation whose C. F. ends in a vowel, have that vowel lengthened before the endings of the sing. in the indic. act.

Subj. The endings of the singular in the past tenses (opt.) are, -ην, -ης, -η (§ 245), instead of the ordinary forms. In the plural both forms are used.

Imper. The 2 p. sing. retains the ending -θῐ; in Attic, however, this is generally rejected and the final vowel lengthened. In the 2 aor. a final ς represents this θῐ.

Infin. The suffix is -ναι, from the earlier -μεναι. In the 2 aor. the root-vowel is lengthened.

Partic. The nominative sing. of the active participle is formed by addition of ς to the C. F.

338. In the Middle and Passive :—

The pres. and past imperf. indic. and the pres. imperat. retain in the 2 p. sing. the old endings, -σαι, -σο, -σο, without elision or contraction.

---

* Or, perhaps, originally, -σαντῐ, σ disappearing, as so often happens, between two vowels of which the first is short (§ 48) : thus, τῐθε-ᾱσῐ, *they are placing*, would be deduced, through τῐθε-αντῐ, from τῐθε-σαντῐ; and -σᾰν, the ending of the 3 pl. in the past tenses, would be related to -σαντῐ of the present, exactly as ο-ν (ο-ντ) of the 1st conj. to -ουσῐ (ο-ντῐ). Hence also may, perhaps, be explained the apparently anomalous εἰξᾱσῐ and ἴσᾱσῐ (i. e. εἰκ-σᾱσι, ἰδ-σᾱσῐ), Attic forms of the 3 pl. present-perfect of Ϝικ- and Ϝιδ-, for ἐοίκᾱσι, *they seem*, and οἰδᾱσι, *they know*. See § 298, n., and Buttmann, *Irreg. Verbs*, p. 82.

339. Some verbs of this conjugation have an increased form in the imperfect tenses made from the C. F. by a reduplication consisting of the repetition of the initial consonant followed by ῐ: thus, στα-, *stand*; θε-, *place*; ἑ-, *let go, send*; δο-, *give*: increased forms ἱστα- (for σιστα-), τιθε-, ἱε-, διδο-.

340. Another class consists of verbs which make their increased form by adding the syllable νυ: as, δεικ- (δῐκ-) *shew*, increased form δεικ-νυ-. Many verbs of this class apparently add νυ to the C. F., but in these words the first ν probably represents a lost final consonant: as, C. F. ἑ-σ- (Ϝεσ-), *clothe*; ζω-σ-, *gird*; σβε-σ-, *quench*: increased forms, ἑν-νυ-, ζων-νυ-, σβεν-νυ-. Compare ἑσ-θητ-, f. *clothing*, Lat. *vesti-*; ζωσ-τηρ-, m. *girdle*; and the 1 aor. ἐσβεσᾰ, *I quenched* (§§ 48, 265, c.).

Words of this class belong to the conjugation of words in μι only in the imperfect tenses: σβε-σ- alone has a 2 aor. (intrans.). Even in the imperfect tenses many forms occur made from the C. F. in νυ after the analogy of verbs in ω. The subj. is formed almost exclusively after that type.

341. The following tables contain those parts of these verbs in which they differ from verbs of the 1st conjugation.

Remarks.

342. In the imperfect tenses of θε- and δο- single forms occur, deduced from the C. F. τιθε-, διδο-, according to the rules of the 1st conjugation. It is not possible to decide, in some cases, on the claims of such forms to be admitted, as they are but of rare occurrence, and the MSS. are far from unanimous.

343. Three verbs of this conjugation—θε-, *place*; ἑ-, *send*; and δο-, *give*—have an anomalous 1 aor. indic. in -κα, ἔθηκᾰ, *I placed*; ἧκᾰ, *I sent*; ἔδωκᾰ, *I gave**: this form is exclusively used in the singular for the 2 aor., sometimes in the 3 p. plur., and yet more rarely in the dual and the other persons of the plur. In the other moods and the participle the 2 aor. alone is used in Attic Greek.

344. In the 2 aor. indic. of στα-, *stand*, the vowel of the root is lengthened throughout the tense. This tense is intransitive,

---

* These forms in -κᾰ, -κᾰς, -κε(ν), should perhaps be viewed as forms of the 2 aor. tense with the person-endings ᾰ, ᾰς, ε (§ 298), κ being then inserted to prevent the concurrence of vowels as in the perf. act. (§ 298). See Ahrens, p. 97.

like the tenses of the same form noticed in § 332. On the signification of the different tenses of στα-, see § 333.

345. In the perfect of στα- an aspirate remains as a trace of the reduplication, ἕστηκᾰ for σεστηκᾰ. In the past-perfect the forms without the augment are more common, ἑστήκη (or -κειν), ἑστήκης (or -κεις), etc.; but εἱστήκη, etc., also occur. Of these tenses many forms are often syncopated, or, rather, are made without the insertion of κ (§ 290) : as, ἕστᾰμεν, ἕστᾰτε, etc., for ἑστήκαμεν, etc., in the present-perf.; ἕστᾰσᾰν for ἑστήκεσᾰν in the 3 p. pl. of the past-perf.; ἑστῶμεν, ἑσταίην, etc., for ἑστήκωμει ἑστήκοιην, etc., in the subjunctive; ἑστᾰναι, for ἑστηκεναι, in the infin.; ἑστωτ-, for ἑστηκοτ-, in the part. (N. S. ἑστως, ἑστωσᾰ, ἑστος). In like manner are made many forms of the perfect tenses of θᾰν-, *die*, and βα-, *go*.

346. As the perfect of στα-, ἕστηκᾰ, *I stand*, has the force of a new present (intrans.), a future is formed from it, ἑστήξω, *I shall stand*.

347. In the perfect of θε- and ἑ-, the vowel is irregularly lengthened into ει, not η. The vowel of στα-, and δο-, remains short in the perf. and 1 aor. passive, and the vowel of θε- and ἑ- in the 1 aor. pass.

348. In the present tenses subj. of δο-, the vowel ο, instead of undergoing contraction with the termination, is lengthened, and then absorbs the following vowel, διδῷς (imperf.), δῷς (indef.) not διδοις, δοις, etc.

Verbal Adjectives.

349. The verbal adjectives are a kind of participles.

350. The first class of verbal adjectives is formed by adding the syllable -το to the C. F. of the verb. In meaning they either correspond to the Latin participles in -*to*, or convey the idea of *possibility*: thus from C. F. λυ-, *loosen*, is formed the verbal adjective λῠτο- (m. n.; λῠτα-, f.), *loosened*, or *able to be loosened* (in Latin *soluto-* or *solubili-*).

351. The second class of verbal adjectives is formed by adding -τεο to the C. F. of the verb. These have the signification of *necessity*, corresponding to the Latin participle in -*ndo* : as, λῠτεο- (λῠτεα-, f.), *solvendo-*, λῠτεον εστῐν, *one must loosen*.

352. Final consonants undergo the usual modifications before these endings: final vowels are, generally, lengthened as before other endings beginning with a consonant.

CONJUGATION OF AN ACTIVE VERB, WITH THE ENGLISH TRANSLATION.*

353.   C.F. γρᾰφ-, *write*.

Principal parts: γρᾰφ-, γραψ-, γεγρᾰφ-, ε-γραψα-.

Indicative Mood.

Present-Imperfect Tense, γρᾰφ-.

As a present-imperfect, *am ——ing*:

Γραμμᾰτᾰ προς τον πᾰτερᾰ μου γρᾰφω,	*I am writing to my father.*
γραμματα προς τον πατερα σου γραφεις,	*You† are writing to your father*
γραμματα προς τον πατερα ἑαυτου γραφει,	*He is writing to his father.*
γραμματα προς τους πατερᾰς ἡμων γραφομεν,	*We are writing to our fathers.*
γραμματα προς τους πατερας ‘ῡμων γραφετε,	*You are writing to your fathers.*
γραμματα προς τους πατερας ἑαυτων γραφουσῐν,	*They are writing to their fathers.*

354. ——— as a present, including past time, *have been ——ing*:

πολῠν ηδη χρονον γραφω,	*I have been writing now a long time.*
πολυν ηδη χρονον γραφεις,	*You have been writing now a long time.*
etc.	etc.

355. ——— as a present of custom:

εγω εν διφθερᾳ γραφω,	*I‡ write on parchment.*
σῠ εν βυβλῳ γραφεις,	*You write on papyrus.*
εκεινος εν πῐνακῐ γραφει,	*He writes on a tablet.*
etc.	etc.

* It has not been thought necessary to include the persons of the Dual in the following sections. The translation will always be the same as that of the corresponding persons of the Plural, with the substitution of *You two, They two*, and (in the Middle and Passive) *We two*, for *You, They, We*.

† Or, *thou art writing to thy father*.

‡ With an emphasis on the pronouns, *I, you, he*, etc. In Greek, as in Latin, the nominatives of the personal pronouns are not generally used, unless by way of emphasis or contrast.

CONJUGATION.   103

356. —— in a dependent clause after a present:

ὁρᾷς ὅτι ταυτὰ σοι γραφω;   *Do you see that I am writing this for you?*
ὁρᾷς ὅτι ταῦτ' ἐμοι γραφεις;   *Do you see that you are writing this for me?*
    etc.   etc.

357. —— in a dependent clause after a past, translated by a past:

ελεγον ὅτι μάτην γραφω,§   *They said that I was writing in vain.*
ελεγον ὅτι ματην γραφεις,   *They said that you were writing in vain.*
    etc.   etc.

358. —— in an indirect question after a present:

ουκ οιδ' ὅ τι γραφω,   *I do not know what I am writing.*
ουκ οισθ' ὅ τι γραφεις,   *You do not know what you are writing.*
    etc.   etc.

359. —— in an indirect question after a past, translated by a past:

ηπορουν τί γραφω,§   *They were in doubt what I was writing.*
ηπορει τι γραφεις,   *He was in doubt what you were writing.*
    etc.   etc.

360.   *Past-Imperfect Tense,* εγράφ-.

As a past-imperfect, *was* —— *ing*:

εγράφον ὅθ' ὁ παις εισηλθεν,   *I was writing when the boy came in.*
εγραφες ὅθ' ὁ παις εισηλθεν,   *You were writing when the boy came in.*
εγραφεν ὅθ' ὁ παις εισηλθεν,   *He was writing when the boy came in.*
εγραφομεν ὅθ' ὁ παις εισηλθεν, *We were writing when the boy came in.*
εγραφετε ὅθ' ὁ παις εισηλθεν, *You were writing when the boy came in.*
εγραφον ὅθ' ὁ παις εισηλθεν,   *They were writing when the boy came in.*

361. —— as a past tense, including time preceding, *had been* —— *ing*:

πολὺν ηδη χρονον εγραφον,   *I had been then writing a long time.*
πολυν ηδη χρονον εγραφες,   *You had been then writing a long time.*
    etc.   etc.

§ The past subjunctive is also frequent in this construction: §§ 379, 380.

362. ——— as a past tense of custom:

εγω εν διφθερᾳ αει εγραφον,	*I always wrote* on parchment.*
συ εν βυβλῳ αει εγραφες,	*You always wrote on papyrus.*
etc.	etc.

363. ——— in hypotheses known to be unreal;

    a. of present time:

ει μη εδει, ουκ ἄν εγραφον,	*If it were not necessary, I should not be writing.*
ει μη εδει, ουκ αν εγραφες,	*If it were not necessary, you would not be writing.*
etc.	etc.

    b. of past time, and implying duration or repetition:

ει θεμῖς ην, εγραφον αν ἀνἄ πᾶσ- ἄν ἡμερᾶν,	*Had it been lawful, I should have written every day.*
etc.	etc.

364.   *Future Tense*, γραψ-.

Translated by *shall, will*, and by a present after ει:

ει παντἄ κἄλως ἑξει, αυριον γραψω,	*If all is well, I shall write to-morrow.*
ει παντα καλως ἑξει, αυριον γραψεις,	*If all is well, you will write to-morrow.*
ει παντα καλως ἑξει, αυριον γραψει,	*If all is well, he will write to-morrow.*
ει παντα καλως ἑξει, αυριον γραψομεν,	*If all is well, we shall write to-morrow.*
ει παντα καλως ἑξει, αυριον γραψετε,	*If all is well, you will write to-morrow.*
ει παντα καλως ἑξει, αυριον γραψουσῖν,	*If all is well, they will write to-morrow.*

365. ——— by *should, would*, in a dependent clause after a past:

ηπειλησἄ ὁτῐ αυτῐκἄ γραψω,†	*I threatened that I should write at once.*
ηπειλησα ὁτι αυτικα γραψεις,	*I threatened that you would write at once.*
etc.	etc.

* Or, *used to write.*
† The future subjunctive is also used in this construction: § 386.

366. ——— by a present after ὅπως:
μελήσει τῷ πατρῖ ὅπως γραψω, My father will see to it that I write·
   etc.   etc.

367.   Present-Perfect Tense, γεγρᾰφ-.
Translated by have ———en:

παντᾰ ακρῑβως γεγρᾰφᾰ,   I have written everything accurately.
παντα ακριβως γεγραφᾰς,   You have written everything accurately.
παντα ακριβως γεγραφεν,   He has written everything accurately.
παντα ακριβως γεγραφᾰμεν,   We have written everything accurately.
παντα ακριβως γεγραφᾰτε,   You have written everything accurately.
παντα ακριβως γεγραφᾱσῐν,   They have written everything accurately.

368.   Past-Perfect Tense, εγεγρᾰφε-.
Translated by had ———en:

ὅτε ταυτ' εγιγνετο, τον λογον εγε-   When this happened, I had
   γρᾰφη,   written the speech.
ὅτε ταυτ' εγιγνετο, τον λογον εγε-   When this happened, you had
   γραφης,   written the speech.
ὅτε ταυτ' εγιγνετο, τον λογον εγε-   When this happened, he had
   γραφει,   written the speech.
ὅτε ταυτ' εγιγνετο, τους λογους εγε- When this happened, we had
   γραφειμεν,   written the speeches.
ὅτε ταυτ' εγιγνετο, τους λογους εγε- When this happened, you had
   γραφειτε,   written the speeches.
ὅτε ταυτ' εγιγνετο, τους λογους εγε- When this happened, they had
   γραφεσᾰν,   written the speeches.

369.   Aorist Tense, ε-γραψα-.
Translated by an English past:

χθες προς τον εμπορον εγραψᾰ, Yesterday I wrote to the merchant.
χθες προς τον εμπορον εγραψᾰς, Yesterday you wrote to the merchant.
χθες προς τον εμπορον εγραψεν, Yesterday he wrote to the merchant.
χθες προς τον εμπορον εγραψᾰμεν, Yesterday we wrote to the merchant.
χθες προς τον εμπορον εγραψᾰτε, Yesterday you wrote to the merchant.
χθες προς τον εμπορον εγραψᾰν, Yesterday they wrote to the merchant.

370. —— by an English past-perfect (after επει, επειδη, etc.) :
επειδη παντ εγραψα, ἀνεπαυσάμην, When I had written all, I rested.
επειδη παντ' εγραψας, ανεπαυσω,   When you had written all, you
                                    rested.
επειδη παντ' εγραψεν, αιεπαυσᾰτο, When he had written all, he rested.
   etc.   etc.

371. —— in hypotheses known to be unreal, of past time :
ει εκελευσᾰς, εγραψ' ἄν,   If you had ordered, I should have written.
ει εκελευσεν, εγραψας αν,   If he had ordered, you would have written.
ει εκελευσᾰ, εγραψεν αν,   If I had ordered, he would have written.
   etc.   etc.

372. —— in an indirect question, by *had* ——*en* (after a past) :
ηρωτᾱ τἵ προς τον εμπορον εγραψα,* He asked what I had written
                                      to the merchant.
   etc.   etc.

373.   SUBJUNCTIVE MOOD.
           Present-Imperfect Tense, γρᾰφ-.
Translated by *may* (object) :
γρᾰφῐδᾰ μοι δῐδωσῐν, 'ἵνᾰ ῥᾳον   He gives me a style, that I may
   γρᾰφω,   write more easily.
γραφιδα σοι διδωσιν, ινα ῥᾳον   He gives you a style, that you
   γραφῃς,   may write more easily.
γρᾰφιδα αυτῳ διδωσιν, ινα ῥᾳον   He gives him a style, that he
   γραφῃ,   may write more easily.
γρᾰφιδᾰς ἡμῐν διδωσιν, ἱνα ῥᾳον   He gives us styles, that we may
   γραφωμεν,   write more easily.
γρᾰφιδας 'ὑμῐν διδωσιν, ινα ῥᾳον He gives you styles, that you
   γραφητε,   may write more easily.
γραφιδας αυτοις διδωσιν, ινα ῥᾳον He gives them styles, that they
   γραφωσῐν,   may write more easily.

374. —— by *might* (object), after a past :
ῥαφιδα μοι εδωκεν, ινα ῥᾳον   He gave me a style, that I
   γραφω,†   might write more easily.
   etc.   etc.

* The past subjunctive of the same tense is (very rarely) found in this construction.

† The past subjunctive is also frequent in this construction : § 381

AN ACTIVE VERB. 107

375. ———— by a present indic. (after ἐάν, etc.):

ἐὰν περὶ πολλῶν γράφω, τάχ' ἀπειρηκὼς ἔσομαι,
If I write about many things, I shall soon be tired.

ὅταν περὶ πολλῶν γράφῃς, ταχ' ἀπᾰγορεύεις,
Whenever you write about many things, you soon grow tired.

ὅστις ἂν περὶ πολλῶν γράφῃ, ταχ' ἀπαγορεύει,
Whoever writes about many things, soon grows tired.

ἕως ἂν γράφωμεν, σῖγωμεν,
As long as we are writing, we are silent.

etc.   etc.

376. ———— by a present indic. (after μή):

φοβοῦμαι μὴ μάτην γράφω,
I fear that I am writing* in vain.

etc.   etc.

377. ———— by *am to* or *to* (deliberative):

πῶς περὶ τούτων γράφω;
How am I to write about this?

οὐδὲν ἔχεις ὅ τι γράφῃς,
You have nothing to write.

πῶς οὖν τίς περὶ τούτων γράφῃ; †
How, then, is any one to write about this?

etc.   etc.

378. ———— by *let me* or *us* (hortative), in the 1st pers. only:

φέρε δή, πάντα πρὸς αὐτὸν γράφω,
Come, then, let me write everything to him.

μὴ γράφωμεν,
Let us not write (be writing).

379.   *Past-Imperfect Tense,* γρᾰφ-.

Translated by a past indic. (convérsion of indic. §§ 356, 357):

εἶπον ὅτι μάτην γρᾰφοιμῐ,
They said that I was writing in vain.

εἶπον ὅτι μάτην γρᾰφοις,
They said that you were writing in vain.

εἶπον ὅτι μάτην γρᾰφοι,
They said that he was writing in vain.

εἶπον ὅτι μάτην γρᾰφοιμεν,
They said that we were writing in vain.

εἶπον ὅτι μάτην γρᾰφοιτε,
They said that you were writing in vain.

εἶπον ὅτι μάτην γρᾰφοιεν,
They said that they were writing in vain.

* Or, less commonly, *shall be writing.*

† This use of the pres. subj. to express deliberation, is confined to the 1st and 3rd persons, except in a dependent sentence. As an interrogative, it is more frequent in the 1st than in the 3rd person.

380. —— by a past indic. in an indirect question (conversion of indic. §§ 358, 359):

ηρωντο ει προς τον γεροντα γραφ-οιμι,   They asked if I was writing* to the old man.
etc.   etc.

381. —— by *might* (object), (conversion of pres. subj. § 373):

γραφιδα μοι εδωκεν, ινα ρᾳον γραφοιμι,   He gave me a style, that I might write more easily.
etc.   etc.

382. —— by a past indic. (conversion of pres. subj. § 375):

προειπεν ὁτι, ει περι πολλων γραφ-οιμι, ταχ' απειρηκως εσοιμην,   He foretold that, if I wrote about many things, I should soon be tired.

ειπεν ὁτι ὁστις περι πολλων γραφ-οι, ταχ' απαγορευοι,   He said that whoever wrote about many things, soon grew tired.
etc.   etc.

383. —— by a past indic., to express repetition (in a secondary clause):

ὁποτε γραφοιμι, ὁ παις επεσκοπει,†   Whenever I was writing, the boy looked on.
etc.   etc.

384. —— by *were to, ... would* (hypothesis):

ει κελευοις, ἡδεως αν γραφοιμι,   If you were to order, I would gladly write.

ει κελευοι, ἡδεως αν γραφοις,   If he were to order, you would gladly write.
etc.   etc.

385. —— by *may*, to express *a wish*:

ἀει τα καλα γραφοιμι!   May I always write good news!
etc.   etc.

386.   *Future Tense,* γραψ-.

Translated by *should, would* (conversion of indic., §§ 364, 365):

ηπειλησα ὁτι αυτικα γραψοιμι,   I threatened that I should write at once.

* Or, *was to write* (conversion of pres. subj. § 377).

† As far as the relative clause is concerned, this is virtually a particular case of the preceding usage. Compare the construction so common in Livy, e. g. xxi. 11: *latius quam qua cæderetur ruebat.*

ηπειλησᾶς ὅτι αυτικα γραψοις, You threatened that you would write at once.
ηπειλησεν ὅτι αυτικα γραψοι, He threatened that he would write at once.
ηπειλησἄμεν ὅτι αυτικα γραψοιμεν, We threatened that we should write at once.
ηπειλησᾶτε ὅτι αυτικα γραψοιτε, You threatened that you would write at once.
ηπειλησᾰν ὅτι αυτικα γραψοιεν, They threatened that they would write at once.

387.   Present-Perfect Tense, γεγρᾰφ-.

After ἐᾱν, etc., to express a completed action:

ἐᾱν γεγρᾰφω αναπαυομαι, If I have finished writing, I rest.
ὅτᾰν γεγραφῃς αναπαυῃ, When you have finished writing, you rest.
ὅς ἄν γεγραφῃ αναπαυεται, Whoever has finished writing, rests.
ἐᾱν γεγραφωμεν αναπαυομεθα, If we have finished writing, we rest.
ὅτᾰν γεγραφητε αναπαυεσθε, When you have finished writing, you rest.
οἱ ἄν γεγραφωσῐν αναπαυονται, Whoever have finished writing, rest.

388.   Past-Perfect Tense, γεγρᾰφ-.

Translated by *had* ——*en* (conversion of a perf. indic., § 367):

ηγγειλᾰν ὅτι παντα γεγρᾰφοιην, They brought word that I had finished writing.
ηγγειλαν ὅτι παντα γεγραφοιης, They brought word that you had finished writing.
ηγγειλαν ὅτι παντα γεγραφοιη, They brought word that he had finished writing.
ηγγειλαν ὅτι παντα γεγραφοιμεν, They brought word that we had finished writing.
ηγγειλαν ὅτι παντα γεγραφοιτε, They brought word that you had finished writing.
ηγγειλαν ὅτι παντα γεγραφοιεν, They brought word that they had finished writing.

389. —— by *had* ——*en* (conversion of a pres.-perf. subj., § 387):

ειπεν ὅτι, ει παντα γεγραφοιην, ανα- He said that, if (when) I had
παυοιμην,   finished writing, I rested.
    etc.   etc.

390   *Present-Indefinite Tense* (Aor. Subj.), γραψα-.

Translated by *may* (object):

γραφιδἄ μοι διδωσἴν, ἵνᾰ προς τον γεροντᾰ γραψω,	*He is giving me a style, that I may write to the old man.*
γραφιδα σοι διδωσιν, ινα προς τον γεροντα γραψῃς,	*He is giving you a style, that you may write to the old man.*
γραφιδα αυτῳ διδωσιν, ινα προς τον γεροντα γραψῃ,	*He is giving him a style, that he may write to the old man.*
γραφιδᾰς ἡμιν διδωσιν, ινα προς τον γεροντα γραψωμεν,	*He is giving us styles, that we may write to the old man.*
γραφιδας ὑμιν διδωσιν, ινα προς τον γεροντα γραψητε,	*He is giving you styles, that you may write to the old man.*
γραφιδας αυτοις διδωσιν, ινα προς τον γεροντα γραψωσἴν,	*He is giving them styles, that they may write to the old man.*

391. —— by *might* (object), after a past:

γραφιδα μοι εδωκεν, ινα προς σε γραψω,	*He gave me a style, that I might write to you.*
etc.	etc.

392. —— by *have* ——*en* (after relative pronouns and conjunctions with ἀν):

επειδᾰν ταυτᾰ γραψω, ἀπειμἴ,	*When I have written this, I shall go away.*
επειδαν ταυτα γραψῃς, απει,	*When you have written this, you will go away.*
επειδαν ταυτα γραψῃ, απεισιν,	*When he has written this, he will go away.*
etc.	etc.

393. —— by a present indic., in a conditional clause with αν.*

εᾰν προς τον ἀδελφον μου γραψω, αυτικα πᾰρεσται,	*If I write to my brother, he will come at once.*
εαν προς τον αδελφον σου γραψῃς, αυτικα παρεσται,	*If you write to your brother, he will come at once.*
etc.	etc.

394. —— by *shall, will* (after μη):

φοβειται μη ματην γραψω,	*He is afraid that I shall write in vain.*
φοβειται μη ματην γραψῃς,	*He is afraid that you will write in vain.*
etc.	etc.

* This is a particular case of the preceding use, though the English translation differs: the Latin would employ the future-perfect, *scripsero*, etc., in both cases.

AN ACTIVE VERB. 111

395. ——— by *am to* or *to* (deliberative):

ἀπορῶ ὅπως γράψω ἅ νοῶ,*   *I am at a loss how to write what I think.*

οὐκ οἶσθ' ὅπως γράψῃς ἃ νοεῖς,   *You do not know how to write what you think.*

etc.   etc.

396. ——— by *let me* or *us* (hortative), in the 1 pers. only:

φέρε δή, πρὸς τὸν γέροντα γράψω,   *Come, then, let me write to the old man.*

φέρε δή, πρὸς τὸν γέροντα γράψωμεν,   *Come, then, let us write to the old man.*

397. ——— as an imperative (only with μή, § 407):

μὴ γράψῃς πρὸς τὸν γέροντα,   *Do not write to the old man.*
μηδεὶς πρὸς τὸν γέροντα γράψῃ,   *Let no one write to the old man.*
μὴ γράψητε πρὸς τὸν γέροντα,   *Do not write to the old man.*
μὴ γράψωσι πρὸς τὸν γέροντα,   *Let them not write to the old man.*

398.   *Past-Indefinite Tense* (Aor. Opt.), γραψα-.

Translated by a past-perfect indic. (conversion of aor. indic., § 369):

ειπεν ὅτι μάτην γράψαιμι,   *He said that I had written in vain.*
ειπας ὅτι μάτην γράψειας,   *You said that you had written in vain.*
ειπον ὅτι μάτην γράψειεν,   *I said that he had written in vain.*
ειπον ὅτι μάτην γράψαιμεν,   *They said that we had written in vain.*
ειπατε ὅτι μάτην γράψαιτε,   *You said that you had written in vain.*
ειπομεν ὅτι μάτην γράψειαν,   *We said that they had written in vain.*

399. ——— by *was to, to* (conversion of pres.-indef. subj., § 395):

ἠπόρουν ὅ τι πρὸς τὸν ἔμπορον γράψαιμι,   *I was at a loss what to write to the merchant.*

ἤροντο εἰ πρὸς τὸν ἔμπορον γράψειεν,   *They asked if he was to write† to the merchant.*

etc.   etc.

---

* Compare § 377: and on the difference between the aorist and the imperfect in this and similar cases, see the Syntax. The introduction of ἀπορῶ, etc., as they are in the present, has no effect on either mood or tense.

† Or, very rarely, *if he had written;* but the aor. indic. is almost invariably used in such a case; see § 372.

400. ——— by *might* (object), (conversion of pres.-indef. subj., § 390):

γραφιδα μοι εδωκεν, ινα προς τον γεροντα γραψαιμι,
etc.

He gave me a style, that I might write to the old man.
etc.

401. ——— by *had* ———*en* (conversion of pres.-indef. subj., § 392):

ὑπεσχετο ὁτι, επειδη ταυτα γραψαιμι, ἀπιοιην,

He promised that, when I had written this, I should go away.

ὑπεσχετο ὁτι, επειδη ταυτα γραψειας, απιοις,

He promised that, when you had written this, you should go away.

etc.
etc.

402. ——— by a past indic., to express repetition in a secondary clause:

ειποτε περι εμαυτου γραψαιμι, εθαυμαζεν,
etc.

If ever I wrote (had written) about myself, he was surprised.
etc.

403. ——— by *were to*, ... *would* (hypothesis):

ει προς τον αδελφον μου γραψαιμι, αυτικ' αν παραγενοιτο,

If I were to write (or, If I wrote) to my brother, he would come at once.

ει προς τον αδελφον σου γραψειας, αυτικ' αν παραγενοιτο,
etc.

If you were to write to your brother, he would come at once.
etc.

404. ——— by *may* (expressing a wish):

ταχα σοι τα καλα γραψαιμι!
μηποτε τα κακα γραψειας!
etc.

May I soon write you good news!
May you never write bad news!
etc.

405. IMPERATIVE MOOD.

Imperfect Tense, γραφ-.

Of a present, or continuous, or repeated action:

γραφε, *Write! or, go on writing!*
γραφετω, *Let him write, etc.*

γραφετε, *Write! etc.*
γραφοντων, *Let them write, etc.*

406. —— with μη :
 μη γράφε, *Don't be writing.*
 μη γράφετω, *Don't let him go on writing.*

407.   Aorist Tense, γραψα-.
Of a single act :
 γραψον ταυτα, *Write this!*
 γραψάτω ταυτα, *Let him write this.*
 γραψάτε ταυτα, *Write this!*
 γραψαντων ταυτα, *Let them write this.*

For prohibitions in the Aorist, see § 397.*

408.   Infinitive Mood.

Imperfect Tense, γράφ-.

Translated by *to* —— :
 αισχῦνομαι πάλιν γράφειν, *I am ashamed to write again*

409. With the article, translated by *to* ——, or ——*ing* :
Nom. το κάλως γραφειν ωφελιμον εστιν, *To write well (or, writing well) is useful.*
Acc. οἱ πολλοι θαυμαζουσῖ το καλως γραφειν, *Most men admire writing well.*
Gen. εκ του καλως γραφειν πολλ' ωφελειται, *He derives much advantage from writing well.*
Dat. τῳ καλως γραφειν παντων ὑπερεχει, *He excels all men in writing well.*

410. —— by an English indic. :
οιμαι καλως γραφειν, *I think (that) I write well* (i. e. *am a good writer*).
οιει καλως γραφειν, *You think you write well.*
ὠμην καλως γραφειν, *I thought I wrote well.*
ὠετο καλως γραφειν, *He thought he wrote well.*

411. —— or with a pronoun in the accusative :
ὁμολογουσῖν εμε καλως γραφειν, *They own that I write well.*
ὡμολογουν σε καλως γραφειν, *I owned that you wrote well.*

---

* The perfect imperative is seldom wanted in the active voice, § 301. In the passive it is regularly used when, not the performance, but the completion of an act is contemplated : as, ταυτα γεγραφθω, *let this be written, let me find this written* (e. g. when I return).

412. ——— by *from* ———*ing* (after words of hindering, etc.):
ουδεν με κωλῡσει γραφειν,   Nothing shall hinder me from writing.

413.   Future Tense, γραψ-.

Translated by *will* (*would*):
ὑπισχνουμαι η μην γραψειν,   I promise that I will really write.
ηλπιζον αυτον πολλᾱκις γραψειν,   I hoped that he would often write.

414.   Perfect Tense, γεγραφ-.

Translated by *has* (*had*) ———*en*:
φησῐ παντᾰ γεγρᾰφεναι,   He says that he has written (i. e. has finished writing) all.
εφη παντα γεγραφεναι,   He said that he had written all.

415.   Aorist Tense, γραψα-.

Of a single act (in contrast with § 409):
αισχρον εστι ταυτα γραψαι, or } It is disgraceful to write this.
το ταυτα γραψαι αισχρον εστιν, }

416. Of an act anterior to the time of the governing verb (in contrast with § 410):
φησιν εμε ταυτα γραψαι,   He says that I wrote this.
εφη εμε ταυτα γραψαι,   He said that I had written this.

417.   PARTICIPLES.

Imperfect Tense, γρᾰφοντ-.

With the article, translated by *the* ———*er*:
Nom. ὁ γρᾰφων (ἡ γρᾰφουσᾰ),   The writer (i. e. The man who is writing, or who habitually writes).
Gen. του γρᾰφοντος,   Of the writer.
     etc.   etc.

418. Translated by ———*ing*:
ταυτα γραφων εσῑγᾱ,   He was silent while writing this.

419. ——— by an English indic. (after verbs of *knowing*, *seeing*, etc.):
οιδᾰ ματην γραφων,   I know that I am writing in vain.
ουκ ηδεσᾰν ματην γραφοντες,   They did not know that they were writing in vain.

——— or with a pronoun in the accus.:
ὁρω σε ματην γραφοντᾰ,   I see that you are writing in vain.

420. *Future Tense,* γραψοντ-.

Translated by *to* ——, *intending to* ——:

παρηλθον τουτο το ψηφισμα γραψ-   *I came forward to write* (i. e.
ων,   *propose*) *this decree.*

421. *Perfect Tense,* γεγραφοτ-.

παντα γεγραφως ἡδεως ἄπειμι,   *Now that I have written all, I will gladly go away.*

422. *Aorist Tense,* γραψαντ-.

With the article:
Nom. ὁ γραψᾶς,   *The writer* (i. e. *the man who wrote*).
Gen. του γραψαντος,   *Of the writer.*
  etc.   etc.

423. Translated by *having* ——*en,* or *after* ——*ing:*

προς τον αδελφον γραψας ἄπηλ-   *After writing to his brother, he*
θεν,   *went away;* or, *He wrote to his brother, and then went away.*

424. ——— by an indic. (after verbs of *knowing,* etc.):

ουκ οιδα ταυτα γραψας,   *I do not know that I wrote that.*
ειδον σε πολλα ματην γραψαντα,   *I saw that you had written much in vain.*

425.   VERBAL ADJECTIVE, γραπτεο-.

γραπτεον εστι μοι ταυτα τα ψη-   *I must write (propose) these de-*
φισματα,   *crees.*
γραπτεον εστι σοι ταυτα τα ψη-   *You must write these decrees.*
φισματα,
γραπτεον εστιν ἡμιν ταυτα τα ψη-   *We must write these decrees.*
φισματα,
  etc.   etc.

CONJUGATION, IN THE FIRST PERSON, OF A REFLECTIVE, OF A DEPONENT, AND OF A PASSIVE VERB, WITH THE ENGLISH TRANSLATION.

426.   τρεπ- (m.), *turn oneself, take to flight.*
δεχ- (m.), *receive.*
λυ- (p.), *be loosened, be released.*

Indicative Mood.

Present-Imperfect.

τρεπομαι, I am turning myself.
δεχομαι, I am receiving.
λυομαι, I am being released.

427 ### Past-Imperfect.

ετρεπομην, I was turning myself.
εδεχομην, I was receiving.
ελυομην, I was being released.

428. ### Future.

τρεψομαι, I shall turn myself.
δεξομαι, I shall receive.
λυσομαι, I shall be (once and again) released.* (Fut.-Imperf.)
λυθησομαι, I shall be released. (Fut.-Indef.)

429. ### Present-Perfect.

τετραμμαι, I have turned myself (am in full flight).
δεδεγμαι, I have received (am in possession of).
λελυμαι, I have been released (am free).

430. ### Past-Perfect.

ετετραμμην, I had turned myself (was in full flight).
εδεδεγμην, I had received (was in possession of).
ελελυμην, I had been released (was free).

431. ### Future-Perfect.

τετραψομαι, I shall have turned myself (shall be in full flight).
δεδεξομαι, I shall have received (shall be in possession of).
λελυσομαι, I shall have been released (shall be free).

432. ### Aorist.

ετραπομην, I turned myself (took to flight).†
εδεξαμην, I received.
ελυθην, I was released.

---

* On the distinction between these two forms of the future passive, see § 281. It has not been thought necessary to give the fut.-imperf. and fut.-perf. in the other moods.

† This verb also possesses a 1st aor. mid., ετρεψαμην, etc., which is used to mean, *I caused to turn from me, I put to flight.*

433.   Subjunctive Mood.*

Present-Imperfect.

φοβειται μη τρεπωμαι,   He is afraid that I am turning myself.
φοβειται μη τἰ δεχωμαι,   He is afraid that I am receiving something.
φοβειται μη λυωμαι,   He is afraid that I am being released.

434.   Past-Imperfect.

ειπον ὁτἰ τρεποιμην,   They said that I was turning myself.
ειπον ὡς ουδεν δεχοιμην,   They said that I was receiving nothing.
ειπον ὁτι λυοιμην,   They said that I was being released.

435.   Future.

προειπον ὁτι τρεψοιμην,   I gave out that I should turn myself.
προειπον ὡς ουδεν δεξοιμην,   I gave out that I should receive nothing.
προειπον ὁτι λὔθησοιμην,   I gave out that I should be released.

436.   Present-Perfect.

εᾱν τετραμμενος ω διωκουσῑν,   If† I have turned myself (am in full flight), they pursue.
εαν τι δεδεγμενος ω θαυμαζουσῑν,   If I have received (am in possession of) anything, they wonder.
εαν λελὔμενος ω λῡπουνται,   If I have been released (am free), they are grieved.

437.   Past-Perfect.

ειπον ὁτι τετραμμενος ειην,   They said that I had turned myself (was in full flight).
ειπον ὡς ουδεν δεδεγμενος ειην,   They said that I had received (was in possession of) nothing.
ειπον ὁτι λελυμενος ειην,   They said that I had been released (was free).

438.   Aorist (Pres.-Indef.).

ουκ εχω ὁποι τρἄπωμαι,   I know not whither to turn myself.
ουδεν εστῐν ὁ τι δεξωμαι,   There is nothing for me to receive.
ἀπορω ὁπως λὔθω,   I am at a loss how I am to be released.

---

* For the various modes of translating the subjunctive, see §§ 373—404.

† i.e. *If ever, whenever.*

439. Aorist (Past-Indef.).

ουκ ειχον όποι τράποιμην,   *I knew not whither to turn myself.*
ουδεν ην ὁ τι δεξαιμην,   *There was nothing for me to receive.*
ηπορουν ὁπως λυθειην,   *I was at a loss how I was to be released.*

440. Imperative Mood.
Imperfect.

τρεπου,   *Turn yourself!*
δεχου,   *Receive!*
λυου,   *Be released!*

441. Perfect.

λελῦσο,*   *Be free!*

442. Aorist.

τράπου,   *Turn yourself!*†
δεξαι,   *Receive!*
λῠθητῐ,   *Be released!*

443. Infinitive Mood.
Imperfect.

τρεπεσθαι,   *To turn oneself.*
δεχεσθαι,   *To receive.*
λυεσθαι,   *To be released.*

444. Future.

ελπις εστιν αυτους τρεψεσθαι,   *There is hope that they will turn themselves.*
ελπις εστιν αυτους δεξεσθαι τι,   *There is hope that they will receive something.*
ελπις εστιν αυτους λυθησεσθαι,   *There is hope that they will be released.*

445. Perfect.

τετραφθαι,   *To have turned oneself (be in full flight).*
δεδεχθαι,   *To have received (be in possession).*
λελυσθαι,   *To have been released (be free).*

---

* Middle verbs, like active verbs, can seldom have a perfect imperative; δεδεξο occurs in a peculiar signification.
† See note *, page 119.

446.   *Aorist.*

  τράπεσθαι,   *To turn oneself.**
  δέξασθαι,   *To receive.*
  λυθῆναι,   *To be released.*

447.   PARTICIPLES.
        Imperfect.

  τρεπομενο-,   *Turning oneself.*
  δεχομενο-,   *Receiving.*
  λυομενο-,   *Being released.*

448.   *Future.*

  τρεψομενο-,   *About to turn oneself.*
  δεξομενο-,   *About to receive.*
  λυθησομενο-,   *About to be released.*

449.   *Perfect.*

  τετραμμενο-,   *Having turned oneself.*
  δεδεγμενο-,   *Having received.*
  λελυμενο-,   *Having been released.*

450.   *Aorist.*

  τράπομενο-,   *Having turned oneself*
  δεξάμενο-,   *Having received.*
  λυθεντ-,   *Having been released.*†

451.   VERBAL ADJECTIVE.

λύτεος εστί μοι ὁ δεσμώτης,   *I must release the prisoner.*‡
λυτεοι εἰσίν ἡμῖν οἱ δεσμῶται,   *We must release the prisoners.*
λυτεά εστι σοι ἡ γύνη.   *You must release the woman.*
λυτεαι εισιν ὑμιν αἱ γυναικες,   *You must release the women.*
   etc.   etc.

---

* For the distinction between the aorist and imperfect of the imperative and infinitive, see the corresponding parts of γραφ-.

† For the distinction between the perf. and aor. participles, compare the following sentences: λελύμενος πάντα τολμᾳ ποιειν, *Now that he is free, he dares to do everything;* λυθεις ἀπῆλθεν οἰκάδε, *On being released, he went away home.*

‡ Literally, *The prisoner is to be released by me.* For the active construction of verbals in τεο-, see § 425.

SOME IRREGULAR AND DEFECTIVE VERBS CONJUGATED.

452. εσ-, *be.*

INDICATIVE.

Pres.-Imperf.	*Past-Imperf.*	*Future.*
S. ειμί, *I am.*	S. ην or η (also ημην) } *I was.*	S. εσομαι, *I shall be.*
ει	ησθα	εση (-ει)
εστι(ν)	ην	εσται
D.2. εστον	D.2. ηστον or ητον	D. εσομεθον
εστον	ηστην or ητην	εσεσθον
		εσεσθον
P. εσμεν	P. ημεν	P. εσομεθα
εστε	ηστε or ητε	εσεσθε
εισι(ν)	ησαν	εσονται

SUBJUNCTIVE.

Pres. S. ω, ης, η. D. ητον, ητον. P. ωμεν, ητε, ωσι(ν).
Past. S. ειην, ειης, ειη. D. ειητον, ειητην. P. ειημεν, ειητε, ειησαν or ειεν. Also, but less commonly, ειτον, ειμεν, etc.
Fut. εσοιμην, εσοιο, etc.
IMPER. S. ισθι, εστω. D. εστον, εστων. P. εστε, εστωσαν or οντων, less commonly εστων.
INFIN. *Imperf.* ειναι. *Fut.* εσεσθαι. PART. *Imperf.* οντ- (N.S. ων, ουσα, ον). *Fut.* εσομενο-.

453. ι- (I. F. ει-), *go.*

INDICATIVE.

Pres.-Imp. S. ειμι, ει, εισι(ν).* D. ιτον, ιτον. P. ιμεν, ιτε, ιασι(ν).
This tense is generally used as a future in the indicative.
Past-Imp. S. ηειν or ηα, ηεις or ηεισθα, ηει(ν). D. ηειτον or ητον, ηειτην or ητην. P. ηειμεν or ημεν, ηειτε or ητε, ηεσαν.
The shorter forms are more common.

SUBJ. *Pres.* ιω, ιης, etc. *Past.* ιοιμι or ιοιην, ιοις, ιοι, etc.
IMPER. S. ιθι, ιτω. D. ιτον, ιτων. P. ιτε, ιοντων or ιτωσαν.
INFIN. ιεναι. PART. ιοντ- (N.S. ιων, ιουσα, ιον).

* Thus accented—ειμι, ει, εισιν; and so distinguished from the identical forms of εσ-, *be*, which are enclitic (ειμι, εισιν), except the 2 p. ει, *thou art.*

454. ἑ- (I. F. ϝἑ-), *let go, send.*

This verb is conjugated like θε- (τίθε-), *place,* save that the ι of the reduplication in the imperf. tenses is generally long in Attic; ἵημι, ἵεναι, ἵεντ-, etc.; and that the 3 plur. indic. pres. is ἱᾶσί(ν), not ἱεᾶσί(ν). In the 2 aor. act. and mid. and the 1 aor. pass. the augment, which, however, is often neglected, is made in ει, not η (§ 251); ἄν-ειμεν, *we sent up;* ἀφείθην (or without augment ἀφέθην), *I was let go.* The simple verb is comparatively rare, and many parts occur only in compounds.

455. ϝιδ-, *see, know.*

This root, in the sense of *see,* only appears in the 2 aor. tense, which is regularly formed: on the syllabic augment ειδον (i. e. εϝιδον), see § 251.

With the signification *know,* the perfect and future tenses are formed: they are as follows:—

INDICATIVE.

	Present-Perfect.	*Past-Perfect.*	*Future.*
S.	οιδα, *I know.*	ηδη or ηδειν, *I knew.*	εισομαι
	οισθα	ηδησθα or ηδεισθα	etc.
	οιδε(ν)	ηδη or ηδει(ν)	
D.2.	ιστον	ηδειτον also ηστον	
	ιστον	ηδειτην	ηστην
P.	ισμεν	ηδειμεν†	ησμεν
	ιστε	ηδειτε	ηστε
	ισᾶσί(ν)*	ηδεσαν	ησαν

SUBJ. *Pres.* ειδω, ειδης, etc. *Past.* ειδειην, ειδειης, etc.
IMPER. ισθι, ιστω, etc. INFIN. ειδεναι. PART. ειδοτ- (N. S. ειδως, ειδυια, ειδος).

456. ϝικ-, *be like.*

INDIC. *Pres.-Perf.* εοικα, *I am like,* etc. 3 pl. εοικᾶσί(ν) or ειξᾶσιν. *Past-Perf.* εῴκειν.
INFIN. εοικεναι. PART. εοικοτ- or εικοτ-.

457. φα-, *say,*

is conjugated like στα-, *stand,* except that it is without reduplication in the imperf. tenses, and that the 2 sing. pres. has an anomalous ι subsc.

---

* The regularly formed οιδας, οιδαμεν, οιδατε, οιδασί(ν) are rare in classical Greek.

† Also ῄδεμεν, ῄδετε, § 298: and in 2 p. sing. ῄδης or ῄδεις

Pres.-Imperf. φημί, φῄς, φησί(ν), φάμεν, etc.

Past-Imperf. ἔφην, ἔφησθα (rarely ἔφης), ἔφη, etc.: this tense is also used as an aorist.

The future φήσω and 1 aor. ἔφησα are only found with the signification *assert*.

458. From a C. F. *α-*, *say*, supposed by some to be φα- with the consonant thrown off, are formed ἠμί, *say I;* ἦν, *said I;* and ἦ, *said he.* These forms are used parenthetically, like the Latin *inquam*, and only occur in a few phrases.

459. From the root χρα- is formed an impersonal verb signifying *necessity* :—

INDIC. *Pres.* χρή, *oportet.* *Past.* ἐχρῆν or χρῆν. *Fut.* χρήσει.
SUBJ. *Pres.* χρῇ. *Past.* χρείη
INFIN. χρῆναι. PART. (τὸ) χρεών.

460. Sometimes two or more verbs, which are conjugated in part only, are used to supply each other's deficiencies. Thus are conjugated

αἱρε- and ἐλ- (Ϝελ-)ς *take.* Pres. αἱρέω ; fut. αἱρήσω ; perf. ᾕρηκα ; 2 aor. εἷλον ; 1 aor. pass. ᾑρέθην.

ἐδ- and φάγ-, *eat.* Pres. ἐσθίω (earlier ἔδω and ἔσθω) ; fut. ἔδομαι ; perf. ἐδήδοκα ; 2 aor. ἔφαγον ; 1 aor. pass. ἠδέσθην.

ἐρχ- (m.), ἰ-, and ἐλυθ-, *come.* Pres. ἔρχομαι ; past-imperf. ᾖα ; fut. ἐλεύσομαι, oftener εἶμι ; perf. ἐλήλυθα ; 2 aor. ἦλθον. In the other moods the forms of ἰ- are used in the imperf. instead of those of ἐρχ-.

ζα- and βιο-, *live.* Pres. ζάω ; fut. ζήσω and βιώσομαι ; perf. βεβίωκα ; 2 aor. ἐβίων.

θρεχ- and δράμ- (or δρεμ-), *run.* Pres. τρέχω ; fut. δραμοῦμαι (rarely θρέξομαι) ; perf. δεδράμηκα ; 2 aor. ἔδραμον (1 aor. ἔθρεξα rare).

ὁρα-, ὀπ-, and ἰδ- (Ϝιδ-), *see.* Pres. ὁράω ; fut. ὄψομαι ; perf. ἑώρακα ; 2 aor. εἶδον ; pass. perf. ἑώραμαι and ὦμμαι ; 1 aor. ὤφθην.

φα-, ἐρ- (ῥε-), and εἰπ- (Ϝεπ-), *say.* Pres. φημί ; fut. ἐρῶ ; perf. εἴρηκα ; 2 aor. εἶπον ; 1 aor. pass. ἐρρήθην. Some forms of the 1 aor. act. εἶπα also frequently occur.

φερ-, οἰ-, and ἐνεκ- (ἐγκ-), *carry.* Pres. φέρω ; fut. οἴσω ; perf. ἐνήνοχα ; 2 aor. ἤνεγκον ; 1 aor. ἤνεγκα. For the variation of usage between the two aorists, consult the Dictionary.

461. In like manner the passive of κτεν-, *kill*, does not occur in Attic prose, the tenses of θἄν- or ἀποθἄν- being used instead— ἀποθνησκουσῖν, *they are being put to death*; τέθνηκεν, *he is killed*; ἀπεθἄνον, *they were killed*. So the fut. and 2 aor. mid. of ἀπο-δο-, ἀποδώσομαι and ἀπεδόμην, are found in connection with πρα-, *sell* (pres. πιπρασκω; perf. πεπρᾱκᾰ): and a 1 aor. ἐπριᾰμην in connection with ὠνε- (m.), *buy*

PRINCIPAL TENSES OF VERBS.

462. In the following Tables of the Principal Tenses of Verbs, the tenses are arranged in the following order,—present-imperfect, future, present-perfect, aorist.* The tenses of the passive are divided from those of the active by a colon (:). The letter M signifies that the middle voice is in use. From the pres.-imperf. act. may be deduced the past-imperf. act., and the pres. and past-imperf. mid. and pass.: from the fut. act. the fut. mid. (and fut.-imperf. pass.); from the pres.-perfect the past-perfect; from the aor. act. the aor. mid. (generally); and from the aor. pass. the fut.-indef. pass. When a middle form is cited among the tenses of the active, or a passive form among the tenses of the middle, etc., it is to be understood as ranging with them in meaning. The verbs are divided into the classes distinguished in §§ 262—270.

A verbal root is often strengthened in two ways, i. e. has two increased forms, some tenses being derived from one, some from the other: as, C. F. λᾰβ- (ἐλᾰβον), I. F. λαμβᾰν- (λαμβᾰνω) and ληβ- (ληψομαι). In this case the word is classified according to the form appearing in the present, and the other form is generally given after the pure C. F.: thus, λᾰβ- (ληβ-); but when the secondary increased form is made by an affixed ε, as, C. F. μᾰθ- (ἐμᾰθον), I. F. μανθᾰν- (μανθᾰνω), and μᾰθε- (μεμᾰθηκα), the C. F. is written μᾰθ-ε-.

* When the 1st and 2nd aorists (or perfects) are both in use, they are both given, without a comma interposed. They are not distinguished by (1) or (2) prefixed, as the learner should recognise them by the formation. They are to be regarded as identical in meaning unless the contrary is stated: but that form is generally placed first which occurs most frequently.

A small stroke prefixed to a form (-διδρασκω, etc.) signifies that that form is only, or at least principally, found in compounds.*

I. The crude form is not increased : § 262.

463. K, Γ, X.

πλεκ-, *plait* πλεκω, πλεξω, πεπλεχα, επλεξα : πεπλεγμαι, επλάκην and επλεχθην. M.

ἡκ-, *come* ἡκω (*I am come*), ἡξω.

διωκ-, *pursue* διωκω, διωξω and -ξομαι, εδιωξα : εδιωχθην. M.

ἑλκ- and ἑλκυ-, *draw* ἑλκω, ἑλξω and ἑλκύσω, εἱλκύκα, εἱλκύσα : εἱλκυσμαι, εἱλκυσθην. M.

δερκ- (m.), *see* δερκομαι, δερξομαι, δεδορκα (= pres.), εδρᾰκον εδερχθην and εδρᾰκην.

ἄγ-, *lead* ἄγω, αξω, ηχα, ηγᾰγον and ηξα (very rare) : ηγμαι, ηχθην. M.

λεγ-, *lay, collect* λεγω, λεξω, -ειλοχα, ελεξα : λελεγμαι and -ειλεγμαι, ελεχθην and ελεγην. M.

———, *tell* λεγω, λεξω, ελεξα : λελεγμαι, ελεχθην. M. with a perf. δι-ειλεγμαι.

φλεγ-, *scorch* φλεγω, φλεξω, εφλεξα : πεφλεγμαι, εφλεχθην and εφλεγην.

ορεγ-, *stretch* ορεγω and ορεγνῡμι, ορεξω, ωρεξα : ορωρεγμαι, ωρεχθην. M.

φθεγγ- (m.), *speak* φθεγγομαι, φθεγξομαι, εφθεγμαι, εφθεγξάμην.

οιγ-, *open*, and ἀν-οιγ- οιγω and οιγνῡμι, οιξω, ᾠξα : also in the compound ἄν-εωχα and ἄν-εωγα (intr.), ἄν-εῳξα : ἄν-εῳγμαι, ἄν-εῳχθην.

στεργ-, *love* στεργω, στερξω, εστοργα, εστερξα.

ειργ- & εἰργ- (Ϝεργ-), *shut* (*out* or *in*)† ειργω and εἰργνῡμι, ειρξω (εἰ-). ειρξα (εἰ-) : ειργμαι (εἰ-), ειρχθην (εἰ-).

μᾰχ-ε-‡ (m.), *fight* μᾰχομαι, μᾰχουμαι and μᾰχεσομαι (Ion.), μεμᾰχημαι, εμᾰχεσαμην.

δεχ- (m.), *receive* δεχομαι, δεξομαι, δεδεγμαι, εδεξάμην : εδεχθην.

* It is not, however, attempted to distinguish *all* those forms which are only so found—a task proper to Dictionaries and special treatises, such as those of Buttmann and Veitch, works from which, and from Ahrens' *Greek Accidence*, great assistance has been derived in drawing up these lists.

† The aspirated forms signify *shut in*, the unaspirated *shut out:* but the distinction is not observed in Homer.

‡ To be read ' μαχ- and μαχε-.'

ἐχ- (σεχ-ε-), *hold,* ἐχω and ἰσχω (§ 485), ἑξω and σχησω, ἐσχηκα,
  have   ἐσχον : ἐσχημαι, ἐσχεθην. M.
θρεχ-, *run* τρεχω, θρεξομαι, εθρεξα. Fut. and aor. rare;
              see § 460.
οιχ-ε- (m.), *be gone* οιχομαι, οιχησομαι, οιχωκα.
αρχ-, *be first,** rule* αρχω, αρξω, ηρξα : ηρχθην.
—— (m.), *begin* αρχομαι, αρξομαι, ηργμαι, ηρξάμην.

464. Τ, Δ, Θ.

πετ- and πετα- (m.), πετομαι (Att.) and πετᾰμαι, πετησομαι and πτη-
  fly   σομαι, πεποτημαι (§ 269), επομην επτᾰμην
               and (poet.) επτην. Late authors have an
               anomalous present ἱπτᾰμαι.
ἀνῠ-τ-, *accomplish* ἀνύτω and ἀνυω, ἀνῠσω, ηνῠκα, ηνῠσα : ηνυσμαι,
                      ηνυσθην. M.
ᾳδ- (αειδ-), *sing.* ᾳδω, ᾳσομαι and ᾳσω, ῃσα : ῃσμαι, ῃσθην. Also
                      αειδω, αεισομαι, etc. in the poets.
εδ-, *eat* εδω (poet.) ; see εδ-, § 460.
ἡδ- (m.), *be pleased* ἡδομαι, ἡσθησομαι, ἡσθην. See ἁδ-, § 477.
κλει-δ- and κλη-δ-, κλειω, κλεισω, κεκλεικα, εκλεισα : κεκλεισμαι and
  shut   κεκλειμαι, εκλεισθην. Also in older Attic
                      κλῃω, κλῃσω, etc.
ψευδ-, *deceive* ψευδω, ψευσω, εψευσα : εψευσμαι, εψευσθην. M.
σπενδ-, *pour*   σπενδω, σπεισω, εσπεισα : εσπεισμαι. M.
περθ-, *destroy* περθω, περσω, επερσα and επρᾰθον (Epic). The
                  common form is πορθε-, § 269.
ἀχθ- (m.), *be vexed* ἀχθομαι, αχθεσομαι, ηχθεσθην.

465. Π, Β, Φ.

ἑπ- (σεπ-), *be busy* -έπω, -έψω, -εσπον. More frequently in
  about   the middle
—— (m.), *follow* ἑπομαι, ἑψομαι, ἑσπομην.†
βλεπ-, *see* βλεπω, βλεψω and -ψομαι, βεβλεφα, εβλεψα.

* Also *be the first to* —, and so *begin*, with reference to others following.

† The aspirate on this 2 aor. is anomalous, as ε is of course augment, and σ represents the ʽ of the root ἑπ- : we should therefore have expected εσπομην = ε-σεπ-ομην : (compare ε-σπον in the active, and ἐσχον, ἑπτομην, 2 aorists of σιχ- and πετ-). Accordingly in the unaugmented forms ἑ disappears, at least in the ordinary language, σπωμαι, σπε-σθαι, etc.

δρεπ-, *pluck*   δρεπω and (late) δρεπτω, δρεψω, εδρεψα. M.
τρεπ-, *turn*   τρεπω, τρεψω, τετροφα and τετρᾰφα, ετρεψα
                   and ετρᾰπον (poet.): τετραμμαι, ετρεφθην and
                   ετρᾰπην. M.
πεμπ-, *send*   πεμπω, πεμψω, πεπομφα, επεμψα: πεπεμμαι
                   (-μψαι), επεμφθην. M.
τερπ-, *gladden*   τερπω, τερψω, ετερψα: ετερφθην and εταρπην
                   (Ep.). M.
σεβ- (m.), *revere* σεβομαι (rarely σεβω), εσεφθην (very rare).
γρᾰφ-, *write*   γρᾰφω, γραψω, γεγρᾰφα, εγραψα: γεγραμμαι,
                   εγρᾰφην. M.
θρεφ-, *nourish*   τρεφω, θρεψω, τετροφα (trans. and intr.),
                   εθρεψα: τεθραμμαι, ετρᾰφην and εθρεφθην. M.
στρεφ-, *twist*   στρεφω, στρεψω, εστροφα, εστρεψα: εστραμ-
                   μαι, εστρᾰφην and εστρεφθην. M.
μεμφ- (m.), *blame* μεμφομαι, μεμψομαι, εμεμψᾰμην and εμεμφθην.

466.   P, Λ, N, M.

δερ-, *flay*   δερω, δερῶ,* εδειρα: δεδαρμαι, εδᾰρην.
φερ-, *bear, carry* φερω; see § 460.
εθελ-ε- and θελ-ε-, εθελω, εθελησω, ηθελησα, ηθελησα. Also θελω,
  will, choose   etc.
μελ-ε-, *be a care* μελω, μελησω, μεμηλα, εμελησα.†
επῐ-μελ-ε- (m.),   επῐμελομαι and -λεομαι, -μελησομαι, -μεμελημαι,
  care for   -εμεληθην. The poets also use the simple
                   μελομαι, etc.
μελλ-ε-, *be going(to)* μελλω, μελλησω, εμελλησα (and ημ-).
βουλ-ε-, *wish*   βουλομαι, βουλησομαι, βεβουλημαι, εβουληθην
                   (ηβ-).
μεν-ε-, *remain*   μενω, μενῶ, μεμενηκα, εμεινα.
νεμ-ε-, *allot*   νεμω, νεμῶ, νενεμηκα, ενειμα: νενεμημαι, ενε-
                   μηθην. M.

467.   A.

τλα-, *suffer, dare* ——, τλησομαι, τετληκα, ετλην.
δρα-, *do*   δραω, δρᾱσω, δεδρᾱκα, εδρᾱσα: δεδρᾱμαι, εδρα-
                   σθην.

* In these contract futures the circumflex accent over the ω is printed
to indicate the inflection.

† The tenses of the active are chiefly used impersonally, μελει,
μελησει, etc.

TENSES OF VERBS.

ὁρα-, *see*   ὁραω, ἑωρᾱκα: see § 460.

χρα-, *give (an oracle)*   χραω, χρησω, κεχρηκα, εχρησα: κεχρησμαι, εχρησθην. M. (*consult an oracle*). See χρα-, § 485.

χρα- (m.), *use (furnish oneself)*   χραομαι (inf. χρησθαι, etc., § 273, *n.*), χρησομαι, κεχρημαι, εχρησάμην.

κτα- (m.), *acquire*   κταομαι, κτησομάι, κεκτημαι and εκτημαι, εκτησάμην: εκτηθην.

δῠνα- (m.), *be able*   δῠνᾰμαι, δῠνησομαι, δεδῠνημαι, εδῠνηθην (ηδ-) εδῠνασθην and εδῠνησᾰμην (Ep.).

επιστα- (m.), *know*   επιστᾰμαι, επιστησομαι, ηπιστηθην.

Other verbs in a (εα, ια, ρα) are conjugated like

τῑμα-, *honour*   τῑμαω, τῑμησω, τετῑμηκα, ετῑμησα: τετῑμημαι, ετῑμηθην. M.

πειρα-, *try*   πειραω, πειρᾱσω, πεπειρᾱκα, επειρᾱσα: πεπειρᾱμαι, επειρᾱθην. M. (= act.) with 1 aor. pass. and mid.

θεα- (m.), *behold*   θεαομαι, θεᾱσομαι, τεθεᾱμαι, εθεᾱσᾰμην.

468. E.

δε-, *bind*   δεω, δησω, δεδεκα, εδησα: δεδεμαι, εδεθην.

δε-ε-, *want, lack*   δεω, δεησω, δεδεηκα, εδεησα. Also impersonally δει, δεησει, etc.

— (m.), *want, ask*   δεομαι, δεησομαι, δεδεημαι, εδεηθην.

αινε-, *praise*   αινεω, αινεσω (-ησω poet.), ηνεκα, ηνεσα (-ησα poet.): ηνημαι, ηνεθην. Chiefly used in the compound επαινε-, (fut. επαινεσω and -σομαι).

αιρε-, *take*   αιρεω, αιρησω, ῃρηκα: ῃρημαι, ῃρεθην. M. See § 460.

Other verbs in ε are conjugated like

αιτε-, *ask*   αιτεω, αιτησω, ῃτηκα, ῃτησα: ῃτημαι, ῃτηθην. M.

ἡγε- (m.), *lead*   ἡγεομαι, ἡγησομαι, ἡγημαι, ἡγησᾰμην.

469. I.

κονι-, *make dusty*   κονῑω, κονῑσω, εκονῑσα: κεκονῑμαι. M.

τι-, *honour*   τῐω, τῑσω, ετῑσα: τετῑμαι.*

χρι-, *rub, anoint*   χρῑω, χρῑσω, εχρῑσα: κεχρισμαι, εχρισθην. M.

* This word is confined to the poets: in prose τῑμα- is used instead. See also τι-, § 478.

παι-, *strike*   παιω, παισω and παιησω, πεπαικα, επαισα. In pass. πλᾰγ- is more used, § 474.

σει-, *shake*   σειω, σεισω, σεσεικα, εσεισα : σεσεισμαι, εσεισθην. M.

δϝει- (δϝι-), *fear*   ———, δεισομαι (Ep.), δεδοικα and δεδια (*I fear*), εδεισα. Homer has also a pres. δειδω (in 1 p. only).

οι-ε- (m.), *think*   οιομαι and οιμαι (so ᾠομην and ᾠμην), οιησομαι, ᾠηθην.

κει- (m.), *lie*   κειμαι, κεισομαι.

470. O.

βιο-, *live*   βιοω, βιωσομαι, βεβιωκα, εβιων and εβιωσα (rare).

ἀνᾱλο- (ἀνᾰ-ϝᾰλο-), *use up*   ἀνᾱλοω and ἀνᾱλισκω, ἀνᾱλωσω, ἀνᾱλωκα (or ανηλ-), ἀνᾱλωσα (ηλ-) : ἀνᾱλωμαι (ηλ-), ἀνᾱλωθην (ηλ-).

ἄρο-, *plough*   αροω, αροσω, ηροσα : αρηρομαι, ηροθην.

Other verbs in o are conjugated like

δουλο-, *enslave*   δουλοω, δουλωσω, δεδουλωκα, εδουλωσα: δεδουλωμαι, εδουλωθην. M.

χειρο- (m.), *subdue*   χειροομαι, χειρωσομαι, εχειοωσᾰμην : κεχειρωμαι, εχειρωθην.

471. Υ.

δυ-, *cause to enter*   -δῡ͂ω, -δῡσω, -εδῡσα : -δεδῠμαι, -εδῠθην.

———, *enter, and (tr.) put on*   δῠ͂ομαι and δῡνω (IV.), δῡσομαι, δεδῡκα, εδῠν and (rarer) εδῡσᾰμην.

θυ-, *sacrifice*   θῡ͂ω, θῡσω, τεθῠκα, εθῡσα : τεθῠμαι, ετῠθην. M.

λυ-, *loosen*   λῡ͂ω, λῡσω, λελῠκα, ελῡσα : λελῠμαι, ελῠθην. M.

κωλυ-, *hinder*   κωλῡω, κωλῡσω, κεκωλῠκα, εκωλῡσα : κεκωλῠμαι, εκωλῡθην. M.

ῥυ- (m.), *rescue*   ῥῡ͂ομαι, ῥῡσομαι, ερρῡσᾰμην.

ερυ- and ειρυ-, *draw*   ερυω and ειρυω, ερῠσω ερυω and ειρῠσω, ειρῠσα : ειρῠμαι and ειρυσμαι, ειρυσθην. M.

φυ-, (tr.) *produce*   φῡ͂ω, φῡσω, εφῡσα.

———, (intr.) *be born*   φῡ͂ομαι, φῡ͂σομαι, πεφῠκα, εφῡν.

παυ- (παϝ-?), *make to cease*   παυω, παυσω, πεπαυκα, επαυσα : πεπαυμαι, επαυθην and επαυσθην. M.

θραυ-, *break*   θραυω, θραυσω, εθραυσα : τεθραυμαι and τεθραυσμαι, εθραυσθην.

κελευ-, *order* κελευω, κελευσω, κεκελευκα, εκελευσα : κεκιλευ-
σμαι, εκελευσθην. M.

Other verbs in ευ are conjugated like

βουλευ-, *deliberate* βουλευω, βουλευσω, βεβουλευκα, εβουλευσα :
βεβουλευμαι, εβουλευθην. M.

ἀκου- (ακοϝ- ?), ἀκουω, ἀκουσομαι, ἀκηκοα, ηκουσα : ηκουσμαι,
hear ηκουσθην.

II. The root-vowel is strengthened : § 263.

472. *a.* Verbs ending in a mute.

τἄκ-, *melt* (tr.) τηκω, τηξω, ετηξα.
—— (intr.) τηκομαι, τετηκα, ετἄκην.
φὔγ-, *flee* φευγω, φευξομαι and -ξουμαι, πεφευγα, εφὔγον.
τὔχ-, *prepare* τευχω, τευξω, τετευχα, ετευξα : τετυγμαι, ετυχ-
θην. M.
πἴθ-, *persuade* πειθω, πεισω, πεπεικα and πεποιθα (intr.), επεισα
and επἴθον (poet.) : πεπεισμαι, επεισθην. M.
σἄπ-, *rot* (tr.) σηπω, σηψω, εσηψα.
—— (intr.) σηπομαι, σεσηπα, εσάπην.
λῐπ-, *leave* λειπω, λειψω, λελοιπα, ελῐπον and ελειψα (rare):
λελειμμαι, ελειφθην. M.
τρῐβ-, *rub* τρῑβω, τριψω, τετρῐφα, ετριψα : τετριμμαι, ετρῐ-
βην and ετριφθην. M.
ἀλῐφ-, *anoint* ἀλειφω, ἀλειψω, ἀληλῐφα, ηλειψα : ἀληλιμμαι,
ηλειφθην. M.

473. *b.* P, N.

ἀϝ ο- (αερ-), *raise* αιρω (αειρω), ἆρῶ (αερῶ), ηρκα, ηρα : ηρμαι,
ηρθην. M. with 1 and 2 aor.
κἄθἄρ-, *cleanse* κἄθαιρω, κἄθἄρῶ, εκαθηρα : κεκἄθαρμαι, εκἄθαρ-
θην. M.
χἄρ-, *rejoice* χαιρω, χαιρησω, κεχαρηκα and κεχἄρημαι, εχἄρην.
ερ-ε. (m.), *ask* ειρομαι (Ion.), ερησομαι, ηρομην.
ἀγερ-, *collect* ἀγειρω, ἀγηγερκα, ηγειρα : ἀγηγερμαι, ηγερθην. M.
εγερ-, *rouse* εγειρω, εγερῶ, εγρηγορα (intr.), ηγειρα : εγηγερ-
μαι, ηγερθην. M.
φθερ-, *spoil, de-* φθειρω, φθερῶ, εφθαρκα and εφθορα (tr. and
stroy intr.), εφθειρα : εφθαρμαι, εφθἄρην. M.
κερ-, *shear* κειρω, κερῶ, εκειρα (κερσω and εκερσα, poet.) :
κεκαρμαι, εκἄρην.

K

TENSES OF VERBS.

περ-, *pierce*	πειρω, επειρα : πεπαρμαι, επάρην.
σπερ-, *sow*	σπειρω, σπερῶ, εσπειρα : εσπαρμαι, εσπάρην.
οδῠρ- (m.), *lament*	οδῠρομαι, οδῠρουμαι, ωδῠράμην.
φᾰν-, (tr.) *shew*	φαινω, φᾰνῶ, πεφαγκα, εφηνα : πεφασμαι, εφανθην.
——, (intr.) *appear*	φαινομαι, φᾰνουμαι, πεφηνα, εφᾰνην.
μιᾰν-, *stain*	μιαινω, μιᾰνῶ, εμιᾱνα : μεμιασμαι, εμιανθην.
κρᾰν-, *accomplish*	κραινω, κρᾰνῶ, εκρᾱνα : εκρανθην. Like these three are conjugated many words in ᾰν (ιαν, ραν).
τε-ν-, *stretch*	τεινω, τενῶ, τετακα, ετεινα . τετᾰμαι, ετᾰθην. M.
κτε-ν-, *kill*	κτεινω, κτενῶ, εκτονα and (later) εκτᾰκα, εκτεινα εκτᾰνον and (poet.) εκτᾰν. In prose ἀπο-κτεν- is used. For the passive, θᾰν- (απο-θαν-) was commonly employed, § 461.
κλῐ-ν-, *bend*	κλῑνω, κλῐνῶ, κεκλῐκα, εκλῑνα : κεκλῐμαι, εκλῐθην (-νθην poet.) and εκλῐνην. M.
κρῐ-ν-, *separate, decide*	κρῑνω, κρῐνῶ, κεκρῐκα, εκρῑνα : κεκρῐμαι, εκρῐθην. M.
ἀπο-κρῐν- (m.), *answer*	ἀποκρῑνομαι, -κρῐνουμαι, -κεκρῐμαι, ἀπεκρῑνάμην and (late) -εκρῐθην.
ἀμῠν-, *ward off*	ἀμῡνω, ἀμῠνῶ, ημῡνα. ⎫ And like these many words in ῠν.
οξῠν-, *sharpen*	οξῡνω, ωξυγκα : ωξυμμαι or ωξυσμαι, ωξυνθην. ⎭
οφελ-,* *owe*	οφειλω and οφελλω (Ep.), οφειλησω, ωφειληκα, ωφειλησα and (in a peculiar sense) ωφελον.

III. ι cons. is added : § 264.

474.   a. K, Γ, X (T).

φῠλᾰκ-, *watch*	φῠλασσω (-ττω), φῠλαξω, πεφῠλᾰχα, εφῠλ ιξα : πεφῠλαγμαι, εφῠλαχθην. M.
ἑλῐκ-, *roll*	ἑλισσω and εἱλισσω, ἑλιξω (εἱ-), εἱλιξα : εἱ- λιγμαι, εἱλιχθην. M.
φρῑκ-, *bristle, shiver*	φρισσω, φριξω, πεφρῑκα, εφριξα.
κηρῡκ-, *proclaim*	κηρυσσω, κηρυξω, κεκηρῠχα, εκηρυξα : κεκηρυγ- μαι, εκηρυχθην.
ἀλλᾰγ-, *exchange*	αλλασσω, αλλαξω, ηλλᾰχα, ηλλαξα : ηλλαγμαι, ηλλαχθην and ηλλᾰγην. M

* For other verbs in λ see § 476

TENSES OF VERBS. 131

πλᾱγ- (πληγ-), πλησσω, πληξω, πεπληγα, επληξα · πεπληγμαι
  strike   επληγην and (Att.) -επλᾰγην. M.
πρᾱγ-, *do*   πρασσω, πραξω, πεπρᾱχα and πεπρᾱγα (intr.)
          επραξα : πεπραγμαι, επραχθην. M.
τᾱγ-, *arrange* τασσω, ταξω, τετᾰχα, εταξα : τεταγμαι, εταχθην. M.
πᾰτᾰγ-, *strike* πᾰτασσω, πᾰταξω, επᾰταξα. Rare in pass.: see
          πλᾱγ-.
σφᾰγ-, *slay* σφαττω and σφαζω, σφαξω, εσφαξα : εσφαγμαι,
          εσφᾰγην and εσφαχθην (rare).
τᾰρᾱχ-, *stir up,* τᾰρασσω, τᾰραξω, τετρηχα (intr.), ετᾰραξα : τε-
  confound   τᾰραγμαι, ετᾰραχθην.
ορῠχ-, *dig*   ορυσσω, ορυξω, ορωρῠχα, ωρυξα : ορωρυγμαι
          and (later) ωρυγμαι, ωρυχθην.
πᾰτ-, *sprinkle* πασσω, πᾰσω, επᾰσα : πεπασμαι, επασθην.
πλᾰτ-, *mould* πλασσω, πλᾰσω, επλᾰσα : πεπλασμαι, επλα-
          σθην. M.
πεπ-, *cook*   πεσσω and (later) πεπτω, πεψω, επεψα : πεπεμ-
          μαι, επεφθην. Compare πεμπ-, § 465.

475.   *b*. Δ.

ϝεργᾰδ- (m.), *work* εργαζομαι, εργᾰσομαι, ειργασμαι, ειργᾰσᾰμην :
          ειργασθην.
δᾰμ-ᾰδ-, *tame* δᾰμαζω and δαμνημι (§ 481, *n.*), δᾰμᾰσω and
          δᾰμῶ, εδᾰμᾰσα : δεδμημαι, εδᾰμασθην and
          εδᾰμην.

          Other verbs in *αδ* are conjugated like
θαυμᾰδ-, *wonder* θαυμαζω, θαυμᾰσομαι, τεθαυμᾰκα, εθαυμᾰσα : τε
          θαυμασμαι, εθαυμασθην.
φρᾰδ-, *tell*   φραζω, φρᾰσω, πεφρᾰκα, εφρᾰσα and (Ep.) πε-
          φρᾰδον : πεφρασμαι, εφρασθην.
ἑδ- (σεδ-),* *sit* chiefly occurring in composition with κᾰτᾰ
κᾰθεδ-   } *seat, sit* κᾰθιζω, κᾰθιῶ, εκᾰθῐσα and κᾰθῖσα.
and κᾰθῐδ- } (m.) *sit* κᾰθιζομαι, κᾰθεδουμαι, εκᾰθεζομην.

   * The simple word is rare. On the connection between the forms
ἱδ- and ἱδ-, and the existence of a present ἱζομαι, see σεδ-, § 485, and
Buttmann, *Irreg. Verbs*, p. 129, etc. From the same root are regularly
made (§ 251) a 1 aor. act. and mid., εἷσα and εἱσᾰμην, and a fut. ἐσομαι·
there is also a perfect ἧμαι, κᾰθημαι, *I sit*.

Verbs in ιδ are conjugated like

νομιδ-, *deem, think*   νομιζω, νομισω (Att. νομιῶ), νενομικα, ενομισα :
                         νενομισμαι, ενομισθην.

χᾰρῐδ- (m.), *do a favour*   χᾰριζομαι, χᾰριουμαι, κεχᾰρισμαι, εχᾰρῐσᾰμην.

ἁρμοτ-, *fit*   ἁρμοζω and ἁρμοττω, ἁρμοσω, ἡρμοκα, ἡρμοσα :
              ἡρμοσμαι, ἡρμοσθην. See σφᾰγ-, § 474.

σωδ- and σω-, *save*   σωζω and σωω (Ep.), σωσω, σεσωκα, εσωσα :
                        σεσωσμαι and σεσωμαι, εσωθην.

ἁρπᾰδ- and ἁρπᾰγ-, *seize*   ἁρπαζω, ἁρπᾰσω and -σομαι, ἡρπᾰκα, ἡρπᾰσα :
                 ἡρπασμαι, ἡρπασθην. Also (but not Attic)
                 ἁρπαξω, ἡρπαξα, etc. occur, and a late 2 aor.
                 pass. ἡρπᾰγην.

παιδ- and παιγ-, *sport*   παιζω, παιξουμαι and -ξυμαι, πεπαικα, επαισα :
                 πεπαισμαι. Later επαιξα, etc.

κρᾰγ-, *scream*   κραζω, κεκραξομαι, κεκρᾱγα, -εκρᾰγον.

ῥεγ- (ϝρεγ-) and ἐργ- (ϝεργ-), *work*   ῥεζω and ερδω, ῥεξω and ερξω, εοργα (ϝεϝοργα) εμρεξα and ερξα (Ion.).

στῐγ-, *prick*   στιζω, στιξω, εστιξα : εστιγμαι.

οιμωγ-, *cry* οιμοι   οιμωζω, οιμωξομαι, ᾠμωξα : ᾠμωγμαι.

νῐβ-, *wash*   νιζω (late νιπτω), νιψω, ενιψα : νενιμμιιι, ενιφθην. M.

476.   c. Λ.

ἁλ- (m.), *leap*   ἁλλομαι, ἁλουμαι, ἡλᾰμην and ἡλομην.

βᾰλ-, *throw*   βαλλω, βᾰλῶ, βεβληκα, εβᾰλον : βεβλημμι, εβληθην. M.

σφᾰλ-, *trip up*   σφαλλω, σφᾰλῶ, εσφαλκα, εσφηλα : εσφαλμαι, εσφᾰλην.

αγγελ-, *report*   αγγελλω, αγγελῶ, ηγγελκα, ηγγειλα : ηγγελμαι, ηγγελθην. M.

-ελ-, *raise, rise*   τελλω, τεταλκα, ετειλα : τεταλμαι. M. (Chiefly in compounds.)

στελ-, *equip*   στελλω, στελῶ, εσταλκα, εστειλα : εσταλμαι εστᾰλην. M.

τῐλ-, *pluck*   τιλλω, τῐλῶ, ετῑλα : τετιλμαι. M.

IV. A consonantal affix is added : § 265.

477.   *a.* ἀν or ν is added.

θῐγ-, *touch*   θιγγᾰνω, θιξομαι, εθῐγον.

λᾰχ- (ληχ-, λεγχ-), λαγχάνω, ληξομαι, ειληχα and λελογχα (Ion.),
  get by lot   ελᾰχον : ειληγμαι, εληχθην.
τῠχ-ε- (τευχ-), *hit,* τυγχᾰνω, τευξομαι, τετῠχηκα, ετῠχον.
  happen
'ἁμαρτ-ε-, *miss the* 'ἁμαρτᾰνω, ἁμαρτησομαι, ἡμαρτηκα, ἡμαρτον :
  mark, err   ἡμαρτημαι, ἡμαρτηθην.
βλαστ-ε-, *grow* βλαστᾰνω, βλαστησω, εβλαστηκα (βεβλ-),
    εβλαστον.
'ᾰδ-ε- (Fαδ-), *please* ἁνδᾰνω, 'ᾰδησω, ἑᾰδα (FεFᾱδα), ἑᾰδον.
χᾰδ- (χενδ-), *hold* χανδᾰνω, χεισομαι, κεχανδα, εχᾰδον.
λᾰθ- (ληθ-), *lie hid* λανθᾰνω and ληθω (IL.), λησω, λεληθα, ελᾰθον :
    λελησμαι.
—— (m.), *forget* λανθᾰνομαι and ληθομαι, λησομαι, λελησμαι,
    ελᾰθομην. (Chiefly in the compound επῐλᾰθ-.)
μᾰθ-ε-, *learn* μανθᾰνω, μᾰθησομαι, μεμᾰθηκα, εμᾰθον.
πῠθ- (πευθ-) (m.), πυνθανομαι and (poet.) πευθομαι (II.), πευσομαι,
  inquire, learn πεπυσμαι, επῠθομην.
αισθ-ε- (m.), *per-* αισθᾰνομαι and (rare) αισθομαι (L), αισθησομαι,
  ceive   ῃσθημαι, ῃσθομην.
ὁλισθ-ε-, *slip* ολισθᾰνω, ολισθησω, ωλισθον.
λᾰβ- (ληβ-), *take* λαμβᾰνω, ληψομαι, ειληφα, ελᾰβον. ειλημμαι,
    εληφθην. M.
αυξ-ε-,* *increase* αυξᾰνω and αυξω, αυξησω, ηυξηκα, ηυξησα : ηυξη-
  (tr.)   μαι, ηυξηθην. M.
οφλ-ε-, *owe* οφλ-ισκ-ᾰνω, οφλησω, ωφληκα, ωφλον.
'ἱκ-, *come* 'ἱκᾰνω and 'ἱκω (II.), see § 479.
κῐχ-ε-, *find* κῐχᾰνω and κιγχᾰνω, κῐχησομαι, εκῐχον.
ἁλῐτ-, *sin* ἁλῐταινω, ηλῐτον.

478.

δᾰκ- (δηχ-), *bite* δακνω, δηξομαι, εδᾰκον : δεδηγμαι, εδηχθην.
κᾰμ-, *toil* καμνω, κᾰμουμαι, κεκμηκα, εκᾰμον.
τεμ-, *cut* τεμνω, τεμῶ, τετμηκα, ετᾰμον and ετεμον : τε-
    τμημαι, ετμηθην. M.
βα-, *go* βαινω, βησομαι, βεβηκα, εβην. The fut. βησω
    and 1 a. εβησα are transitive.
φθα-, *outstrip* φθᾱ´νω, φθησομαι, εφθᾰκα, εφθην and εφθᾰσα.
ελα-, *drive* ελαυνω and ελαω (rare), ελᾰσω and ελῶ (for
    ελαω), εληλᾰκα, ηλᾰσα : εληλᾰμαι, ηλᾰθην.

* Αυξ- from αυγ-σκ-? Compare ἀλεξ- for ἀλεκ-σκ-. § 484, and the
Latin *aug-e-*.

φθι-, *decay* φθἴνω and φθιω (Ep.), φθῖσομαι, εφθῖμαι, εφθῖμην. The fut. and 1 a. φθῖσω (φθιῶ) and εφθῖσα are trans.

πι- and πο-, *drink* πῑνω, πῑομαι and (rare) πῖουμαι, πεπωκα, επιον πεπομαι, εποθην.

τι-, *pay* τ˘ῑνω, τῑσω, τετῑκα, ετῑσα : τετισμαι, ετισθην. M.

479. *b.* νε is added.

'ἰκ- (m.), *come* ἰκνεομαι, ἰξομαι, ἰγμαι, 'ἰκομην. (Chiefly ἀφἰκ-.)

'ὑπο-ἐχ- (m.), *promise* 'ὑπισχνεομαι, 'ὑποσχησομαι, 'ὑπεσχημαι, 'ὑπεσχομην.

480. *c.* νυ is added.

δεικ-, *shew* δεικνῡμι and δεικνυω,* δειξω, εδειξα : δεδειγμαι, εδειχθην. M.

ϝᾱγ-, *break* αγνῡμι, αξω, εᾱγα (intr.), εαξα : εᾱ´γην.†

πᾱγ- (πηγ-), *fix* πηγνῡμι, πηξω, πεπηγα (intr.), επηξα : επᾰγην. M.

ῥᾱγ- (ῥηγ-), *break, burst* (tr.) ῥηγνῡμι and (poet.) ῥησσω, ῥηξω, ερρηξα : ερρηγμαι. M.

—— (intr.) ῥηγνῡμαι, ερρωγα, ερρᾰγην.

μῐγ-, *mix* μιγνῡμι and μισγω, μιξω, εμιξα : μεμιγμαι, εμῐγην and εμιχθην. M.

ζῠγ- (ζεῦγ-), *join* ζευγνῡμι, ζευξω, εζευξα : εζευγμαι, εζῠγην and εζευχθην. M.

ἀρ- (m.), *win* ἀρνῠμαι, ἀρουμαι, ηρομην.

ορ-, *rouse* ορνῡμι, ορσω, ορωρα (intr.), ωρσα and (redup. 2 a.) ωρορον. M. ορωρεμαι, ωρομην.

ολ- (tr.), *destroy* ολλῡμι, ολεσω and (Att.) ολῶ, ολωλεκα, ωλεσα.

— (intr.), *perish* ολλῠμαι, ολουμαι, ολωλα, ωλομην.

ομ-ο-, *swear* ομνῡμι, ομουμαι, ομωμοκα, ωμοσα : ομωμομαι and -σμαι, ωμοθην and -σθην.

481.

σκεδ-ᾰσ-, *scatter* σκεδαννῡμι,‡ σκεδᾰσω and (Att) σκεδῶ, εσκεδᾰσα : εσκεδασμαι, εσκεδασθην.

* As this double form of the present tense is common to almost all the verbs of this class, the second form is not given in the verbs which follow.

† So ἑᾱλων from 'ἀλο-. Ahrens explains ᾱ by the supposition of a double augment, as in ἑωρων.

‡ Some of these presents in ν-νῡμῐ coexist with forms in νημῐ (from a C. F. in να), which are for the most part poetical. The syllable ᾰσ

TENSES OF VERBS.

κρεμ-ἀσ-, *suspend*	κρεμαννῦμι, κρεμάσω and κρεμῶ, εκρεμάσα : εκρεμασθην. M. pres. κρεμᾰμαι.
κερ-ᾰσ-, *mingle*	κεραννῦμι and (poet.) κεραω, κερᾰσω, εκερᾰσα : κεκρᾰμαι, εκρᾰθην and εκερασθην.
πετ-ᾰσ-, *spread*	πεταννῦμι, πετᾰσω and πετῶ, επετᾰσα : πεπτᾰμαι and πεπετασμαι, επετασθην.
ἑσ- (ϝεσ-), *clothe*	ἕννῦμι and (Ion.) εἱνῦμι, ἑ(σ)σω, ἑ(σ)σα : εἱμαι. M. Prose writers use the compound
αμφι-εσ-,	αμφιεννῦμι, αμφιεσω and αμφιῶ, ημφιεσα : ημφιεσμαι. M. (On the augment see § 256.)
σβε-σ-, *quench*	σβεννῦμι, σβεσω, εσβεσα : εσβεσμαι, εσβεσθην.
——— (intr.), *go out*	σβεννῦμαι, σβησομαι, εσβηκα, εσβην.
κορ-εσ-, *satiate*	κορεννῦμι, κορεσω, εκορεσα : κεκορεσμαι, εκορεσθην. M.
στορ-εσ- and στρω-σ-, *strew*	στορνῦμι and στρωννῦμι, στορεσω στορῶ and στρωσω, εστορεσα and εστρωσα : εστρωμαι, εστρωθην.
ζω-σ-, *gird*	ζωννῦμι, εζωσα : εζωσμαι. M.
ῥω-σ-, *strengthen*	ῥωννῦμι, ερρωσα : ερρωμαι, ερρωσθην.
χο-σ- and χω-σ-, *heap up*	χοω and later χωννῦμι, χωσω, κεχωκα, εχωσα. κεχωσμαι, εχωσθην.

482.   *d.* τ is added to p- sounds.

σκεπ- (m.), *look at, examine*	σκεπτομαι*, σκεψομαι, εσκεμμαι, εσκεψᾰμην.
κλεπ-, *steal*	κλεπτω, κλεψω and -ψομαι, κεκλοφα, εκλεψα : κεκλεμμαι, εκλᾰπην and (rare) εκλεφθην.
κοπ-, *cut*	κοπτω, κοψω, κεκοφα, εκοψα : κεκομμαι, εκοπην. M.
τῠπ-, *beat*	τυπτω, τυπτησω, ετυψα and (rare) ετῠπον : τετυμμαι, ετῠπην. M.
βλᾰβ-, *hurt*	βλαπτω, βλαψω, βεβλᾰφα, εβλαψα : βεβλαμμαι, εβλᾰβην and (rare) εβλαφθην.
κᾰλῠβ-, *cover*	κᾰλυπτω, κᾰλυψω, εκᾰλυψα : κεκᾰλυμμαι, εκᾰλυφθην. M.
'ἀφ-, *touch*	ἀπτω, ἀψω, ἡψα : ἡμμαι, ἡφθην. M.
βᾰφ-, *dip*	βαπτω, βαψω, εβαψα : βεβαμμαι, εβᾰφην. M.

is wanting, and the root-vowel undergoes a change. Thus are found σκιδνημι, κρημνημι, κιρνημι, and πιτνημι.

* In the pres. and past imperf. the Attics generally use σκοπεω or σκοπουμαι (§ 269): the 1 aor. of this form, εσκοπησα, is late.

θᾰφ-, *bury*   θαπτω, θαψω, εθαψα : τεθαμμαι, εταφην. M.
σκᾰφ-, *dig*   σκαπτω, σκαψω, εσκᾰφα, εσκαψα : εσκαμμαι, εσκᾰφην.
ῥᾰφ-, *sew*   ῥαπτω, ῥαψω, ερραψα : ερραμμαι, ερρᾰφην. M.
ῥῐφ- (ῥιπ-?), *hurl*   ῥιπτω and ῥιπτεω, ῥιψω, ερριψα : ερριμμαι, ερρῐφην and ερριφθην.
κυφ-, *stoop*   κυπτω, κυψω and -ψομαι, κεκῡφα, εκυψα.
κρῠφ-, *hide*   κρυπτω, κρυψω, κεκρῠφα, εκρυψα : κεκρυμμαι, εκρυφθην and (rare) εκρῠφην. M.

483.   e.   εθ is added.

φλεγ-, *scorch*   φλεγω and φλεγεθω (poet.), φλεξω, etc. See φλεγ-, § 463.
τελ-, *rise, be*   τελεθω (poet.) = τελλω, which however is chiefly trans. See τελ-, § 476.
εδ-, *eat*   εσθω (i. e. εδ-θω) and more commonly εσθιω, (also εδω poet.), etc. See § 460.
πλα-, *be full*   πληθω, πεπληθα (chiefly poet.). See πλα-, § 485.
πρα-, *burn* (tr.)   πιμπρημι and (very rare) -πρηθω. See πρα-, § 485.
νε-, *spin*   νεω and νηθω, νησω, ενησα : νενημαι and νενησμαι.

484.   V.   ισκ (εσκ) or σκ is added : § 266.

ἀλεκ-, *ward off*   ἀλεξω (i. e. αλεκ-σκ-ω), αλεξησω, ηλεξησα and (very rare) ηλεξα, also (Ep. redup. 2 a.) ηλαλκον. M.
δῐδᾰχ-, *teach*   δῐδασκω,* δῐδαξω, δεδῐδᾰχα, εδῐδαξα: δεδῐδαγμαι, εδῐδαχθην. M.
πᾰθ- (πενθ-), *suffer*   πασχω (i. e. παθσκω), πεισομαι, πεπονθα, επᾰθον.
ἀρ-, *please*   ἀρεσκω, ἀρεσω, ηρεσα : ηρεσμαι, ηρεσθην. M.
στερ-ε-, *deprive*   στερισκω and στερεω, στερησω, εστερηκα, εστερησα : εστερημαι, εστερηθην. In prose ἀποστερεω is the ordinary form. A pass. pres. στερομαι means *I am deprived* (orbatus sum).
θορ-, *leap*   θρωσκω (§ 46), θορουμαι, εθορον.

* Δῐ-δα-σκω is evidently formed, after the analogy of the verbs given in § 486, from the poet. root δα-, *teach, learn*, whence εδαην, *I learnt*; but that διδαχ- was practically viewed as a new verbal root is plain not only from the tenses of the verb, but from the derived substantive δῐδᾰχα-, f. *instruction*.

TENSES OF VERBS. 137

ευρ-ε-, *find*   ευρισκω, ευρησω, ευρηκα, ευυον : ευρημαι, ευρεθην. M.

μολ-, *go*   βλωσκω,* μολουμαι, μεμβλωκα, εμολον.

θαν-, *die*   θνησκω, θανουμαι, τεθνηκα, εθανον. In Attic prose the compound αποθαν- is usual, except in the perf.

χαν-, *yawn*   χασκω, χανουμαι, κεχηνα, εχανον. The pres. χαινω is very late.

ηβα-, *be at one's prime*   ηβασκω, I *grow manly*, and ηβαω, I *am at my prime*, ηβησω, ηβηκα, ηβησα.

ἱλα- (m.), *appease*   ἱλασκομαι (also ἱλεομαι), ἱλᾰσομαι, ἱλᾰσᾰμην.

γηρα-, *grow old*   γηρασκω and γηραω, γηρᾱσω and -σομαι, γεγηρᾱκα, εγηρᾱσα and (in some forms) εγηρᾶν.

φα-, *say, affirm*   φασκω and φημι, past-imperf. εφασκον, φησω, εφησα. For the usage in the simple sense of *saying*, see § 460.

ἁλ-ο- (Fᾰλ-ο-), *be captured*   ἁλισκομαι, ἁλωσομαι, ἑᾱλωκα (FεFαλ-) and ηλωκα, ἑᾱ́λων† and ηλων. See αναλο-, § 470.

485.   VI. Reduplication is used: § 267.

τεκ-, *bring forth*   τικτω (for τιτκω), τεξομαι and -ξω, τετοκα, ετεκον. M.

σεχ- (ἐχ-), *hold*   ισχω,‡ σχησω, etc. See ἐχ-, § 463.

πετ-, *fall*   πιπτω, πεσουμαι, πεπτωκα, επεσον.§

σεδ- (ἐδ-), *seat*   ἱζω, etc. See ἐδ-, § 475.

γεν- (m.), *become, be*   γιγνομαι (and γινομαι), γενησομαι, γεγενημαι and γεγονα, εγενομην.

μεν-, *remain*   μιμνω‖ (poet.). See μεν-, § 466.

ονα-, *benefit*   ονινημι (for ονονημι), ονησω, ωνησα : ωνηθην. M. 2 aor. ωνημην (but inf. ονασθαι).

πλα-, *fill*   πιμπλημι, πλησω, πεπληκα, επλησα : πεπλησμαι, επλησθην. M.

* i. e. μλωσκω, or, rather, μβλωσκω. Compare the perfect μεμβλωκα, and see § 42.

† In the indic. ᾱ, in the other moods ᾰ. See § 480, n.†

‡ The presents ισχω, ἱζω, ἱστημι are, of course, for σισχω, σιζω, σιστημι, initial σ being softened into ', § 47, b : in ισχω even the aspirate is lost in obedience to the well known rule, § 44.

§ In Doric επετον ; in the common forms επεσον and πεσουμαι, τ is softened into σ. § 47, σ.

‖ On the loss of ε in this and the five words preceding, see § 49.

πρα-, *burn* πιμπρημι,* πρησω, επρησα : πεπρημαι, επρησθην.
χρα-, *lend* κιχρημι, χρησω, εχρησα : κεχρημαι. M. (=*borrow*).
στα-, *stand* (tr.) ἱστημι, στησω, εστησα : ἐστᾰμαι, εστᾰθην. M.
—————— (intr.). ἱστᾰμαι, στησομαι, ἑστηκα, ἑστηξω, εστην.
ἑ-, *let go, send* ἱ̃ημι, ἡσω, εἱκα, ἡκα, etc. See § 454.
θε-, *place* τἰθημι, θησω, τεθεικα, εθηκα (εθεμεν, etc. § 343): τεθειμαι, ετεθην. M.
δο-, *give* δἰδωμι, δωσω, δεδωκα, εδωκα (εδομεν, etc.) : δεδομαι, εδοθην. M.

486. σκ is added to the reduplicated root.

ἀρ-, *fit* ἀρᾰρισκω, ἀρᾱρα (intr.), ηρσα and (redup. 2 a.) ηρᾰρον. See ἀρ-, *win*, and ἀρ-, *please*, §§ 480 and 484.
μνα-, *remind* μιμνησκω, μνησω, εμνησα : μεμνημαι (*I remember*), εμνησθην.
δρα-, *run away* -διδρασκω, -δρᾱσομαι, -δεδρᾱκα, -εδρᾱν.
πρα-, *sell* πιπρασκω, πεπρᾱκα : πεπρᾱμαι, επρᾱθην. See § 461.
γνω-, *examine, think* γιγνωσκω, γνωσομαι, εγνωκα, εγνων† : εγνωσμαι, εγνωσθην.
βρω-, *eat* βιβρωσκω, βεβρωκα : βεβρωμαι, εβρωθην.
τρω-, *wound* τιτρωσκω, τρωσω, ετρωσα : τετρωμαι, ετρωθην.

487. VII. ε is added : § 268.

δοκ-, *seem* δοκεω, δοξω, εδοξα : δεδογμαι. The poets also use δοκησω, etc.
πᾰτ- (m.), *feed* πᾰτεομαι, πᾰσομαι, επᾰσᾰμην : πεπασμαι.
γηθ-, *rejoice* γηθεω, γηθησω, γεγηθα, εγηθησα.
ωθ-, *push* ωθεω, ωσω (and ωθησω poet.), εωσα : εωσμαι, εωσθην.
κῠρ-, *chance* κῠρεω and κῠρῳ (II.), κυρσω, εκυρσα. Also κῠρησω, etc.

* The μ before πρ, πλ, in these words is euphonic: compare μεσημβ-ρια-, *mid-day* (§ 42). and μεμ-β-λωκα, perf. of μολ- in the last §, where β is inserted between μ and ρ, etc. The compounds with εν are εμπιπλημι, εμπιπρημι, but again ενεπιμπλην, etc., in the augmented tense.

† A 1 aor. active, of course with a causative meaning, exists in the Ionic compound ἀν-εγνωσα. *I persuaded.*

καλ-, *call*	κηλεω, καλεσω and (Att.) καλῶ, κεκληκα, εκάλεσα: κεκλημαι, εκληθην. M. Compare βαλ-, § 476.	
γαμ-, *take to wife*	γαμεω, γαμῶ, γεγαμηκα, εγημα. M. Late γαμησω, etc.	

VIII. Verbs in ϝ or σ : § 270.

488   F.

καϝ-, *burn*	καιω and κάω, καυσω and -σομαι, κεκαυκα, εκαυσα and εκηα (Ep.) εκεα (Trag.): κεκαυμαι, εκαυθην and εκαην (Ion.).
κλαϝ-, *weep*	κλαιω and κλάω, κλαυσομαι and κλαιησω (ā), εκλαυσα : κεκλαυμαι. M.
θεϝ-, *run*	θεω, θευσομαι.
πλεϝ-, *set sail*	πλεω, πλευσομαι and -σουμαι, πεπλευκα, επλευσα: πεπλευσμαι.
νεϝ-, *swim*	νεω, νευσομαι and -σουμαι, νενευκα, ενευσα.
πνεϝ-, *breathe*	πνεω, πνευσομαι and -σουμαι, πεπνευκα, επνευσα.
ῥεϝ-, *flow,*	ῥεω, ῥευσομαι and ῥυησομαι, ερρυηκα, ερρυην and (rare) ερρευσα.
χεϝ-, *pour*	χεω, χεω, κεχῠκα, εχεα: κεχῠμαι, εχῠθην. M.

489.   Σ.*

ἀγάσ-, *wonder at*	ἄγαμαι, ἀγάσομαι, ηγασθην and ηγασάμην.
χαλάσ-, *slacken*	χαλαω, χαλάσω, κεχάλακα, εχάλασα : κεχάλασμαι, εχάλασθην.
γελάσ-, *laugh*	γελαω, γελάσομαι, εγελάσα : γεγελασμαι, εγελασθην.
κλάσ-, *break*	κλαω, εκλάσα : κεκλασμαι, εκλασθην.
σπάσ-, *draw*	σπαω, σπάσω, εσπάκα, εσπάσα : εσπασμαι, εσπασθην. M.
εράσ-, *love*	εραω and εράμαι, ερασθησομαι, ηρασθην and ηράσάμην.
αιδ-εσ- (m.), *feel shame. respect*	αιδεομαι and αιδομαι, αιδεσομαι, ηδεσμαι, ηδεσθην and ηδεσάμην.
ζεσ-, *boil*	ζεω, ζεσω, εζεσα : εζεσμαι.
ἀκεσ- (m.), *heal*	ἀκεομαι, ηκεσάμην.
αρκεσ-, *aid, suffice*	αρκεω, αρκεσω, ηρκεσα : ηρκεσθην.
τελεσ-, *complete*	τελεω, τελεσω and (Att.) τελῶ, τετελεκα, ετελεσα : τετελεσμαι, ετελεσθην. M.
ξεσ-, *polish*	ξεω, εξεσα : εξεσμαι.

* For other verbs in σ see § 481

490. Many active verbs have a future middle. The most important of these will be found in the Tables: others are ἀπανταω, *I meet*, ἀπαντησομαι (-σω); ἀπολαυω, *I enjoy*, ἀπολαυσομαι; βἄδιζω, *I walk*, βἄδιουμαι; βοαω, *I shout*, βοησομαι; επιορκεω, *I swear falsely*, επιορκησομαι (-σω); κολαζω, *I chastise*, κολᾰσομαι (Att. κολῶμαι; also κολᾰσω); πηδαω, *I leap*, πηδησομαι; σῑγαω, *I am silent*, σῑγησομαι; σιωπαω, *I am silent*, σιωπησομαι; σκωπτω, *I mock*, σκωψομαι; σπουδαζω, *I am eager*, σπουδᾰσομαι (-σω); χωρεω, *I withdraw*, χωρησομαι (-σω).

491. Many middle verbs have an aorist passive (deponents passive). Some of these have already been given in the Tables: others are ἁμιλλαομαι, *I compete*, ἡμιλληθην; αρνεομαι, *I deny*, ηρνηθην (Ep. ηρνησᾰμην); διᾰλεγομαι, *I discuss*, διελεχθην (Ep. διελεξᾰμην); διᾰνοεομαι, *I purpose*, διενοηθην (also ἀπον-, εν-, προν-); εναντιοομαι, *I oppose*, ηναντιωθην; ενθῡμεομαι, *I lay to heart*, ενεθῡμηθην (also προθ-); ευλᾰβεομαι, *I am cautious*, ευλᾰβηθην; πορευομαι, *I travel*, επορευθην; φῐλοτῑμεομαι, *I am ambitious*, εφῐλοτῑμηθην. Some of these have also a fut.-indef. derived from the aorist root.

ADVERBS.

492. On adverbs derived from adjectives and pronouns, see § 175, etc., § 204, etc., and § 210.

493. Adverbs are formed from substantives by means of the suffix δον (ἄδον, ηδον): as, from

βοτρυ-, *bunch of grapes*, βοτρῡ-δον *like a bunch of grapes*.
ἰλα-, *troop*, ἰλ-ἄδον, *in troops, abundantly*.
κῠν-, *dog*, κῠν-ηδον, *like a dog*.
ἱππο-, *horse*, ἱππ-ηδον, *like a horse*.

494. Adverbs are formed from verbs by means of the suffixes δον, δᾰ, δην (ἄδην): as, from

ἀνᾰφᾰν-, *shew forth (up)*, ἀνᾰφαν-δον and ἀνᾰφαν-δᾰ, *openly*.
σχ-(ἐχ-), *hold, hold on by*, σχ-ε-δον, *hardly, nigh, nearly*.
κρῠφ-, *hide*, κρυβ-δην and κρυβ-δᾰ (also κρῠφ-α), *secretly*.
γρᾰφ-, *scratch, write*, γραβ-δην, *in a scraping manner, by writing*
σπερ-, *sow, scatter* σπορ-ἄδην, *scatteredly*.

495. Adverbs in ει or ῑ (rarely ῐ), are formed from adjectives, mostly compounds: as, πανδημ-εί or πανδημ-ί, *with the whole people*; ἀμάχ-ει, *without a battle*; ἀκλαυτ-ί, *without weeping*. These are probably modifications of the dative case.

496. Adverbs are formed from verbs by means of the suffix τί: as, from

ὀνυμάδ-, *name*,   ὀνομασ-τί, *by name*.
Περσιδ-, *hold with the Persians*, Περσισ-τί, *in Persian fashion, speak Persian*,   *in the Persian tongue*.

497. A few adverbs in ξ or αξ are formed principally from substantives signifying some part of the body: as, from

ὀδοντ-, *tooth*,   ὀδάξ, *with the teeth*.
πυγ-μα-, *fist*,   πύξ, *with the fist*.
γονυ-, *knee*,   γνύξ, *on the knee*.
   λάξ, *with the heel*.
also μουνο-, *alone*,   μούναξ, *singly*.
ἀλλάγ-, *change*,   ἀλλάξ, *by turns*.

498. Adverbs in (σ)θεν or (σ)θε are formed from prepositions: as, προ-σθε(ν), *before*, from προ, *before*; ὑπερ-θε(ν), *from above, above*, from ὑπερ, *over*; ὀπισθε(ν) or ὀπίθε(ν), *behind*; ἐνερ-θε(ν) or νερ-θε(ν), *from beneath, beneath*, connected with ἐνεροι=*inferi*. From ἐκ, *out from*, are derived ἐκ-τος, *without*, and ἐκτοσ-θε(ν), *from without*: from ἐν, *in*, are derived ἐν-τος, *within*, and ἐντοσ-θε(ν), *from within*; also ἔνδον and ἐνδοθῖ, *within, at home*, and ἔνδοθεν. Some of these words are also employed as prepositions. Compare the table of pronominal adverbs, § 204.

PREPOSITIONS.

499. The prepositions of the Greek language, with the primary significations of each, are as follows:—

a. Followed by the accusative only:
εἰς or ἐς, *into, to* (Lat. *in*, with acc.).

b. Followed by the genitive only:
ἀντί, *over against, instead of*.   ἐξ, ἐκ, *out of, from*.
ἀπο, *from* (away from).   προ, *before*.

c. Followed by the dative only·
ἐν (Ep. ἐνί, ἐιν), *in* (Lat. *in* with abl.)
σύν or ξύν, *with*.

d. Followed by the accusative or genitive :
 διά, *through* (between).   ὑπερ (Ep. ὑπειρ), *over*.
 κατά, *down.*

e. Followed by the accusative or dative :
 ἀνά, *up.*

f. Followed by the accusative, genitive, or dative :
 αμφί, *about* (on both sides of).   περί, *around.*
 επί, *upon.*   προς (Ep. προτί, ποτί), *up to*
 μετά, *amidst.*   ὑπο (Ep. ὑπαι), *under.*
 παρά (Ep. παραι), *by* (by the side of).

The use of αμφί, ἀνά, and μετά with the dative is confined to the poets.

500. The prepositions were all originally adverbs of place : many of them are often so employed by the poets, and προς is so used even in Attic prose. In general usage, they either stand in connection with some case of a noun, in order to define the relation between the several words of a sentence more closely than could be done by means of the cases alone; or they are compounded with verbs, to express the direction of the action of the verb. They are also used in the formation of compound adjectives.

501. In connection with the cases of nouns prepositions undergo some change of their original signification, yet rather in appearance than reality; as the widely different translations which one preposition must often receive are due solely to the case which accompanies it. Thus, παρά meaning *by the side of*, παρά τον βασιλεᾱ is *to* (the side of) *the king;* παρά του βασιλεως, *from* (the side of) *the king;* and παρά τῳ βασιλει, *by* (the side of), or *near, the king :* the difference of meaning in each instance being caused by the proper force of the accus., gen., and dat. cases respectively (§ 61, *b.*).

502. In composition with verbs the prepositions retain their adverbial character: hence the place of the augment and the reduplication is between the preposition and the verbal root, and in the earlier language the preposition was readily separated from the verb by one or more words—a process commonly, but incorrectly, treated as a violent license under the name of *Tmesis* (τμησίς, *cutting*).

503. All the prepositions given in § 499 are used in composition with verbs : the following, some of which are rather adverbs,

are not so used : ἄνευ (and poet. ἄτερ), *without, apart from;* αχρῐ(ς) and μεχρῐ(ς), *until;* ἕνεκᾰ (ἕνεκεν, εἵνεκᾰ), *for the sake of,* all of which are followed by the genitive ; and ἅμᾰ, *together with,* which takes the dative. The particle ὡς is sometimes used with the accus. to express motion *to,* for the most part with persons only.

504. The usual place of the preposition, as the name implies, is immediately before the noun which it accompanies ; it is, however, sometimes separated from the case by the particles μεν, δε, γᾰρ, etc. Περῐ and ἕνεκᾰ even in prose, the others in the poets, occasionally follow their noun.

505. The prepositions sometimes seem to be used as verbs, with an ellipsis of ἐστῐ or εἰσῐ;—πᾰρᾰ for πᾰρεστῐ or πᾰρεισῐ, ἐνῐ for ἐνεστῐ, etc.

CONJUNCTIONS.

506. The conjunctive particles μεν*——δε (—δε) are used to contrast two or more words or clauses which are either opposed to, or merely distinguished from, each other. They are regularly placed after the contrasted words, or the first words of the contrasted clauses. Their force may be rendered by *on the one hand—on the other;* but generally μεν may be passed over in the English sentence, and δε be rendered by *and,* or (if the contrast is one of opposition) *but:* as, ελεγε μεν ὡς το πολῠ, τοις δε βουλομενοις ἐξην ἀκουειν, *he usually spoke, and those who liked might listen;* λεγεις μεν ευ, πραττεις δ'ουδεν, *you speak well, but do nothing.*

507. The copulative conjunctions are και, *and;* τε (encl.), *and;* ἤ, *either, or;* ουδε (μηδε),† *and not, not even;* ουτε (μητε), *neither, nor.* These may be used in pairs : as, και κᾰτᾰ γην και κᾰτᾰ θᾰλασσᾰν, *both by land and by sea;* εγω τε και σῠ, *both I and you;* ανδρων τε θεων τε, *both of men and of gods;* ἤ τῐς ἤ ουδεις, *either one or no one;* ουτε ταυτᾰ ουτε τἀλλᾰ, *neither this nor the other.*

508. Particles of emphasis are γε (encl.), *at least;* περ (encl.), *just;* ἤ, *verily;* μην, *assuredly;* δη, *certainly, of course;* μεντοι, *however,* etc.

* Apparently weaker forms of μην and δη.
† On the distinction between the negative particles ου and μη, and their compounds, see the Syntax.

509. For the interrogative and conditional particles, and for those conjunctions which serve to attach subordinate to principal clauses, see the Syntax.

DERIVATION AND COMPOSITION.

510. Words are either *simple*—i. e. derived from a single root, as μάχ-ομαι, *I fight*, from μάχ-, *fight;* γράφ-ω, *I write*, from γράφ-,* *write;* λογο-, m. *speech*, from λεγ-, *speak*—or *compound*, i. e. formed from two or more roots, as λογο-γραφο-, m. *a writer of narratives.*†

511. Simple words are either *primary derivatives*—i. e. formed immediately from the root, as, φυγ-α-, f. *flight*, from φυγ-, *flee;* αρχ-α-, f. *beginning*, from αρχ-, *begin*— or *secondary derivatives*, i. e. formed through some simpler derivative, as αρχ-α-ιο-, *ancient*, from αρχ-α-, *beginning*. The term *derivative* is, however, usually restricted to words of the latter class.

512. Nouns, whether primary (primary derivatives), or derived (secondary derivatives), are usually formed by the addition of a syllable, called the suffix, which serves to determine the precise relation in which the word stands to the root. Thus, from γράφ-, *write*, are formed γράφ-ευ-, m. *writer;* γράφ-ιδ-, f. *writing instrument;* γραμ-μάτ-, n. *a writing;* γραμ-μα-, f. *line:* from δικα-, f. *equivalent, right*, are formed δικα-ιο-, *righteous;* and from this again, δικα-ιο-σύνα-, f. *righteousness*.

513. Many primary verbs, and a few substantives, are made without any suffix: as, μάχ- (m.), *fight;* λεγ-, *speak;* ἀγ-, *lead;* 'ἀλ-, m. f. *salt, sea:* or with a slight change of vowel, as φλογ-, f. *flame*, from φλεγ-, *burn*. Such substantives, of course, belong to the inseparable declension.

514. For the changes to which consonants and vowels are subject in the derivation and composition of words, consult the sections on letter-changes.

* Such words as γράφ-, *write;* αρχ-, *begin*, are classed among primary roots, as not admitting of any further analysis within the limits of the Greek language. They are probably not *pure* roots, but made by the addition of some affix.

† Care must be taken not to confound compound words and derivatives from compounds: ὁμοφρον-, *of one mind*, is a compound adjective; ὁμοφρονε-, *be of one mind*, is a verb derived from the compound adjective.

515. *Of the Derivation of Nouns.*

The following Tables exhibit the most important suffixes of substantives and adjectives.

MASCULINE SUFFIXES.

Suffix	Added to	Gives a substantive meaning	Thus, from	English	Is derived	English
ϵϝ	verbs	one who —s	φεν-	slay	φον-ευ-	slayer
ϵϝ	nouns	person	γραμματ-	a writing	γραμματ-ευ-	scribe
			ἱππο-	horse	ἱππ'-ευ-	horseman
ϵϝ[1]	town	inhabitant	Μεγαρο-	Megara	Μεγάρ'-ευ-	a Megarian
τα	verbs	one who —s	κυβερνα-	steer	κυβερνη-τα-	steersman
τ ρ	verbs	one who —s	ῥε-	speak	ῥη-τορ-	speaker
τηρ	verbs	one who —s	καλ-ε-	summon	κλη-τηρ-	summoner
τα	nouns	person	τοξο-	bow	τοξο-τα-	bowman
ῑ-τα	nouns	person	ὁδο-	way	ὁδ'-ῑτα-	traveller
ω-τα	nouns	person	στρατια-	army	στρατι'-ωτα-	soldier
τυ[1]	town	inhabitant	Αἰγινα-	Ægina	Αἰγῑνη-τα-	an Æginetan
ῑ-τα }	or	inhabitant	Ἀβδηρο-	Abdera	Ἀβδηρ'-ῑτα-	an Abderite
ω-τα }	country	inhabitant	Σικελια-	Sicily	Σικελι'-ωτα-	a Sicilian Greek
τηρ-[2]	verbs	means	ζωσ-	gird	ζωσ-τηρ-	girdle
o[3]	verbs	person	ἀειδ-	sing	ἀοιδ-ο-	singer
o	verbs	act?	λεγ-	speak	λογ-ο-	speech
α[4]	—	person	τρῑβ-	wear, practise	παιδο-τρῑβ-α-	trainer of boys
ιδη[5]	parent	son of	Νεστορ-	Nestor	Νεστορ-ιδα-	son of Nestor
ιον	parent	son of	Κρονο-	Cronus	Κρον'-ιον- or Κρον-ιων-	son of Cronus
ιων	parent	son of				
ι-σκο-	nouns	little	παιδ-	child, boy	παιδ-ισκο-	young boy
μο[6]	verbs	act	ὀδυρ-	lament	ὀδυρ-μο-	lamentation
(θ)μο	verbs	act	κλαϝ-	weep	κλαυ-θμο-	weeping
(σ)μο	verbs	act	θε-	place	θε-σμο-	statute
ων	nouns	place for	γυναικ-	woman	γυναικ-ων-	women's apartment
ἀκ[7]	nouns	little	κλων-	twig	κλων-ἀκ-	little twig
ἀκ	nouns	——	πορπα-	buckle	πορπ-ἀκ-	shield-handle
ηκ	nouns	——	μυρμο-	ant	μυρμ'-ηκ-	ant
ὐχ[7]	nouns	——	βοτρυ-?	bunch of grapes	βοστρ-ὐχ-	lock of hair

Remarks on the Suffixes.

[1] This suffix is, of course, only a special case of that immediately above.

[2] Nouns masc. in τηρ, and nouns fem. and neut. in τρα and τρο, signifying the means, are probably to be regarded as adjectives used substantively.

[3] Some of these nouns in o are masc. and fem.; as, ἀοιδο- m. and f.

[4] The few nouns of this class are, mostly, compounds.

[5] This suffix also appears as ἀδα and ιαδα. When it is added to words whose C. F. ends in ϵϝ, ϝ disappears, and ι of the suffix forms a diphthong with the pre-

ceding ε: thus, from Πηλεϝ- or Πηληϝ, *Peleus*, are made Πηλειϝα- (or Πηλεϊδα-) an Πηληϊάδα-, *son of Peleus;* similarly from Ατρεϝ- are formed Ατρειδα- and Ατρειων

[6] But of many words in θμο and σμο the initial consonant of the suffix seems du rather to a lost final consonant in the root.

[7] Also fem., as ῥοδ-ἀκ-, f. *dwarf-rose;* πτυχ-, f. *fold;* αμπ-υχ-, m f. *band, circle* (from αμφί). These suffixes, ἄκ, ᾱκ, ηκ, ὔχ, as also ἀγ(λᾰλ-ᾰγ-, *bubbler*), ὔγ (πτερ ὔγ-, f. *pinion*), ἴκ (ἑλ-ῐκ-, f. *a spiral*), are varieties of one suffix, and all seem to hav been originally diminutive. Some of them are also adjectival.

516.   Feminine Suffixes.

Suffix	Added to	Gives a Substantive meaning	Thus, from	English	Is derived	English
α[1]	verbs	act	φῠγ-	*flee*	φῠγ-α-	*flight*
μα	verbs	act	μνα- (m.)	*remember*	μνη-μα-	*remembrance*
ια[2]	adj.	quality	ευδαιμον-	*prosperous*	ευδαιμον-ια-	*prosperity*
σ-ῠνα[3]	adj.	quality	αφρον-	*senseless*	αφροσῠνα-	*senselessness*
			δικαιο-	*righteous*	δικαιο-σῠνα-	*righteousness*
ο-να	verbs		ἡδ- (m.)	*enjoy*	ἡδ-ονα-	*joy, pleasure*
τητ-	adj.	quality	τᾰχυ-	*swift*	τᾰχῠ-τητ-	*swiftness*
τι[4]	verbs	act	φα-	*speak*	φᾰ-τι-	*speaking*
σι	verbs	act	πραγ-	*do*	πραξι-	*doing*
σια	verbs	act	δοκιμᾰδ-	*prove*	δοκιμᾰ-σια	*proving*
ια[5]	male	female	ἱερεϝ-	*priest*	ἱερεια-	*priestess*
σα	male	female	ἄνακτ-	*king*	ἄνασσα-	*queen*
αινα	male	female	λε-οντ-	*lion*	λε-αινα-	*lioness*
ῐδ	parent	daughter of	Δᾰναο-	*Danaus*	Δανα'-ῐδ-	*daughter of Danai*
ῐδ-[6]	male	female	Ἑλλην-	*a Greek*	Ἑλλην-ῐδ-	*a Greek woman*
ῐδ	—	—	γρᾰφ-	*write*	γρᾰφ-ῐδ-	*writing instrumen*
ᾰδ	nouns	collective	φυλλο-	*leaf*	φυλλ'-ᾰδ-	*heap of leaves*
τειρα[7]	verbs	female agent	δο-	*give*	δο-τειρα-	*female who give*
τρια	verbs	female agent	ποιε-	*create*	ποιη-τρια-	*poetess*
τρῐδ	verbs	female agent	αυλε-	*play the flute*	αυλη-τρῐδ-	*female flute-playe*
τῐδ[7]	nouns	female person	πολι-	*city*	πολῑ-τῐδ-	*female citizen*
τρα	verbs	means	κᾰλῠβ-	*hide*	κᾰλυπ-τρα-	*veil*
τρα	verbs	place	πᾰλαι-	*wrestle*	πᾰλαι-σ-τρα-	*wrestling-school*
ι-σκα	nouns	little	παιδ-	*child*	παιδ-ισκα-	*little girl*

Remarks.

[1] Feminines in α are also used as collective nouns: thus, from φῠλᾰκ-, *watcl* φῠλᾰκ-α-, f. is both *watching* and *a guard*, like the Latin *custodia-*. Similarly, som words in ια are collectives: as, γερουσ-ια- (γεροντ-ια-), *a senate;* ἐκκλησ-ια- (fron ἐκκλητο-, *summoned*), *an assembly*.

[2] Substantives in ια, from adjectives chiefly, are very numerous; it is important t to attend to the necessary letter-changes: thus, from σοφο-, *wise;* ἄληθεσ-, *true* ἀθᾰνᾰτο-, *immortal*, are derived σοφ'ια-, *wisdom;* ἀληθεια-, *truth;* ἀθᾰνᾰσια-, *im mortality*.

[3] Most words of this class are derived from adjectives in ον, as αφροσῠνα-, *foll*

from αφρον-; μνημοσύνα-, remembrance, from μνημον-, mindful; so that υνα should, probably, be regarded as the original suffix, σ being due to ν final of the adj.

⁴ τι and σι are the same suffix.

⁵ The suffixes σα and ια are probably identical, σσα being due to the concurrence of ι with a preceding guttural or dental; so μέλισσα-, bee, from μελῖτ-, n. honey. See § 45, a.

⁶ This use of the suffix ιδ is obviously related to the preceding: ιδ also appears as a termination of feminine adjectives: thus, θουρο-, m. θουρἰδ-, f. impetuous; Περσα-, a Persian, Περσἰδ-, f. (sc. γα-), the land of the Persians, Persia.

⁷ These fem. nouns in τειρα (τερ-ια), τρια, τρἰδ, and τἰδ, should rather be considered as formed through masc. nouns in τηρ, τορ, and τα. Compare the Latin victr-ic- through vict-or-; doctrina- through doctor-; textrina- through textur-.

517.   NEUTER SUFFIXES.

Suffix	Added to	Gives a substantive meaning	Thus, from	English	Is derived	English
μᾰτ	verbs	thing done	πραγ-	do	πραγ-μᾰτ-	deed
εσ¹	verbs	{ act { thing done	πενθ- βᾰλ-	grieve throw	πενθ-εσ- βελ-εσ-	grief dart
εσ	adj.	property	ευρ-υ-	broad	ευρ-εσ-	breadth
ο	verbs	—	ζὔγ-	join	ζὔγ-ο-	yoke
το²	verbs	thing done	πο-	drink	πο-το-	draught
τρο³	verbs	{ means { wages for	ἄρο- λυ-	plough set free	ἄρο-τρο- λυ-τρο-	a plough ransom
τηρ-ιο⁴	verbs	place	βουλευ-	deliberate	βουλευ-τηριο-	senate-house
(ε)ιο	nouns	place	χαλκεϝ-	coppersmith	χαλκε-ιο-	coppersmith's shop
ιο	nouns	little	παιδ-	child	παιδ-ιο-	little child
ἴδιο	nouns	little	κὔν-	dog	κὔν-ἴδιο-	little dog
ἄριο	nouns	little	παιδ-	child	παιδ-ἄριο-	little child
(ᾰ)νο	verbs	—	τεκ-	bring forth	τεκ-νο-	child

Remarks.

¹ Varieties of this suffix are ᾰσ, ᾰτ, ᾰρ, as: σελᾰσ-, blaze; τερᾰτ-, portent; θεναρ-, the flat of the hand.

² These nouns in το are probably neuters of adjectives in το.

³ The price for which anything is bought is a sort of instrument.

⁴ These words in τηριο and ειο (αιο, etc.) are rather to be regarded as the neuters of adjectives in τηρ-ιο and ε-ιο: the true suffix is ιο, the syllables τηρ and ε (εϝ) denoting the agent. The compound suffix would grow to be regarded as a simple, and thus be added to nouns agent of a different form: thus, from διδασκάλο-, teacher was made διδασκαλειο-, n. a school. Compare the Latin audi-tor-io- with the Greek κροᾱ-τηρ-ιο-, place of audience. Some nouns in τηριο and ειο also signify the means.

518. Suffixes of Adjectives.

Suffix	Added to	Gives an adjective meaning	Thus, from	English	Is derived	English
o^1	verbs	state	λειπ-	leave	λοιπ-ο-	left
$ιο^2$	nouns	belonging to	ἁλ-	sea	ἁλ-ιο-	marine
ιο	adj.	—ly	κᾰθᾰρο-	clean	κᾰθᾰρ'-ιο-	cleanly
εο	nouns	made of	χρῡσο-	gold	χρῡσ'-εο-	golden
ειο	nouns	belonging to	γῠναικ-	woman	γῠναικ-ειο-	feminine
λο	}		δει-	fear	δει-λο-	timid
η-λο	}	state ?	ὑψ-εσ-	height	ὑψ-ηλο-	high
ω-λο	}		φειδ-	spare	φειδ-ωλο-	thrifty
ᾰ-λεο			θαρσ-εσ-	courage	θαρσ-ᾰλεο-	courageous
ρο	nouns	full of	αισχ-εσ-	shame	αισχ-ρο-	shameful
ε-ρο	nouns	full of	φοβο-	fear	φοβ'-ερο-	frightful, oft
η-ρο	nouns	full of	μοχθο-	hardship	μοχθ'-ηρο-	full of hards
νο	verbs	state	σεβ-	worship	σεμ-νο-	revered
νο	nouns	like, etc.	ερεβεσ-	gloom	ερεβεν-νο-	gloomy
ῐ-νο	nouns	like, etc.	ανθρωπο-	man	ανθρωπ'-ινο-	human
ῐ-νο	nouns	made of	ξῠλο-	wood	ξῠλ'-ινο-	wooden
ερ-ιο	nouns	belonging to	χειμ-ων-	winter	χειμ-εριο-	wintry
ερ-ῐνο	nouns	belonging to	νυκτ-	night	νυκτ-ερῐνο-	belonging to ?
ῐ-νο	town	belonging to	Τᾰραντ-	Tarentum	Ταραντ-ινο-	of Tarentum
η-νο	town	belonging to	Κυζικο-	Cyzicus	Κυζικ'-ηνο-	of Cyzicus
ᾱ-νο	town	belonging to	Σαρδι-	Sardis	Σαρδι-ᾱνο-	of Sardis
ῐμο	verbs	fit to (act. or pas.)	ωφελ-ε-ια- (m.)	serve	ωφελ-ῐμο-	serviceable
σ-ῐμο	verbs		ια- (m.)	heal	ιᾱ-σῐμο-	curable
ῐμο	nouns	like, etc.	νομο-	custom	νομ'-ῐμο-	customary
ῐκο	verbs	fit to	αρχ-	rule	αρχ-ῐκο-	fit to rule
τ-ῐκο	verbs	fit to	πραγ-	do	πρακ-τῐκο-	fit for busine
κο	nouns	belonging to	Λιβῠ-	a Libyan	Λιβῠ-κο-	Libyan
ῐκο	nouns	belonging to	Ἑλλην-ιππο-	a Greek horse	Ἑλλην-ῐκο-ιππ'-ῐκο-	Grecian of horses
ᾰκο	nouns	belonging to	Κορινθιο-	a Corinthian	Κορινθι'-ᾰκο-	of the Corinth
τα		male agent, etc.	στεφᾰνο-	wreath	στεφᾰν-ῐ-τα-	{ belonging to
τ-ῐδ		female			στεφᾰν-ῐ-τῐδ-	{ wreaths
το	verbs	{ —ed	γνω-	know	γνω-το-	known
		{ —able	θᾰν-	die	θνη-το-	liable to die
τεο	verbs	to be —d	ποιε-	make	ποιη-τεο-	to be made
τερο	{ adj. or prep.	of two	[πο-;]	which ?	πο-τερο-;	which of two
			προ	before	προ-τερο-	former
τηριο³	verbs	fit to	σω-	save	σω-τηρ-ιο-	saving
v^4			ἡδ-	delight-	ἡδ-υ-	delightful, su
μον	verbs	full of	μνα-	remember	μνη-μον-	mindful
(ϝ)εντ	nouns	full of	δολο-	craft	δολο-εντ-	crafty
ηρεσ⁵	nouns	fitted with, etc.	χαλκο-	copper	χαλκ'-ηρεσ-	fitted with co
ωδεσ⁶	nouns	full of	κινδῡνο-	danger	κινδῡν'-ωδεσ-	dangerous

Remarks.

¹ This suffix is much used in compound adjectives.

² In appending the suffix attention must be paid to the final letter of the C. F. Thus, from δῐκα-, *right*; βᾰσῐλεϝ-, *king*; θερεσ-, *summer* Μῐλητο-, *Miletus*, are derived δῐκαιο-, βᾰσιλειο-, θερειο-, Μῐλησιο-; and from αλγεσ-, *pain*, with suffix νο, αλγεινο-, *painful*, for αλγεσ-νο-, through αλγεν-νο-; compare the co-existing forms φαεννο- and φαεινο-, *shining*, from φαεσ-, *light*, and the feminines χᾰριεσ-σα- (adj.) and τῠπει-σα- (part.) from the C. F. χᾰριεντ- and τῠπεντ-.

³ These are strictly to be viewed as adjectives in ιο from nouns in τηρ; but many adjectives in τηριο occur without any corresponding substantive in τηρ.

⁴ Perhaps this suffix carries with it a diminutive force. Compare the English adjectives in *ish*; and for the form the numerous Latin adj. in *i*, as *suavi-*, *sweet*.

⁵ Adjectives in ηρεσ are perhaps to be regarded as compounded with the root ἄρ-, *fit*.

⁶ This suffix possibly contains the element ειδ-εσ-, *form, shape*: compare such words as μηνο-ειδεσ-, *moon-shaped*.

Of the Derivation of Verbs.

519. Frequently a pure root, without the addition of any suffix, is used as the C. F. of a verb: as, ἄγ-, *lead*; τᾰγ- (σσ), *arrange*; μᾰθ-, (μανθᾰν-), *learn*; ῥε-, *flow*; φῠγ- (φευγ-), *flee*.

520. Many crude forms of substantives and adjectives are, without any additional suffix, employed as verbal crude forms: as, πτῠχ-, f. *a fold*, and πτῠχ- (σσ), *fold up*; παιδ-, m. f. *child*, and παιδ- (ζ), *play like a child*; φῠλᾰκ-, m. *watchman*, and φῠλᾰκ- (σσ), *watch*; ἑλῐκ-, *twisted*, and ἑλῐκ-(σσ), *twist*; κηρῡκ-, m. *herald*, and κηρῡκ- (σσ), *proclaim*. The suffixes, thus transferred, often came to be viewed as original verb-suffixes, and were then appended to roots of different form.

521. Thus from substantives in α arise verbs in α: as,

Subst.	Verb.
θηρα-, f. *hunting*,	θηρα-, *hunt*.
τῑμα-, f. *honour*,	τῑμα-, *honour*.
τολμα-, f. *daring*,	τολμα-, *be daring*.

And then from words of a different form: as,

γοο-, m. *wailing*,	γοα-, *bewail*.
νεμεσι-, f. *indignation*,	νεμεσα-, *be indignant*.

522. From substantives in o arise verbs in o: as,

δουλο-, m. *slave,* δουλο-, *enslave.*
χρυσο-, m. *gold,* χρυσο-, *gild.*

And then from words of a different form: as,

ῥιζα-, f. *root,* ῥιζο-, *cause to take root.*

523. From substantives and adjectives in εσ arise verbs in εσ, or more frequently in ε, σ being dropped (§ 48): as,

τελεσ-, n. *end,* τελεσ- or τελε-, *fulfil.*
ἀκεσ-, n. *remedy,* ἀκεσ- or ακε- (m.), *heal.*
θαρσεσ-, n. *courage,* θαρσε-, *be bold.*
εὐτυχεσ-, *fortunate,* εὐτυχε-, *be fortunate.*

And then from words of a different form: as,

φιλο-, m. f. *friend,* φιλε-, *be a friend, love.*
οἰκο-, m. *house,* οἰκε-, *dwell.*
φωνα-, f. *voice,* φωνε-, *speak.*
εὐδαιμον-, *happy,* εὐδαιμονε-, *be happy.*

Verbs in ε from subst. and adj. in o are very numerous.

524. From nouns in ι and υ arise a few verbs in ι and υ: as,

μηνι-, f. *wrath,* μηνι-, *be wroth.*
ἰθυ-, *straight,* ἰθυ-, *go straight.*

525. From substantives in ευ arise verbs in ευ: as,

βασιλευ-, m. *king,* βασιλευ-, *be king.*
ἱππευ-, m. *horseman,* ἱππευ-, *ride, serve in cavalry.*

And, more frequently, from words of a different form: as,

βουλα-, f. *counsel,* βουλευ-, *give counsel.*
δουλο-, m. *slave,* δουλευ-, *be a slave.*
ἡγεμον-, m. *guide, leader,* ἡγεμονευ-, *guide, rule.*

526. From substantives in μ-ατ arise verbs in μ-αν (αιν):* as,

ονοματ-, n. *name,* ονομαν-, *give a name to.*
σηματ-, n. *sign, token,* σηματ-, *give a sign.*

And then from words of a different form; more readily, however, from words which show some resemblance to the original form: as,

ποιμεν-, m. *shepherd,* ποιμαν-, *tend sheep.*
ευφρον-, *glad,* ευφραν-, *gladden.*

* For this substitution of ν for τ, compare the adjectives α-πραγ-μον-, *easy;* α-πημ-ον-, *unharmed,* from πραγ-ματ-, πημ-ατ-; also the Latin neuter substantives in *men* and *mento,* which evidently correspond in form and meaning to the Greek neuters in μᾰτ.

θερμο-, *hot*,   θερμᾶν-, *make warm.*
λευκο-, *white*,   λευκᾶν-, *whiten.*

527. From adjectives in υ arise verbs in ῠ-ν (ῡν): as,
ἡδυ-, *sweet*,   ἡδῡν-, *sweeten.*
βᾰρυ-, *heavy*,   βᾰρῡν-, *make heavy.*

And then from words of a different form: as,
λαμπρο-, *bright*,   λαμπρῠν-, *brighten.*

In some instances, the adj. in υ has disappeared in the positive, traces of the formation surviving, however, in the compar. and superl., and in a derived verb in ῠν: thus, with αισχ-ρο-, *ugly*, etc., are connected the compar. and superl. αισχιον- and αισχιστο-, and a subst. αισχεσ-, suggesting an adjectival C. F. αισχυ-, whence is derived a verbal C. F. αισχῠν-, *shame.* Similarly, we have αλγ-εινο-, *painful*, αλγῑον-, αλγιστο-, αλγεσ-, [αλγυ-], αλγῠν-. κρᾰτ-ερο-, *strong*, κρεισσον-, κρᾰτιστο-, κρᾰτεσ-, [κρᾰτυ-], κρᾰτῠν-.

528. From substantives in ῐδ arise verbs in ῐδ (ζ): as,
παιδ-, m. f. *child*,   παιδ-, *play like a child.*
ελπῐδ-, f. *hope*,   ελπῐδ-, *feel hope.*
ερῐδ-, f. *strife*,   ερῐδ-, *strive.*

And, more frequently, from words of a different form: as,
Ἑλλην-, m. *a Greek*,   Ἑλληνῐδ-, *speak Greek*, etc.
ὁπλο- (pl.), n. *arms*,   ὁπλῐδ-, *furnish with arms.*

529. From substantives in ᾰτ (μ-ατ) are made verbs in ᾰδ (ζ): as,
θαυμᾰτ-, n. *wonder*,   θαυμᾰδ-,* *feel wonder*
δελεατ-, n. *bait, enticement*,   δελεᾰδ-, *entice.*

And, more frequently, from words of another form: as,
δῐκα-, f. *justice*,   δῐκᾰδ-, *give judgement.*
εργο-, n. *work*,   εργᾰδ- (m.), *work.*

530. A few verbs called *desideratives* are formed in α (or ια) from nouns, and in σει from verbs (through the future): as,
φονο-, m. *bloodshed*,   φονα-, *thirst for blood.*
θᾰνᾰτο-, m. *death*,   θᾰνᾰτα- & θᾰνᾰτια-, } *long to die.*
πολεμε-, *make war*,   πολεμη-σει-, *wish for war.*
γελα-σ-, *laugh*,   γελᾰ-σει-, *wish to laugh.*

531. On *inceptive* verbs in σκ (ι-σκ), see § 266.

* As well as θαυμᾶν-, an older form.

Connected with this formation in σκ is a peculiar form of the past-imperfect and aorist tenses, active and middle, made by means of a suffix σκ or ε-σκ with the person-endings of the past-imperf., and signifying the repetition of an act in past time; the augment is usually dropped: thus, from τρεπ-, *turn*, are formed (past-imp. 1 sing.) τρεπεσκον and τρεπεσκομην; (1 aor.) τρεψασκον and τρεψασκομην; (2 aor.) τραπεσκον and τραπεσκομην. The use of these tenses is confined to the Ionic dialect; in Attic the same meaning was conveyed by means of the ordinary tenses with ἄν: as, ειδον ἄν, *I would* (repeatedly) *see*, = ἴδεσκον.

532. Verbs in α, αδ, ε, ευ, generally denote *a state*, or *the possession or exercise of some faculty, etc.*, implied by the simple word; thus, they are both transitive and intransitive: as, from νῑκα-, f. *victory*, arises the verb νῑκα-, *be victorious, conquer*. But verbs in ε and ευ are generally intransitive.

533. Verbs in ο, ἄν, ὔν, have usually a *factitive* signification: as, δουλο-, *make a slave of*; θερμᾶν-, *warm*; ἡδῠν-, *sweeten*.

534. Verbs in ἴδ belong to both classes: as, ελπῐδ-, *be hopeful, hope*, but ἀγνῐδ-, *render pure*. Many verbs in ἴδ derived from proper names are *imitative*: as, Φιλιππῐδ-, *belong to Philip's party*; Ἑλληνῐδ-, *act the Greek*.

Of Composition.

535. The first member of a compound word may be either a noun (substantive or adjective), a verb, or some particle. The second member may be either a noun or a verb.

536. If the first member of a compound be a substantive or adjective, it is prefixed (in the crude form) with no other change or addition than such as may be required for euphony: thus are derived

from πῠρ-, *fire*, and φερ-, *bear*, πυρ-φορ-ο-, *fire-bearing*.

σᾰκεσ-, *shield*, πᾰλ-, *brandish*, σᾰκεσ-πᾰλ-ο-, *brandishing a shield*.

χορο-, *chorus*, δῐδασκᾰλο-, *teacher*, χορο-δῐδασκᾰλο-, *teacher of a chorus*.

πολυ-, *many*, γλωττα-, *tongue*, πολυ-γλωττ-ο-, *many-tongued*.

Final *a* is usually changed to *o*: as,
from ἡμερα-, *day*, and φῠλᾰκ-, *watcher*, ἡμερο-φῠλᾰκ-, *watching by day*.

Final ο is dropped if the second word begin with a vowel: as,
from ιππο-, *horse*,   and αρχ-, *command*. ιππ-αρχ-ο-, *commander of cavalry*.
  κωμα-, *village*,   αρχ-, *command*,   κωμ-αρχ-ο-, *head of a village*.

But, if the second word begin with ϝ or σ subsequently lost, the final vowel of the first word is generally retained, and crasis often takes place: as,

from κᾰκο-, *bad*,   and ηθεσ- (ϝηθεσ-), *disposition*, κᾰκο-ηθεσ-, *ill-disposed*.
  κᾰκο-, *bad*,   εργο- (ϝεργο-), *deed*,   κᾰκουργο-, i. e. κᾰκο-εργο-, *evil-doer*.
  ῥαβδο-, *staff*,   ἐχ- (σεχ-), *hold*,   ῥαβδουχ-ο-, i. e. ῥαβδο-οχ-ο-, *holding a staff*.

If the first word end with a consonant and the second begin with a consonant, ο is used as connecting vowel: as,

from θαυμᾰτ-, *wonder*, and ποι-ε-, *do*, θαυμᾰτ-ο-ποι-ο-, *wonder-worker*.
  πᾰτερ-, *father*,   κτεν-, *kill*, πατρ-ο-κτον-ο-, *father-killer*.

Also after the weak vowels ι and υ, ο is inserted: as,
from φῠσι-, *nature*, and λεγ-, *speak*, φῠσι-ο-λογ-ο-, *natural philosopher*.
  ιχθυ-, *fish*,   φᾰγ-, *eat*,   ιχθυ-ο-φᾰγ-ο-, *fish-eater*.*

But of neuters in εσ and ατ (ματ) those syllables are often dropped; or, rather, an earlier stage of the root is recurred to: as,

from ανθ-εσ-, *flower*, and νεμ-, *feed*, ανθ-ο-νομ-ο-, *feeding on flowers*.
  σπερμ-ατ-, *seed*,   λεγ-, *gather*, σπερμ-ο-λογ-ο-, *picking up seeds*.

537. If the first member of a compound be a verb, it is annexed without change, or, if euphony requires, with the insertion

---

* At least, such is the usual but not altogether satisfactory explanation of this ο. On the other hand, it has been suggested that in such compounds originally a genitival or other secondary form constituted the first element, of which the so-called connecting vowel ο is a relic. Thus, for instance, ιχθυοσ-φαγο- would have been the original form of this word. Compare Πελοποννησο-, *island of Pelops*, which is admitted to be for Πελοποσ-νησο-, just as ερεβεννο- is from ερεβεσ-νο- (§ 48). In such words as πῠρῐ-γενεσ-, *wrought by fire*; ορεσι-τροφο- (or ορει-τροφο-), *reared on the mountains*, a dative case is usually recognised in the former element.

of a short vowel, ε, ῐ or ο, as connecting vowel: thus are derived—

from πειθ- (m.), *obey*, and αρχ-, *command*, πειθ-αρχ-ο-, *obedient to orders.*

δᾰκ-, *bite*, θῡμο-, *heart*, δᾰκ-ε-θῡμο-, *heart-consuming.*

αρχ-, *command*, τεκτον-, *artificer*, αρχ-ῐ-τεκτον-. *chief artificer.*

λῐπ-, *leave*, στρᾰτο-, *army*, λῐπ-ο-στρᾰτ-ια-, *desertion from the army*

But not unfrequently the syllable σῐ (before vowels σ) is inserted: as,

from λυ-, *loosen*, and πονο-, *toil*, λῡ-σῐ-πονο-, *ending toil.*

πληγ-, *strike*, ιππο-, *horse*, πληξ-ιππο-, *steed-spurring.*

This syllable σι (earlier τι, as βω-τῐ-ᾰνειρα-, *man-feeding*) is doubtless the same as the suffix σι of feminine nouns signifying an *act*.

538. Many compound adjectives are formed by aid of certain inseparable particles prefixed: the most important of these prefixes are—

a. The negative particle ᾰν-, before consonants ᾰ- (*Alpha privativum*): thus,

from ᾰν- and αιτιο-, *cause*, is made ᾰν-αιτιο-, *guiltless*, etc.

ελευθερο-, *free*, ᾰν-ελευθερο-, *unfree, slavish.*
πᾰτερ-, *father*, ᾰ-πᾰτορ-, *fatherless.*
μᾰθ-, *learn*, ᾰ-μᾰθ-εσ-, *stupid.*

If the second member of the compound began with ϝ, α was used according to the rule; in Attic contraction sometimes ensued: thus,

from ᾰ- and (ϝ)εργο-, *work*, was made α-εργο-, Att. αργο-, *idle.*

(ϝ)εκοντ-, *willing*, α-εκοντ-, ᾱκοντ-, *unwilling.*
(ϝ)εικ-, *seem*, α-εικ-εσ-, αικεσ-, *unseemly.*

Similarly from ὑπνο-, *sleep*, originally συπνο-, was formed α-ῠπνο-, *sleepless*, not ᾰυπνο-.

The particle νη-, apparently another form of ᾰν-, has the same signification: it is used in poetical compounds; as, νηλεεσ-, *pitiless*, from ελεεσ-, *pity*.*

---

* With the inseparable negative particle ᾰν-, ᾰ-, or νη-, compare the preposition ᾰνευ, *without*, the Latin conjunction *nē* and particle *in-*, the German *ohne* and *un-*, and the English *un-*: also consult Prof. Key, *Phil. Soc.*, iii. p. 52.

b. The particle δυσ-, conveying the notion of *difficult, bad*, and corresponding to the English *mis-* in *misfortune*: thus,

from δυσ- and θῡμο-, *heart*, was made δυσ-θῡμο-, *despondent*.

ἁλο-, *be captured*,   δυσ-άλω-το-, *difficult to capture*.

Compare with these the numerous compounds of ευ, *well*; as, ευ-θῡμο-, *cheerful*; ευ-άλω-το-, *easy to capture*, etc.

c. The copulative particle ἁ-, or, without the aspirate, ἀ-, of ἅμᾰ, *at one, together (Alpha copulativum)*: thus,

from ἁ- and παντ-, *all*, was made ἅ-παντ-, *all together*.

     κελευθο-, *road*,   ἀ-κολουθο-, *attendant on*.
     τᾰλαντο-, *balance*,   ἀ-τᾰλαντο-, *equivalent*.*

539. Compound adjectives expressing *intensity*, are made with the inseparable particles ἀγᾰ-, ζᾰ-, ἀρῐ-, and ερῐ-: as, ἀγα-κλῠτο-, *very famous*; ζα-πλουτο-, *very rich*; ἀρῐ-δηλο-, *very plain*; ἐρῐ-δουπο-, *loud-sounding*. These words are not found in Attic prose.

540. Compound adjectives are also made with prepositions and adverbs prefixed: as, προ-θῡμο-, *forward-minded, eager*; ἀπο-δημο-, *away from one's country*; συν-δῐκο-, *advocate*; ευ-θῡμο-, *cheerful*; οψῐ-μᾰθευ-, *late in learning*.

541. The second member of a compound may be either a noun or a verb: the termination must be adapted, if necessary, to the class of words to which the compound belongs. Hence,

a. If the second member of a compound adjective be a noun, it often remains quite unchanged: thus,

from σᾰφεσ-, *clear*,   is made   ἀ-σᾰφεσ-, *obscure*.
     πολι-, *state*,   ἄ-πολι-, *outlaw*.
     σθενεσ-, *strength*,   ἀ-σθενεσ-, *weak*.
     Ϝετεσ-, *year*,   δεκα-ετεσ-, *ten years old*.
     παιδ-, *child*,   ευ-παιδ-, *with good children*.
     εργο-, *work*,   φῐλ-εργο-, *industrious*.

b. Feminine substantives in *a* give rise to compound adjectives in o: thus,

from τῑμα-, *honour*, is made φῐλο-τῑμο-, *ambitious*.

---

* On the so-called *Alpha intensivum*, see Lobeck, *Pathologiae Graeci Serm. Elementa*, pp. 32—36. In many of the words usually given as compounded with this particle, the *a* is evidently the *a copulative*; in others the initial *a* seems to be the moveable euphonic *a*, or at most a formative letter without signification.

c. Nouns of the syncopated declension in ερ, and φρεν-, *heart, mind*, change ε into ο: thus,

from μητερ-, *mother*, is made ἀ-μητορ-, *motherless.*
    ἀνερ-, *man*,   πολυ-άνορ-, *populous.*
    φρεν-, *mind*,   σω-φρον-, *sound-minded.*

d. Neuters in μᾰτ form adjectives in μον, less frequently in μο: thus,

from πραγμᾰτ-, *deed*, is made πολυ-πραγμον-, *busy.*
    σημᾰτ-, *sign*,   ἄσημον-, *without sign* (or ἄσημο-, see § 526.)

e. Words of the separable declension not unfrequently take the suffix ο: thus,

from λῐμεν-, *harbour*, is made ἀ-λῐμεν-ο-, *harbourless.*
    ἀνερ-, *man*,   Αλεξ-ανδρ-ο-, *Alexander.*

Sometimes two forms coexist, one in a consonant and one in ο; as, πολυ-ανδρο- and πολυ-άνορ-, *populous*; ευ-τειχεσ- and ευ-τειχεο-, *well-walled.*

542. If the second member of a compound adjective be a verb, the verbal root may remain unchanged: but more frequently some suffix is added, as ο, εσ, το, or less frequently τ: thus,

from πληγ-, *strike*, is made κᾰτα-πληγ-, *timid.*
    ζῠγ-, *yoke*,   συζῠγ- (also συζῠγ-ο-), *yoked together.*
    κτεν-, *kill*,   πατρο-κτον-ο-, *killing one's father.*
    μᾰθ-, *learn*,   ἀ-μᾰθ-εσ-, *stupid.*
    δυ-, *enter*,   ἀ-δῠ-το-, *not to be entered.*
    γνω-, *know*,   α-γνω-τ-, *unknown.*

In such compounds the verb is generally, but not exclusively, passive or intransitive. Sometimes the adjective is ambiguous*; thus, πατροκτονο- means also *killed by one's father*; α-βλᾰβ-εσ-, is *unharmed* and *harmless*; ἀ-πειθ-εσ-, *disobedient* and *not-persuasive*; ἀ-ποτο-, *not drinkable* and *never drinking.*

543. Compound substantives, partaking of the nature of substantives and adjectives, are made from verbal roots by addition of the suffixes denoting *agents*: as, νεφελ-ηγερε-τα-, *cloud-col-*

---

* In accentuated Greek such ambiguous words are sometimes distinguished: as, πατροκτόνος (N. S.), *killing one's father*, but πατρόκτονος, *killed by one's father*: in the genitive, however, both become πατροκτόνου. The number of the words in which the distinction is made is, moreover, very limited.

lecting, from νεφελα-, *cloud*, and ἄγερ-, *collect*; μηλο-βο-τηρ-, *sheep-feeding*. But these are chiefly poetical.

544. Feminine substantives of an abstract signification may be compounded with prepositions without undergoing any change of form: thus, from the fem. nouns βουλα-, *counsel*; δἴκα-, *right, suit at law*; ὁδο-, *road*, are formed the compounds ἐπῐ-βουλα-, *plot*; κᾰτᾰ-δῐκα-, *sentence*; σῠν-οδο-, *assembly*. In composition with other words than prepositions such feminines usually take the suffix ια, as αει-φῠγ-ια-, *perpetual banishment*, from φῠγα-, *flight*. Thus such words as συν-θε-σι-, *putting together*; ναυ-μᾰχ-ια-, *sea-fight*, may be regarded either as *derived* from the compound words, συν-θε-, *put together*; ναυ-μαχο-, *fighting at sea*, or *compounded* of σῠν and θεσι-, ναυ- and μᾰχα-. They are usually treated as *derivatives*.

545. Compound verbs are only made by prefixing some preposition to a simple verb: the verb undergoes no change. Thus, from βᾰλ-, *throw*; θε-, *put*, are made the compounds ἄπο-βᾰλ-, *throw away*; συν-θε-, *put together*.*

546. The very numerous verbs apparently compounded of verbs and other words not prepositions are really derived from compound adjectives or substantives: thus,
from *a* priv. and δῠνᾰτο-, *able*, is made ἀ-δῠνᾰτο-, *unable*;
and thence is derived the verb ἀδῠνᾰτε-, *be unable*.
from ναυ-, *ship*, and μᾰχ-, *fight*, is made ναυ-μαχ-ο-, *fighting by sea*;
and thence ναυμᾰχε-, *fight by sea*.
ευ, *well*,   εργ-, *work*,   ευ-εργ-ετα-, *benefactor*;
and thence ευεργετε-, *be a benefactor*.
σω-, *sound*,   φρεν-, *mind*,   σω-φρον-, *sound-minded*;
and thence σωφρονε-, *be sound-minded*.
The only exceptions to this statement are found in a few Epic participles, such as δακρυ-χεοντ-, *shedding tears*, from δακρυ-, *tear*, and χε-οντ-, *pouring*.

547. If the first syllable of the second element of a compound was short, it was sometimes lengthened, originally to avoid the concurrence of too many short syllables, and the practice was then extended to cases in which no such reason appears: thus, ἱππ-ηλᾰτα-, *driver of horses*; επ-ωνῠμο-, *surnamed*; ἀν-ωμοτο-, *un-*

---

* This process is less composition, strictly so called, than juxta-position: see § 502.

sworn; φῐλ-ηρετμο-, *fond of rowing*; ευ-ωδεσ-, *sweet-smelling*, are compounded of ελα-, *drive*; ονομ-ᾰτ-, *name*; ομο-, *swear*; ερετμο-, *oar*; οδ-, *smell*. To the same principle are due the long vowels in such words as ελᾰφη-βολο-, *shooting deer* (for ελᾰφο-βολο-).

LATIN AND GREEK GRAMMARS.

A GRAMMAR OF THE LATIN LANGUAGE, from Plautus to Suetonius. By H. J. ROBY, M.A. In Two Parts. Second Edition. Part I. Crown 8vo. 8s. 6d.—Part II. 10s. 6d.

"Marked by the clear and practical insight of a master of his art. A book that would do honour to any country."—*Athenæum*.

A LATIN GRAMMAR FOR SCHOOLS. By H. J. ROBY, M.A. Crown 8vo. 5s.

EXERCISES IN LATIN SYNTAX AND IDIOM. Arranged with reference to Roby's "School Latin Grammar." By E. B. ENGLAND, M.A., Owens College, Manchester. Crown 8vo.
[*In the press.*

FIRST LATIN GRAMMAR. By M. C. MACMILLAN, M.A., Assistant Master in St. Paul's School, London. Extra fcap. 8vo. 1s. 6d.

"Quite the best book of the kind for little boys that we have seen."—*Athenæum*.

AN ELEMENTARY GREEK GRAMMAR. By Professor W. W. GOODWIN, Professor of Greek in Harvard University. New Edition, revised. Crown 8vo. 6s.

"The best Greek grammar of its size in the English language."—*Athenæum*.

SYNTAX OF THE MOODS AND TENSES OF THE GREEK VERB. By Professor W. W. GOODWIN. New Edition, revised. Crown 8vo. 6s. 6d.

A FIRST GREEK GRAMMAR. By W. G. RUTHERFORD, M.A., Assistant Master in St. Paul's School, London. New Edition, enlarged. Extra fcap. 8vo. 1s. 6d.

"Throughout commendably clear and succinct."—*Saturday Review*.

SHORT EXERCISES IN LATIN PROSE COMPOSITION, and Examination Papers in Latin Grammar. By Rev H. BELCHER, M.A., Assistant Master at King's College, London. In Two Parts. Part I. 1s. 6d. Key, for Teachers only, 2s. 6d.—Part II. 2s.

MYTHOLOGY FOR LATIN VERSIFICATION: a Brief Sketch of the Fables of the Ancients, prepared to be rendered into Latin Verse for Schools. By F. HODGSON, late Provost of Eton. New Edition. 18mo. 3s.

PARALLEL EXTRACTS, arranged for Translation into English and Latin; with Notes on Idioms. By J. E. NIXON, M.A. Part I. Historical and Epistolary. New Edition, revised and enlarged. Crown 8vo. 3s. 6d.

MACMILLAN AND CO., LONDON.

WORKS BY ALEXANDER POTTS, M.A., LL.D.,
LATE FELLOW OF ST. JOHN'S COLLEGE, CAMBRIDGE.

HINTS TOWARDS LATIN PROSE COMPOSITION. New Edition. Extra fcap. 8vo. 3s.

PASSAGES FOR TRANSLATION INTO LATIN PROSE. Edited, with Notes and references to the above. Extra fcap. 8vo. 2s. Key, for Teachers only, 2s. 6d.

EXERCISES IN LATIN PROSE, with Introduction, Notes, &c., for Middle Forms of Schools. Extra fcap. 8vo.
[In preparation.

SYNTHETIC LATIN DELECTUS. A First Latin Construing Book, arranged on the Principles of Grammatical Analysis, with Notes and Vocabulary. By E. RUSH, B.A., with a Preface by the Rev. W. K. MOULTON, M.A., D.D. Extra fcap. 8vo. 2s.

FIRST STEPS TO LATIN PROSE COMPOSITION. By the late Rev. G. RUST. M.A., of Pembroke College, Oxford, Master of the Lower School, King's College, London. New Edition. 1s. 6d.

FIRST STEPS TO GREEK PROSE COMPOSITION. By BLOMFIELD JACKSON, M.A., Assistant Master in King's College School, London. New Edition, revised and enlarged. 18mo. 1s. 6d.

SECOND STEPS TO GREEK GREEK COMPOSITION. Consisting of Passages for translation, Examination Papers in Grammar and Composition, &c. By BLOMFIELD JACKSON, M.A. 18mo. 2s. 6d.

Key to the above, for use of Teachers only. *[In preparation.*

EXERCISES IN COMPOSITION OF GREEK IAMBIC VERSE. By translation from English Dramatists. By Rev. H. KYNASTON, M A., Principal of Cheltenham College. With Introduction, Vocabulary, &c. Extra fcap. 8vo. 4s. 6d.

Key to same, for Teachers only, 4s. 6d.

A TABLE OF IRREGULAR GREEK VERBS classified according to the arrangement of Curtius's Greek Grammar. By J. M. MARSHALL, M.A., one of the Masters in Clifton College. 8vo. Cloth. New Edition. 1s.

FIRST GREEK READER. Edited, after KARL HALM, with corrections and large additions, by Professor JOHN E. B. MAYOR, M.A., Fellow of St. John's College, Cambridge. New Edition, revised. Fcap. 8vo. 4s. 6d.

GREEK FOR BEGINNERS. By Rev. J. B. MAYOR, M A., Professor of Classical Literature in King's College, London. Part I., with Vocabulary, 1s 6d. Parts II. and III., with Vocabulary and Index, 3s. 6d. Complete in One Vol. New Edition. Fcap. 8vo. Cloth. 4s. 6d.

FIRST LESSONS IN GREEK. Adapted to Goodwin's Greek Grammar, and designed as an Introduction to the Anabasis of Xenophon. By Professor J. W. WHITE. Crown 8vo. 4s. 6d.

MACMILLAN AND CO., LONDON.

www.ingramcontent.com/pod-product-compliance
Lightning Source LLC
Chambersburg PA
CBHW031815220426
43662CB00007B/665